Small business dynamics

Central to the study of small business is an understanding of the processes by which different businesses change, grow and in some cases decline. *Small Business Dynamics* provides an economic and inter-regional analysis of the birth, death and changes within smaller firms over time, with an emphasis on the extent of 'turbulence' which exists and on the causes of variation in business dynamics.

The contributors, who represent leading authorities from Europe and the USA, bring to the question different national and industrial perspectives. Overall the chapters examine small business dynamics from two main perspectives: first, a national perspective which looks at the impact of broad macro-economic trends; second, a regional perspective which highlights the effect of variations across different sectors within the broad economic picture.

Each contribution is followed by a short section of discussants' comments, which give the reader both a view of the main critiques to arise in response to the contributor's analysis and a summary of the key themes that link up with other chapters in the volume.

The findings presented in the volume will provide students and researchers in small business studies with wide-ranging new data, along with sophisticated techniques for interpreting it. The resulting analyses will also be of interest to policy-makers.

Charlie Karlsson is at the Jönköping International Business School Foundation, Sweden. **Bengt Johannisson** is at the Department of Business Administration, Economics and Law, Vaxjö University and Institute for Economic Research, Lund University, Sweden. **David Storey** is at the Centre for Small and Medium Sized Enterprises, Warwick Business School, University of Warwick. He is currently the national co-ordinator of the ESRC Small Business Initiative.

Small business dynamics

International, national and regional perspectives

Edited by
Charlie Karlsson, Bengt Johannisson
and David Storey

London and New York

338.642
S6358

First published 1993
by Routledge
11 New Fetter Lane, London EC4P 4EE

Simultaneously published in the USA and Canada
by Routledge
29 West 35th Street, New York, NY 10001

Typeset in Times by Solidus (Bristol) Ltd, Bristol
Printed and bound in Great Britain by
Biddles Ltd, Guildford and King's Lynn

British Library Cataloguing in Publication Data
A catalogue record for this book is available from the British Library

Library of Congress Cataloging in Publication Data
has been applied for

ISBN 0-415-09625-1

Contents

v

vi   *Contents*

Figures

Tables

Contributors

Dr David B. Audretsch, WZB, Reichpietschufer 50, D-100 Berlin 30, Germany.

Dr Will Bartlett, School for Advanced Urban Studies, Rodney Lodge, Grange Road, Bristol BS8 4EA, England.

Professor Bengt Johannisson, Department of Business Administration, Economics and Law, Vaxjö University, and Institute for Economic Research, Box 5053, S-351 95 Vaxjö; Lund University, Box 7080, S-220 07, Sweden.

Dr Charlie Karlsson, Jönköping International Business School Foundation, c/o Jönköping Chamber of Commerce, Elmiavagen, 554 54 Jönköping, Sweden.

Professor Leif Lindmark, Department of Business Administration, Umeå University, S-901 87 Umeå, Sweden.

Dr Mette Mønsted, Copenhagen School of Economics and Business Administration, Howitzvej 60 DK-2000 Fredriksberg, Denmark.

Professor Ray Oakey, Manchester Business School, University of Manchester, Booth Street West, Manchester M15 6PB, England.

Professor Christer Olofsson, Swedish University of Agricultural Sciences, Department of Economics, Box 7013, S-75007 Uppsala, Sweden.

Professor Paul Reynolds, Coleman/Fannie May Candies Chairholder in Entrepreneurship, College of Business Administration, Marquette University, Milwaukee, Wisconsin 53233, USA.

Professor David Storey, SME Centre, Warwick Business School, University of Warwick, Coventry CV4 7AL, England.

Robert Watson, Manchester School of Management, University of Manchester Institute of Science Technology (UMIST), PO Box 88, Manchester M60 1QD, England.

Professor Joop Vianen, EIM, Research Institute for Small and Medium-Sized Business, PO Box 7001, 2701 AA Zoetermeer, The Netherlands.

Introduction

eds

SOME ISSUES

This book reproduces a selection of papers presented in Jönköping, Sweden in September 1991. The papers, which each form a chapter, relate to the theme of small business dynamics, defined as the study of the birth, death and changes within smaller firms over time.

A multi-disciplinary approach to the topic is employed. The role of smaller firms in the economy has interested those with a background in economics, with contributions also made by geographers. The perspective adopted has been broadly quantitative, in terms of counting the number of births and deaths of firms, but only recently has work using more sophisticated quantitative techniques been undertaken. Other disciplines which favour a more qualitative approach have not been major contributors to this subject area.

Our purpose in this volume is to develop the broadly quantitative study of small business dynamics. Included here are chapters which are enumerations of numbers of firm births and firm deaths, generally at a regional level. Their contribution is to quantify the extent of 'turbulence' which exists, even when there is only a very modest change in either small-firm employment or in the total stock of firms over time. Most of the chapters in this volume, however, try to explain variations in business dynamics. Some use statistical analysis to examine the changes at both national and regional levels, but the focus of each is different. Some, for example, relate small business dynamics to macro-economic conditions, others to sectoral changes, whilst others are interested in inter-regional comparisons within the same country.

There are two frequent (and justified) criticisms made by reviewers of edited books which emerge from conferences. The first is that the range of topics covered is too wide to provide coherence. The second is that, although the papers are reproduced, there is little of the flavour of the discussion which took place. In planning this volume our purpose has been to overcome both these problems. First, a number of papers presented (including one by one of the editors) were deemed to be insufficiently related to the issue of small business dynamics to be included in the current volume. Second, the programme at Jönköping was organized so that a discussant for each paper was nominated and a significant period of time was allocated for subsequent discussion by all participants. In this volume we have included the discussants' comments at the end of the individual chapters, so as to provide the reader with an indication of the critique which they provided. In addition, this introduction attempts to pull together several of the themes which emerged consistently throughout the conference.

An examination of the Contents page of this volume indicates that a wide international perspective was adopted. Contributors came from seven countries, but most were interested in small business dynamics within their own countries. All these countries are 'developed' so that the lessons learnt from this research are not necessarily applicable either to the less developed countries, or to those emerging from the planned economies of Eastern Europe into a market economy for the first time.

Existing work on small business dynamics has focused on private capitalist enterprises, but it is reasonable to ask whether the factors which influence the formation and death of cooperatives are the same as those which explain small business dynamics more generally.

Overall, this volume will examine small business dynamics from two main perspectives. The first relates to national factors, and the second to regional factors. Taking the national perspective first, there is considerable interest in the question of whether macro-economic circumstances influence the birth and death rate of new enterprises. Several alternative, and even conflicting, explanations may be provided. The first is that conditions of prosperity are likely to lead to high rates of new-firm formation, but may also lead to increased death rates of firms (Lane and Schary 1990). Whether they lead to an increase in stock of businesses (births minus deaths) is less clear cut. An alternative explanation is that depressed macro-economic conditions may lead to high rates of new-firm formation, but again the impact on the stock of firms is less clear (Cuthbertson and Hudson 1990). Finally, there must also be questions raised relating to causation in these matters since it is equally possible to argue that higher rates of new-firm formation cause improved economic conditions as it is to argue that improved economic conditions lead to higher rates of new-firm formation.

In many respects it is easier to examine these issues at a regional, rather than a national level. Data are more likely to be available which distinguish one region from another so that the impact of different influences may be identified. For example, the sectoral structure of employment will vary from one region to another and it is therefore possible to compare the birth and death rates of firms between regions taking account of this component, but at the same time holding macro-economic conditions constant. This is the focus of several of the chapters in this volume, but even here there may be differences between regions relating to more qualitative factors. A classic illustration of this is a recognition within Sweden of 'Gnosjö spirit'. This appears to reflect a perception that the Gnosjö region has had an unusually high level of entrepreneurial activity for several generations.

SMALL BUSINESS DYNAMICS AND NEW-FIRM FORMATION

One of the key developments from the late 1970s onwards in developed economies was the relative increase in the importance of small firms. Loveman and Sengenberger (1991) demonstrate that in most developed countries there has been a rise in the proportion of total employment provided by the small-firm sector. This may occur for several reasons:

(a) an increase in the birth rate of new firms;
(b) a decline in the death rate of small firms;
(c) an increase in the stock of small firms;
(d) net employment creation amongst established small firms;
(e) a contraction in employment of established larger businesses, so that they become smaller firms.

The purpose of studies of business in dynamics is to identify the contribution of each of these components and therefore to provide a better understanding of the factors which influence each component. It is clearly important for policy makers to understand both the quantitative significance of each of the components and the factors which influence their magnitude. At the most simple level policies may be adopted which are effective in increasing the birth rate of new firms, but if this merely leads to an increase in the death rate, with the total stock of firms remaining unchanged, then the effectiveness of the policy must be open to question. Equally, if policies to encourage the rate of formation of firms are implemented, and this also leads to an increase in the total stock of firms, but to no net increase in employment, then again the effectiveness of such policies is also open to question.

There have been a number of reviews of the factors which influence the increased importance of small firms (Keeble and Wever 1986, Storey and Johnson 1987). The latter identify three models which they call the Birmingham, Boston and Bologna models. Each of these reflects an increased importance of smaller firms in an economy, but for very different reasons. The Birmingham model reflects the declining importance of larger firms and the pressure upon former workers in these firms to become self-employed, small business owners in order to avoid unemployment. The Boston model reflects the recent growth in importance of new high technology firms which become major wealth creators, leading to increased local employment opportunities in small service sector firms. The Bologna model reflects the growth of smaller firms in north-east central Italy which have merged through the development of flexible specialization (Piore and Sabel 1984). They observe that highly competitive smaller firms have developed through a combination of small family-based production units specializing in particular tasks, such as the production of soles or upper parts of shoes. The flexibility is provided by the capacity of these subcontractors to change their products as the design of the completed product changes. The interdependent system of small firms is able to adapt quickly to market changes.

Over the past five years a number of new explanations have been provided for the increased importance of smaller firms in the economies of developed Western countries. It is our purpose here to review these explanations very briefly so as to provide some context for the chapters on small business dynamics in this volume. For purposes of simplicity a total of seven explanations are presented. These should not be interpreted as necessarily independent of one another, and it is certainly possible that either national or regional economies may experience a growth among small firms which can be attributed to more than a single explanation.

Market and entry barriers

Economists view new firm formation as relating to factors influencing the entry of new units of production. In simple terms it is argued that entry would be expected to take place when expected post-entry profitability increases, and/or when entry barriers fall. Unfortunately, it is often difficult, from official data, to distinguish between existing firms which choose to enter a new industry (cross entry) and the creation of wholly new businesses. From official data it is also often difficult to obtain data on births as opposed to that on net entry (births minus deaths). Nevertheless, it is likely that increased rates of new-firm formation are associated with a lowering of entry barriers and/or an increase in post-entry profits. To demonstrate, however, that the increased importance of small and medium enterprises (SMEs) reflects higher entry rates of firms would imply that entry barriers have fallen over time.

One helpful test of this was conducted by Bradburd and Ross (1989) who examined the theories outlined by Porter (1980). Bradburd and Ross show that whilst it is generally true in the United States that firms with a large market share (generally larger firms) do have higher rates of profit than smaller firms, the nature of the industry provides an important qualification to this finding. They show that in heterogeneous industries there is no evidence that larger firms have higher profits than smaller firms, indeed the reverse may be the case. These results suggest that if heterogeneous industries constitute an increasing share of the industrial sector then it is to be expected that smaller firms will become increasingly important – or at least that entry rates would be expected to increase.

Income growth

There has been an argument presented at least since the early 1970s (Bolton Committee 1971) that smaller firms are more likely to be effective in supplying niche markets. Indeed, it is this argument which was developed by Porter (1980). As incomes rise it is likely that expenditure will move away from 'standardized' goods, which are more likely to be provided by larger firms, towards more differentiated products and services. Because of this ability to product-differentiate and create niches the smaller firm is likely to benefit more than the large. These arguments will apply both to the service and to the manufacturing sector, and are again likely to lead to higher entry rates over time.

Labour market explanations

In the Birmingham model discussed above increased rates of new-firm formation may be related not to positive attraction factors, but instead to a lack of alternative employment opportunities for individuals.

Recent work by Robson (1991) in a review of time series studies of business formations and dissolutions in the United Kingdom attempts to disaggregate the influence of 'unemployment-push' from 'prosperity-pull' forces. He concludes that whilst it is mistaken to see these forces as mutually exclusive the UK data provide stronger support for the 'unemployment-push' hypothesis, than for the 'prosperity-pull'. These results, however, apply only to time series analysis and the reverse results appear to emerge from the cross-sectional studies in Britain (Ashcroft, Love and Malloy 1990).

Innovation and technical change

One of the key findings relating to small firm performance is that such firms tend to be a major source of new innovations. United States data analysed by Acs and Audretsch (1988) suggest that it is the innovative potential of small firms which is at the heart of their superior performance, compared with large firms. In the UK the work conducted at the Science Policy Research Unit (SPRU) shows that small firms are a major source of new innovations. Pavitt *et al.* (1987) showed that although firms with fewer than one thousand employees account for only 3 per cent of R&D expenditure, they are responsible for about one-third of all significant innovations. They also showed that small firms increased their share of significant innovations consistently from the late 1950s onwards. Although there clearly are problems in comparing research activities in small and large firms, such as the difficulties in distinguishing R&D costs within a small firm, the findings are quite persuasive.

In studies of small business dynamics, factors influencing the death rate of firms are important. In this context the work by Audretsch (1991) is particularly important since he finds that amongst other influences new-firm survival is positively related to small-firm innovative activity, defined as the total number of innovations recorded in 1982 divided by industry employment. Audretsch shows that the two variables, small-firm innovation rate and small firm/total innovation rate, are positively associated with new-firm survival rates in the United States between 1976 and 1986.

There is also evidence that in certain key industrial sectors, scale economies, as a result of technological change, may be falling. The classic example of this is reviewed by Acs (1984) who examines the development of mini-mills which have begun to compete effectively with the large, steel producing establishments. Here technological change has fundamentally shifted, and lowered, the minimum efficient scale of production. Similar illustrations are available from the computing and related sectors where scale economies can now be reaped at a much lower level of output than has been the case in the past.

Large/small firm relations

It is not always possible to distinguish the relative growth in the small-firm sector from changes in medium and large firm groups. Johnson (1989) shows that in the UK between 1975 and 1983, although small firms increased their share of manufacturing employment, this was at least partly because of the decline in employment in firms that had previously been larger. What happens therefore to the large-firm sector must inevitably influence smaller firms and vice versa. Hence it is essential to examine key developments amongst larger firms in order to better understand the small-firm sector.

The two most important developments here relate first to sub-contracting or 'outsourcing' and second to the sale of large-firm divisions either to their managers or to other smaller organizations.

Empirical evidence on the changing importance of subcontracting in the UK is provided by Lyons (1992). He shows there is evidence of increased subcontracting within the engineering sector with one-half of firms having increased outsourcing over the last five years, compared with only one-third which has decreased. He also shows that the average size of increase was 47 per cent whereas the average decrease was only 26 per cent.

The 1980s was also characterized, at least in the United Kingdom, by a major growth in the number of management buy-outs and buy-ins, numbers rising from less than fifty in 1980 to more than 500 in the peak year of 1989 (Wright *et al.* 1990).

Governments

A central role in promoting and encouraging the development of small firms has been played by the governments of many developed countries. For example, in the United Kingdom Mrs Thatcher came to power in 1979 with a clear commitment to roll back the powers of the state and promote the creation of an 'enterprise culture'. The lowering of personal tax rates and the explicit encouragement of entrepreneurial activities during the 1980s in Britain was associated with a substantial increase in the total number of business units. Daly (1991) shows that between 1980 and 1990 there was a net increase in the number of businesses registered for VAT of approximately 420,000 or 32 per cent.

The precise contribution of government is difficult to quantify since increases in the number of small firms were also occurring simultaneously in other countries which did not have such vigorous policies. Nevertheless, the fact is that the UK government was active in promoting the small business sector, passing more than one hundred measures to support the sector during the decade. These included the introduction of a Loan Guarantee Scheme, an Enterprise Allowance Scheme and a Business Expansion Scheme. The Enterprise Allowance Scheme was also introduced, with modifications, in several other countries including France and Ireland (Bendick and Egan 1987).

Entrepreneurial spirit

One of the most difficult aspects of small business dynamics to explain is the clear difference in attitudes to enterprise between geographical areas within the same country which may only be a few miles apart. Perhaps the classic example of this lies in Italy where a long-established tradition of small enterprise development exists in the towns and cities of Bologna, Modena, etc. Here the economy for much of the 1980s thrived on the growth of small enterprises at a time when southern Italy continued to experience major economic difficulties. In the south, regional development continued to focus on the attraction inwards of large branch plants rather than the development of small indigenous firms. The transfer of entrepreneurial spirit could clearly not easily be undertaken from one part of Italy to another.

Similar illustrations are available elsewhere in Europe. As we shall show, the region of Gnosjö in Sweden is one that has thrived at a time when much of Swedish manufacturing has, in employment terms, been in decline. Explaining the reasons for the presence of these highly enterprising areas provides a challenge to researchers. In many respects the most satisfactory explanations are provided by those such as Johannisson (1986) and Birley *et al.* (1991) who have been interested in aspects of networking. Highly enterprising areas and individuals are shown to have frequent networking involvement with other key factors in the economy.

THE FOCUS

This section relates the above general discussion to the focus of the nine chapters which make up this volume. The purpose is to provide the reader with a very brief synthesis of each chapter and also to provide both a flavour of the discussion around the themes and an insight into some of the issues relevant to policy.

The arrangement of the chapters reflects an initial coverage of the influence which macro-economic conditions have on small business dynamics. The first three chapters by Vianen, Audretsch and Bartlett all cover studies of individual countries. The remaining ones focus on entrepreneurship and small business dynamics at a regional level. The interest of these chapters is to assess the differing impact of regions on small business dynamics.

The chapter by Vianen focuses on the impact of the business cycle on employment and output of small and medium-sized enterprises (SMEs), in comparison with larger firms. The data which it uses are from the Netherlands and cover the period of the 1980s. The crucial conclusion of the paper is that SMEs have a different pattern from larger firms throughout the business cycle, with SMEs acting as a 'built-in employment stabilizer' throughout the business cycle. Thus it is the fluctuations in employment in larger firms that are most strongly associated with upswings and downswings of the business cycle.

In many respects, as David Audretsch in the role of discussant pointed out, these findings are surprising because the familiar role of smaller firms has been to respond 'flexibly' to changes in demand. It might therefore be expected that smaller firms, in the upswing of the cycle, would be most likely to expand output and employment, but during the downswing such firms would be most vulnerable. Hence the large-firm sector is expected to demonstrate greater stability over the cycle, whereas smaller firms would be expected to fluctuate. The Vianen results, however, do not support this view, but this could be a consequence of the other central finding of his chapter, which is that during the 1980s there was a significant structural change in the Dutch economy, favouring smaller firms.

The issues raised by Vianen are then developed by Audretsch himself, who asks the simple question of whether there is evidence from the United States that new firm formation rates are higher in times of depressed demand or in times of tight demand. He uses the distinction between 'push' and 'pull' factors. The 'push' thesis is that new-firm formation is especially influenced by a large supply of unemployed workers, whereas 'pull' factors reflect the demand for additional goods and services. Audretsch's time series and cross-sectional analysis for the United States between 1976 and 1986 indicates no support for the 'push' thesis. Instead it suggests that new-firm formation is related to conventional economic theory whereby entry takes place in response to an increase in anticipated profitability.

Audretsch does qualify these findings by pointing out that the data relate only to the manufacturing sector; he also suggests that the negative coefficient on the unemployment variable could reflect the existence of a simultaneous relationship, and also the fact that six time period observations may be too few to test for any lagged relationships. To this one might add that the measure of formation rates could also exert an influence. Thus the measures used by Audretsch reflect the total number of formations, normalized by the stock of businesses in the industry. 'Push' factors have been shown to be important where the number of entries is normalized by the working population. It is also the case that, as was pointed out earlier, time series studies show a consistently greater impact for 'pull' factors than is the case for cross-sectional studies (Robson 1991).

The third national/country study is provided by Bartlett. He shifts the focus away from small capitalist enterprises and instead examines cooperative enterprises in Italy, Spain and Portugal. His interest relates to how these businesses change over the business cycle. He argues that cooperative enterprises will be created in a counter-cyclical manner, i.e., formations will be highest at the low point in the cycle. The empirical evidence suggests there are differences between Italy and Spain. In the former there is evidence of procyclical evolution, but in Spain evolution appears to be counter-cyclical. In this sense Bartlett regards cooperatives as converging towards capitalist enterprises with which they co-exist in southern Europe.

In many respects, therefore, the results for cooperatives can be seen to parallel those of other SMEs. This is reflected in the comments made by Mette Mønsted as discussant, where she points to similar issues associated with the growth of cooperatives as with SMEs. She highlights the importance of leadership structures and the formation of supplementary organizations. Thus it may be argued that, whilst the ownership and decision-making structure of cooperatives may be more complex than is the case for capitalist SMEs, the outcomes in terms of formation, survival and growth may differ less than might be expected.

We now turn to the remaining chapters which focus on small business dynamics at a regional level. The first of these is by Reynolds *et al.* who examine regional characteristics which affected business volatility in the United States between 1980 and 1984. Reynolds' analysis is particularly helpful since it relates many of the hypotheses discussed in the previous section to data on 382 labour market areas in the United States. Despite the complexity of the task of data assembly, and the variety of influences examined, some simple, yet powerful, conclusions emerge. These are that areas exhibiting high firm birth rates are those with a high proportion of employment in smaller firms, those where population growth in the prior period has been rapid and where personal wealth is highest. Reynolds finds no support for the view that firm birth rates are high when unemployment is high. Indeed, like Audretsch, who uses the identical data base from the US Small Business Administration, he finds the reverse, i.e. firm birth rates are lowest in regions with high unemployment, *ceteris paribus*. It is somewhat reassuring that two researchers, Reynolds with a spatial perspective and Audretsch with an industrial perspective, reach broadly similar conclusions.

The chapter by Johannisson examines issues for Sweden similar to those which Reynolds examined for the United States. The key limitation of the Swedish analysis is that whereas Reynolds was able to conduct his statistical analysis for 382 labour markets, Johannisson is restricted to 24 regions/counties. Nevertheless, the chapter compensates by linking the testing procedure explicitly to models of business formation deriving directly from existing literature. It argues that there are four basic models influencing formation. These are:

(a) market conditions;
(b) resource availability;
(c) milieu;
(d) career structures.

The first two can be considered as fairly conventional approaches, with market variables of demand and resources relating primarily to the availability of finance. The final two variables introduce new dimensions to the analysis. Johannisson includes within the milieu model sources of creativity, such as the presence of artisans and social networks. Within the career model Johannisson includes elements such as the availability of role models. He then examines policies which could lead to a strengthening of these networks.

The comments by Reynolds, acting as a discussant for this chapter, are interesting since both he and Johannisson are trying to identify the determinants of business volatility across regions. They reflect the key data constraint of having only twenty-four regions within Sweden with which to conduct the analysis. Reynolds suggests a number of useful ways to increase the degrees of freedom such as breaking the period 1986–9 into three one-year periods and distinguishing birth rates according to sector. He might also have suggested that it would be possible to use other statistical methods, such as the creation of principal components, as he does in his own contribution, to determine whether the variables included in four groups identified by Johannisson indicated strong internal coherence. The real value of the Johannisson chapter is therefore that it is tightly theorized, although restricted in its empirics by data limitations.

In many respects, therefore, the chapter by Davidsson *et al.* provides an escape from the constraints of data for Sweden. Their paper represents a pilot study for the area of Linköping Labour Market Area, designed to replicate the methodology employed by Reynolds for the United States. For the whole of Sweden eighty such areas have been defined and comprehensive data will be available for all of them. This will be a significant improvement upon the number of observations used by Johanisson.

The pilot study by Davidsson *et al.* for Linköping means it is difficult to analyse cross-regional patterns. Even so, the importance of small business dynamics is illustrated in this case study, with two-thirds of establishments reporting changes in employment over the 1985/6–1988/9 period. Despite the commonly held view of stability within the Swedish economy, these authors conclude that births, deaths, expansions and contractions are the rule, rather than the exception, in the Linköping Labour Market Area.

In our discussion of factors influencing small business dynamics in the previous section, we emphasized the importance of qualitative factors such as the existence of an entrepreneurial spirit and the establishment of networks and linkages between firms. It is particulary appropriate that the conference took place in Sweden since this country has one prime example of an area which is significantly different from other parts of the country in this respect. The region of Gnosjö has traditionally performed significantly better than other areas in Sweden. In an unpublished paper Wiklund (1991) shows that between 1985 and 1990 employment in this region has significantly out-performed that for the Swedish economy as a whole. He quotes the work of Orjasatter who says 'The Common belief is that the "entrepeneurial spirit" of Gnosjö explains the successful development of the community. The small business men are psychologically different from small business men in other municipalities'. This theme is taken up by Karlsson and Larsson in their chapter, which attempts to investigate the long-run sustainability of the Gnosjö phenomenon.

Their conclusions are somewhat pessimistic, suggesting that the region's comparative expertise in labour intensive industries is likely to be eroded in future years. In essence they argue that the presence of an entrepreneurial spirit, is insufficient to achieve the adjustment to an economy needing to rely on knowledge-intensive industries. The structure and nature of firms in this area are therefore likely to change significantly.

The ability of an area to adjust to changes in economic conditions is likely to be influenced by the extent and strengths of networking. Johannisson's (1986) work on the importance of networking in the Gnosjö area suggests that the area is likely to make the necessary structural adjustments.

The question of networking is also developed in the chapter by Mønsted. She states that small business networks may be divided into three, each with different purposes and rationales: service/assistance, information and innovation. Mønsted also points out that networks, because of power relationships, may even constitute a hindrance to the venturing process.

The final chapter, by Oakey, examines the implications for regions of the development of high technology small firms. There are a number of reasons why high technology small firms may differ from those in more conventional technologies: these relate to the high likelihood of introducing new innovations, the generally high levels of educational attainment of the founders, the possible conservative nature of the banking and financial system in responding to proposals from such firms, and finally the high levels of uncertainty associated with their development of new products and processes.

Given that high technology small firms may be regarded as an important, but nevertheless different, case from small firms as a whole, Oakey argues for the creation of a technology policy for the United Kingdom. He argues that such a policy is necessary to combat the 'short-termism' of the private sector which has characterized much of the 1980s. He argues that such a policy has to focus on both small and large firms since the two groups closely interact with one another.

THE POLICIES

It is a characteristic of many democratic governments that their economic policies are often implemented prior to well-established research being in place. In part this reflects the unwillingness of researchers to indicate the potential policy dimensions of their research. Of course, it is also the case that only once policies have been implemented is it possible to evaluate their success or otherwise. Nevertheless, the contributors to this volume do offer, to a differing degree, insights into policy issues. It is our purpose here to identify some such issues briefly.

Probably the most important finding is the extent to which there are real variations in the performance of small and large firms in many economies throughout the 1980s. A second key finding is that, even within the same country, there are particular regions or sectors which have performed much better than others. Finally, factors which seem to be important in influencing small business dynamics in one country, appear very much less significant in another – the classic examples being the fact that unemployment in the United States does not seem to be associated with higher rates of new firm formation.

Perhaps the main policy issue which emerges from these pages is the extent to which the economic performance of countries or regions is associated with small business dynamics. The associated question is whether it is possible to influence, through public policy, the factors which affect small business dynamics. In this regard the results generated by Reynolds *et al.* do focus upon policy. They argue that the birth rate of firms is influenced by the industrial and size structure of firms, of population growth, of personal wealth and unemployment. However, it is difficult to interpret any of these factors directly into implications for public policy. If, instead, they had shown that areas which pay low taxes or which provide a wide range of public services were also those with high (or low) formation rates, it would have been more easily incorporated within public policy.

A similar set of problems emerges in teasing out the policy implications from observations of the characteristics of highly enterprising areas such as the Gnosjö area. The area is clearly characterized by strong networking ties between firms but, if Karlsson and Larsson are to be believed, the advantages which the area has had in the past may prove to be only temporary, unless appropriate policy measures are taken. Improvements of Gnosjö's infrastructure seems, for example, to have a strong positive impact on the productivity of manufacturing industry in the region and hence on its competitive power (Johansson and Karlsson 1991).

Despite these reservations the various contributors generally indicate a role for public policy in promoting SMEs. The most vigorous case is provided by Oakey in his plea for a technology policy in the United Kingdom, but others attest to the potential importance of public intervention. This is clearly important in macro-economic decisions made by central government, as is illustrated by Vianen in the case of the Netherlands. More subtle illustrations of this are presented by Mønsted who demonstrates the role which the public sector can play in the strengthening of networks both between firms themselves and between firms and support organizations. As Johannisson notes, the strength of these networks is an important indicator of the long-term health of an economy.

THE UNCERTAINTIES

Despite the work reported here, significant uncertainties remain. The area of small business dynamics is only in its infancy, which is reflected in the absence of genuinely internationally comparable work. There remains a tendency, reflected in this volume, for researchers to concentrate on their own areas of interest, making strict comparability impossible.

The uncertainties which remain are to identify the extent to which it is possible to influence small business dynamics and the subsequent impact upon the prosperity of an economy. At this stage we are able to highlight the factors which will influence these changes, but we are less confident about our ability to predict, in a particular country or region, the effectiveness of specific policy changes.

As pointed out earlier, we would not feel confident in applying even the provisional results here either to less developed countries, or to those emerging into a market economy from communist rule.

A more relevant consideration is the extent to which the factors influencing small business dynamics differ in the smaller Scandinavian countries or in the Netherlands, compared with, for example, the United States. We also know, at least from Dutch experience, that the trade cycle is a key factor in influencing changes, but this, too, may have a 'country size' effect.

It is our view that the next step in providing a better understanding of these matters is to conduct genuinely comparable international studies, in which both independent and dependent variables are measured in a comparable manner, and over similar periods of time.

REFERENCES

Acs, Z.J. (1984) *The Changing Structure of the US Economy: Lessons from the Steel Industry*, New York: Praeger.

Acs, Z.J. and Audretsch, D.B. (1988) 'Innovation in Large and Small firms: An Empirical Analysis', *American Economic Review* 78: 678–90.

Ashcroft, B., Love, J.H. and Malloy, E. (1990) 'New Firm Formation in the UK Countries, with Special Reference to Scotland', Fraser of Allander Institute, Paper 90/7.

Audretsch, D.B. (1991) 'New Firm Survival and the Technological Regime', *Review of Economics and Statistics* August 60(3): 441–51.

Bendick, M. and Egan, M. (1987) 'Transfer Payment Diversion for Small Business Development: British and French Experience', *Industrial and Labour Relations Review* July 40: 132–57.

Birley, S., Cromie, S. and Myers, A. (1991) 'Entrepreneurial Networks: Their Emergence in Ireland and Overseas', *International Small Business Journal* 9(4): 56–74.

Bolton Committee (1971) *'Report of the Committee of Inquiry on Small Firms'*, Cmnd 4811, London: HMSO.

Bradburd, R.M. and Ross, D.R. (1989) 'Can Small Firms Find and Defend Strategic Niches? A Test of the Porter Hypothesis', *Review of Economics and Statistics* 258–62.

Cuthbertson, K. and Hudson, J. (1990) 'The Determinants of Compulsory Liquidations in the UK 1972–1988', University of Newcastle upon Tyne.

Daly, M. (1991) 'VAT Registrations and Deregistrations in 1990', *Employment Gazette* November 579–88.

Johannisson, B. (1986) 'Network Strategies: Management Technology for Entrepreneurship and Change', *International Small Business Journal* 5(1): 19–30.

Johansson, B. and Karlsson, C. (1991) 'Technology Development and Regional Infrastructure', Paper presented at the 38th North-American Regional Science Association International meeting in New Orleans, November.

Johnson, P.S. (1989) 'Employment Change in the Small Establishment Sector in UK Manufacturing', *Applied Economics* 21: 251–60.

Keeble, D. and Wever, E. (1986) *New Firms and Regional Development in Europe*, London: Croom Helm.

Lane, S. and Schary, M. (1990) 'Understanding the Business Failure Rate', *Contemporary Policy Issues* October 9(4): 93–105.

Loveman, G. and Sengenberger, W. (1991) 'The Emergence of Small Scale Production: An International Comparison', *Small Business Economics* March 3(1): 1–38.

Lyons, B. (1993) 'Small Subcontractors in UK Engineering', *Small Business Economics* forthcoming.

Pavitt, Robson, M. and Townsend, J. (1987) 'The Size Distribution of Innovating Firms in the UK: 1945–83', *Journal of Industrial Economics* 35: 297–306.

Piore, M. and Sabel, C. (1984) *The Second Industrial Divide: Possibilities for Property*, New York: Basic Books.

Porter, M.E. (1980) *Competitive Strategy*, New York: Free Press.

Robson, M.T. (1991) 'A Survey of Recent Time Series Studies of Business Formations and Dissolutions in the United Kingdom', University of Newcastle upon Tyne (September).

Storey, D.J. and Johnson, S. (1987) *Job Generation and Labour Market Change*, London: Macmillan.

Wiklund, J. (1991) 'A Micro View of the Gnosjö Entrepreneurial Spirit', paper presented at workshop on 'Formation, Management and Organisation of Small and Medium Enterprises', Jönköping, Sweden (25–7 September).

Wright, M., Thompson, S., Chiplin, B. and Robbie, K. (1990) *Buy-outs and Buy-ins: New Strategies in Corporate Management*, London: Graham and Trotman.

L11 L16 E32   18-38

1 Small business developments in the long run and through the business cycle: lessons from the past in the Netherlands

Joop Vianen

INTRODUCTION

Is there a difference in the way business-cycle fluctuations affect the economic performance of small and medium-sized businesses compared with large companies? What impact does the business cycle have on such important economic variables as the employment and production of small and medium-sized enterprises? Does the small and medium-sized enterprise (SME) send out impulses that lead the economy to recovery or further into a downward spiral? This chapter will examine the relation between small-scale private enterprise and the business cycle. It will also consider the – partly related – question of the share of SMEs over the past thirty years. The empirical data presented will be for the Netherlands.

In their interesting essay about the structural development of small and medium-sized enterprises in some industrialized countries, Sengenberger, Loveman and Piore argue that 'The business cycle has almost certainly affected the size distribution, but the evidence does not favour an exclusive or dominant role for the business cycle'. Their argument rests on the following findings:

1   the higher employment shares have remained for small units well into the expansion in the 1980s;
2   the shift took place in countries with widely variant macro-economic conditions, such as Japan, the United Kingdom and Hungary;
3   the recent business cycle downturn was coincident with an institutional crisis. Therefore the coincidence of changes in the size structure with recession does not necessarily imply a stable historical response by the size structure to business cycle fluctuations.

(Sengenberger, Loveman and Piore 1990)

18

Apart from hinting that statistical errors may have distorted the figures, the authors suggest that the following factors may have contributed to the shift of employment to smaller production units in the last ten or twenty years: small-firm cost advantages; government and managerial liberalization; flexible specialization. The influence of these factors has not been thoroughly tested but none of them provide, alone or jointly, a comprehensive and accurate explanation for the movement towards small-scale enterprise.

The focus of this chapter is to relate the business cycle to the development of small- and large-scale private enterprises (LSEs) in the Netherlands. The structural position of SMEs over a longer period will also be considered. My main hypothesis is that through the phases of the business cycle, production and employment develop differently in small-scale and large-scale enterprises. The underlying arguments can be distinguished as:

1   Structural aspects:
   (a) market orientation;
   (b) supply relations;
   (c) cost structure.
2   Behavioural aspects:
   (a) labour adjustments;
   (b) price-setting.

Structural aspects

Market orientation

SMEs generally have different markets from large firms. They produce relatively more for the domestic markets of consumption goods, investment goods and suppliers' products and services, whereas large firms produce mainly for foreign markets (Table 1.1). This distinction is particularly clear in a small country such as the Netherlands. Their divergent market orientations can be explained partly, but not in full, by different sectoral compositions. Manufacturing, for example, supplies more consumption and investment goods to the domestic than to the foreign market.

The business cycle does shows synchronous fluctuations on the domestic and foreign markets. Hence, because of their divergent market orientation, small and large firms experience different cyclical effects on production and employment.

Table 1.1 Composition of sales by size class, the Netherlands, 1990

	SMEs* %	LSEs %
Domestic sales		
consumption	24	16
investments	17	8
intermediate	40	33
Foreign sales (exports)	19	43
Total	100	100

Source: EIM, Kleinschalig Ondernemen 1990, Zoetermeer
Note: *SMEs defined as private enterprises with less than 100 employees.

Supply relations

Another cause of differences in development between large and small firms can be the asymmetrical contractor–subcontractor (input–output) relationship (see Table 1.2). A growth impulse reaching SMEs through LSEs will be different from one initiated in SMEs. In other words, the input–output coefficients are different. For the Netherlands, the average input–output coefficients between SMEs and LSEs are approximately known. If the production of LSEs increases, the direct production effect for SMEs through intermediate deliveries is less (11.4 per cent) than where the production of SMEs

Table 1.2 Input–output coefficients for SMEs and LSEs in the Netherlands, 1990

	SMEs	LSEs	Non-private enterprises
SME	17.3	11.4	8.6
LSE	12.5	10.4	13.5
Non-private enterprises	6.8	8.2	8.6
Total intermediate inputs	36.6	30.0	30.7
Import/value added	63.4	70.0	69.3
Total production	100	100	100

Source: EIM

increases (17.3 per cent). The same holds for the direct effects on the intermediate deliveries of the LSE.

The above data enable us to examine how far the development of SMEs in the Netherlands differed from large firms in the 1980s throughout the full range of the business cycle (see pp. 23–9). Before that, however, I shall sketch the structural development of small and medium-sized enterprises over a somewhat longer period.

Cost structure

The nature of the cost structure of small enterprises is another reason why cyclical influences could affect SMEs differently from LSEs. Table 1.3 shows SMEs' production is characterized by relatively high wage costs and profit margins, but they spend less than large firms on raw materials, semi-finished products and other products and services supplied to them.. Through the phases of the business cycle, prices of supply goods and services and wage and interest rates show different patterns, and the expenses and sales prices of large and small companies will vary accordingly.

Table 1.3 Percentage cost structure by size class in the Netherlands, 1990

	SMEs %	LSEs %
Intermediate consumption	51	58
Wages	27	25
Other exploitation costs	8	8
Interest	2	1
Profit	12	8
	100	100

Source: EIM

Behavioural aspects

Labour adjustment

Thurik and Kleijweg (1985) showed that, in either upswings or downswings, small firms tend to be slower than large firms to adjust their labour capacity to production. Consequently, SME labour productivity drops quickly during the downswing and rises more rapidly during the upswing. Taylor (1974) suggested that the following may explain SMEs' sluggish adjustment.

(a) legal constraints on dismissing employees;
(b) technical constraints arising from the indivisibility of functions;
(c) the need for entrepreneurs to keep dismissal and recruitment expenses within strict limits;
(d) entrepreneurs' aversion to laying off their employees, with whom they share a strong sense of commitment;
(e) the psychological effects of lay-offs on the motivation of the remaining employees;
(f) the entrepreneurs' lack of insight into future developments.

Price-setting

Small, autonomous entrepreneurs, having relatively low capital costs, and mostly operating in highly competitive markets, can exhibit more flexible price-setting behaviour than larger firms. By not having to enter into time-consuming internal consultations, they are more able to respond to opportunities in a contracting market, and adjust their prices to reflect cost changes. Furthermore, lower overhead costs enable small entrepreneurs to implement price reductions earlier than large companies, without immediately risking serious losses.

On average, small firm profit margins are higher than those of larger firms. This means that, in recessionary times, the small firm is able to cut margins and hence prices sharply, in order to survive, even if this means a severe cut in income to the business owner. Several investigations have shown that price-cost margins tend to be more pro-cyclical in concentrated, large-scale industries, than in deconcentrated, small-scale industries (Domowitz *et al.* 1986a, 1986b; Prince and Thurik 1992). In other words, during recessions profit margins have a tendency to rise, especially in the more concentrated sectors. So, when demand falls, sales prices will drop more slowly in the large-firm dominated sectors. On the other hand, when the economy picks up and demand increases, prices in high concentration sectors will rise less quickly, and will rise faster in the small-firm dominated sector.

This suggests that slow labour adjustment together with a flexible price policy lead to very low profitability in recession but in an upswing to higher profits.

LONG-TERM DEVELOPMENTS OF THE SIZE DISTRIBUTION OF FIRMS

As in several other countries, the Netherlands saw a revival of SMEs after the mid-1970s. In 1950, virtually 70 per cent of private sector employment was in small and medium-sized firms. This fell to nearly 55 per cent in the early 1970s, but rose slightly to 57 per cent by 1990. Admittedly, the increasing share of SMEs coincided with an increase in small companies' average size from 8.7 persons in 1963 to 9.2 in 1970. Since then, however, the increased number of companies have once more reduced their average sizes to 6.2 persons in 1990. this is not a spectacular growth, but it does obscure a significant rise in labour productivity and a corresponding concentration of production.

The above indices reflect several different developments. The first is a growth in sectors that are naturally small-scale, such as services and trade. On the other hand, a significant increase in concentration within the sectors has occurred, most notably within the retail trades. Overall, the share of small companies in private sector employment is still smaller than in 1960.

Small and medium-sized firms now take a similar contribution to the Dutch economy as they made in the 1950s and early 1960s. In the 1960–75 period it was the smallest firms (fewer than ten employees) where the greatest relative decline took place but, since that time, it is this group of firms which has shown the most rapid increase. New entrepreneurship, the increasing need for specialized products and services, the technical opportunities for creating smaller production units, and the growing interest in subcontracting, are some of the factors that have stimulated small-scale enterprise.

However, some SME sectors show an opposite movement. In manufacturing, SMEs are expanding their market share, but in the retail trades SMEs are losing ground to a proliferation of chains with many establishments. Here the firms are large, but the establishments are small.

A tendency towards larger units can also be observed in the increasingly important business services sector. Mergers, takeovers, and strong autonomous growth are occurring in many branches of business services. Software houses, accountancy and organization consultants are sectors where concentration has increased sharply – particularly the creation of cross-national groupings.

Shift-and-share analysis can be used to distinguish the effects of sectoral developments from those of the enlargement of scale or the concentration or deconcentration within the sectors.

The so-called sector effect indicates what the difference in employment growth between SMEs and all private enterprise (SMEs + LSEs) would have been if the sectoral shifts only were taken into account, and the changing scales neglected. The scale effect indicates the difference between SMEs and overall private enterprise if the sectoral shifts were neglected and only scale modifications or the (de)concentrations within sectors considered.

As Table 1.4 shows, SME employment growth in the entire 1960–90 period was an average 0.2 per cent a year lower than that of all private enterprises.

Because of the unequal development of sectors, the sector effect for SMEs was 0.2 per cent a year. In other words, given a constant concentration in the sectors, SME employment would have increased by 0.2 per cent a year, but this was cancelled out by the effects of concentration and deconcentration in the sectors. If (de)concentration in the sectors was considered and differences in growth neglected, then SME employment would have been an average 0.4 per cent a year below that of total private enterprises.

In other words, taking the entire thirty-year period from 1960 to 1990 we find that the tendency to larger scale caused SME employment to grow slower than that of total private sector employment, but that shifts in sectoral structure prevented SMEs from a more serious shortfall.

Further examination of the table shows this shortfall occurred entirely in the 1960s, when the scale effect was slowing down the growth of SMEs; it was a period of sizeable scale enlargements in nearly all sectors. In the 1970s and 1980s, the scale effect was slightly positive, indicating an average scale reduction in the sectors. It will be recalled that scale enlargement was dominant in trade, whereas scale reduction took place in manufacturing and building.

With the exception of the period 1980–5, the sectoral shifts appear to have benefited SMEs with the decline of relatively large-scale industries and the proliferation of small shops and services being the main causes.

THE BUSINESS CYCLE IN THE 1980s

The 1980s was a decade of fluctuating economic fortunes in the Netherlands. In the early years of the decade, the country was hit by a major recession. After that the economy, if somewhat haltingly at first, experienced significant growth.

Table 1.4 Evolution of employment in SMEs: sector and scale effects 1960–90, the Netherlands (in annual percentages)*

	Employment growth, all enterprises (1)	Employment growth, SME (2)	Total effect, SME (3)=(2)−(1)	Sector effect	Sector effect
1960–5	1.3	0.3	−1.1	0.1	−1.2
1965–70	+0.0	−0.3	−0.2	0.1	−0.3
1970–5	−1.0	−0.9	0.1	0.1	0.0
1975–80	0.1	0.6	0.5	0.3	0.2
1980–5	−1.6	−1.6	0.0	−0.1	0.1
1985–90	2.4	2.5	0.2	0.1	0.1
1960–90	0.3	0.1	−0.2	0.2	−0.4

Source: EIM
Note: *Shift-and-share analysis is based on six sectors

The pattern was as follows:

1980–3	recession
1983–5	upswing
1985–7	slowdown
1987–90	continued upswing

The period 1985–7 was one in which the so-called third oil crisis affected the Dutch chemical exporting sector and EC policy damaged the agriculture sector. Moreover, the non-private sector, depending on government expenditures, contributed to a slowing of national growth rates. After 1987, however, growth improved again because of the increase in world trade, exports and private consumption expenditure.

The principal macro-economic indexes for this phase of the business cycle are presented in Table 1.5 (see also Annex).

For the Dutch economy, like most other West European countries, the 1980s began with a serious recession (see Annex), largely due to the sharp decline of world trade growth in the 1980–3 period. From then on, world trade gradually recovered, to reach a peak in 1985, and then continued to grow, but at a declining rate.

Production in the Netherlands is highly dependent on world trade. Thus the Dutch economy emerged from recession in 1983 because of the growth in exports. Only in 1985, when the growth of exports was already past its peak, did private consumption expenditure also begin to show significant growth.

Table 1.5 Macro-economic data for the Netherlands by cyclical phase, 1980–90 (average annual growth figures in percentages)

	1980–3	1983–5	1985–7	1987–90
World trade	−0.1	5.7	5.2	7.1
Production volume of enterprises	−0.4	3.3	1.5	3.8
Export volume	1.6	6.8	3.5	6.3
Volume of private consumption	−0.9	1.7	3.1	2.5
Volume of company's gross investments in fixed assets	−3.9	6.9	5.4	6.1

Source: CPB (Centraal Planbureau)/EIM

From 1985–7, the export performance of Dutch private firms was slightly below that both of the previous years, and the volume of world trade. Nineteen eighty-eight was again a peak year for the growth of exports, followed by a slight reduction. Private consumption expenditure continued to grow after a slow-down in 1988.

Under the influence of alternating growth in the export sector and in the domestic market, the growth of private investment in fixed assets accelerated gradually from 1983 to 1986, when a steep decline set it. Nineteen eighty-eight was once more a year of record growth, ut by the end of the decade growth was clearly falling.

A tentative conclusion may be that the Dutch economy receives alternate impulses from the evolution of world trade and exports and from that of private consumption, impulses that are reinforced by investment.

Figure 1.1, reproducing the evolution of production of all enterprises (private and non-private) through the entire period, clearly reflects the fluctuations of the Dutch economy. As will be shown in the next section, the fluctuations of Dutch SMEs are markedly different.

SMALL AND MEDIUM-SIZED ENTERPRISES AND THE BUSINESS CYCLE IN THE 1980s

General

It has already been shown that in the 1980s employment grew slightly faster in SMEs than in large firms. Table 1.6 illustrates that in those

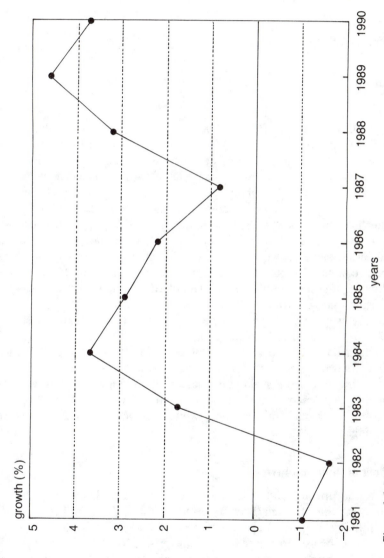

Figure 1.1 Volume of real production growth, all enterprises, business cycle indicator

Source: EIM.

Table 1.6 Some key figures for SMEs and LSEs 1980–90 (in annual percentages)

	SMEs	*LSEs*
Employment (in labour years)	0.5	0.3
Production	2.5	2.7
Labour productivity	2.0	2.4
Number of companies	2.3	1.0

Source: EIM

years employment (measured in labour years) grew by an annual average of 0.5 per cent in small firms and by 0.3 per cent in large. However, because large companies increased labour productivity faster, their output grew faster than that of SMEs. Thus, between 1980 and 1990, the production volume of large firms grew by an annual average of 2.7 per cent, compared with 2.5 per cent in SMEs.

The literature has paid little attention to the divergent development of employment and production in SMEs and large firms. As noted earlier, Sengenberger *et al.* (1990), looking only at employment figures, conclude that SMEs are increasingly important. Dutch production figures, unlike employment data, however show a decreasing share contributed by SMEs.

So, are we really observing a 're-emergence of the small enterprise'? In an international context, it is vital also to analyse production data by size of firm. But how should we interpret the persistently trailing development of SME labour productivity?

The 1980s did see a striking increase in the number of firms, and particularly of small firms; employment per firm was decreasing, mostly amongst the smaller ones, while production per firm was increasing.

Production and employment

Tracing the upward and downward movements, as sketched in the previous section, through the sub-periods, Table 1.7 shows that small firms follow the general cyclical patterns far less closely than large ones. In contrast to large-scale enterprises, SMEs' production declined during the recession. In the upswing after 1983, growth was fast in SMEs, accelerating through the next slowdown (1985–7), and levelling off in the period of continued recovery. In sum, after the

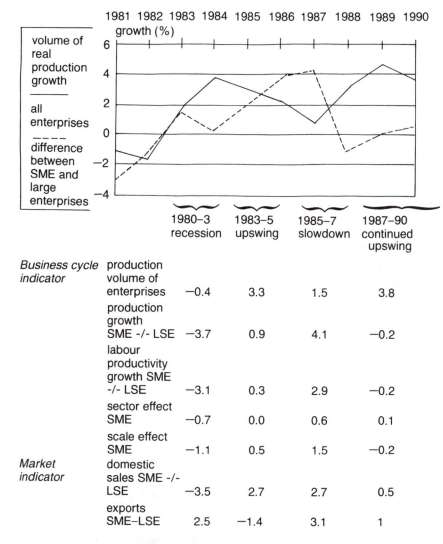

Figure 1.2 Comparisons of the developments in SMEs and LSEs in separate phases of the business cycle

1983 recovery, SMEs developed contrary to the economic cycle rather than following it. Large-scale production reflected cyclical movements much more closely.

The pattern of SME employment is closely associated with that of production, in the sense that in the first recession (1980-3) SMEs

Table 1.7 SMEs and LSEs in the Netherlands, by cyclical stage, 1980–90
(real development in percentages)

	1980–3 recession	*1983–5 upswing*	*1985–7 slowdown*	*1987–90 continued upswing*
Production				
SMEs	−3.0	4.1	6.0	4.9
LSEs	0.7	3.2	1.9	5.1
Employment				
SMEs	−3.6	1.4	3.0	2.5
LSEs	−3.0	0.8	1.9	2.5
Labour productivity				
SMEs	0.7	2.7	2.9	2.4
LSEs	3.8	2.4	0	2.6
Gross investment in fixed assets				
SMEs	−7.9	19.7	8.9	4.8
LSEs	−3.2	14.8	6.5	0.2
Wage rate				
SMEs	4.7	2.0	3.0	2.7
LSEs	5.7	1.4	2.0	2.2
Wage costs per unit of production				
SMEs	3.4	−0.2	0.9	0.7
LSEs	1.8	−1.1	2.0	−0.3

Source: EIM

were more able than LSEs to maintain employment. During that period, the increase in labour productivity of SMEs was well below that of LSEs and also lower than its own average throughout the 1983–90 period. Emerging from the recession, SMEs then increased their labour-productivity much faster than LSEs. This continued until 1987, throughout the second downswing. These labour productivity figures, and consequently the employment creation, are slightly distorted by the fact that some temporary labour in small firms is hired through employment agencies. For administrative reasons this employment is not allocated to the SMEs, but to the employment agencies themselves, which are LSEs. This serves to under-estimate employment in SMEs and so inflate labour productivity figures.

Nevertheless, this is unlikely to have a major effect.

The first part of this chapter suggested some size-related factors that could explain the divergence of labour productivity in small and large firms. To those, we will now add some explanatory factors of a more macro-economic nature. For instance, the above-average increase in SME labour productivity between 1983 and 1987 is easier to understand if we consider that during this period SMEs invested relatively more than LSEs in fixed assets. Moreover, from 1983 onwards, wages appear to have risen faster in SMEs than in LSEs, which have encouraged the substitution of capital for labour and thus investment, a development that again boosted labour productivity in SMEs. Even so, in spite of the growth of SME labour productivity, wage costs per unit of product still exceed those in LSEs.

Looking at the cyclical movements of SMEs alone, we observe a new decline in labour productivity growth in small firms from 1987 onwards. In the final years of the decade, labour productivity growth, as well as production and employment growth in SMEs, were lower than in the previous sub-period. As in the early 1980s, the SME is protecting the economy from the rates of unemployment that would correspond to decreasing production growth. On the other hand, during economic upswings, the SME tends to be slightly lagging in the creation of job opportunities. This suggests that SMEs act as a 'built-in employment stabilizer' of employment through economic fluctuations.

Sectoral and scale developments

Throughout the 1980s SMEs showed a slower growth in production, but a faster rate of employment creation than LSEs. Sectoral shifts during the 1980s were, on balance, to the disadvantage of the smaller firms. Both in terms of production and employment, the sector effect is almost nil. In terms of employment, the entire period shows a slight scale reduction, in keeping with that of the previous decade. In terms of production, on the contrary, scale increases are observed.

During the first recession (1980–3), shifts in the overall sectoral structure as well as increased concentration within the sectors led to distinct scale enlargement in terms of both production and employment. The two effects were mutually reinforcing. The second phase after the recession had a positive effect on production as well as on employment in SMEs. The changing sectoral structure also benefited SMEs.

Scale effects on production and employment were generally

Table 1.8 Production and employment in SMEs and LSEs (total effect),
sector and scale effects by cyclical phase, 1980–90*

	1980–3 recession	1983–5 upswing	1985–7 slowdown	1987–90 continued upswing
Production: total effect	−1.8	0.5	2.1	−0.1
Sector effect	−0.7	0.0	0.6	0.1
Scale effect	−1.1	0.5	1.5	−0.2
Employment: total effect	−0.2	0.3	0.5	0.0
Sector effect	−0.1	−0.0	0.1	0.0
Scale effect	−0.1	0.3	0.4	0.0

Source: EIM
Note: *Shift-and-share analysis is based on six sectors

positive following the recession. As the economy recovered scale
reduction occurred, and increased during the next period of halting
growth and slight decline of the economy. It will be recalled that in
that period (1985–7) SMEs did not suffer a downturn, but that the
slight overall decline of the Dutch economy was induced by the oil
crisis, the production controls on agriculture and government policy
designed to reduce the budget deficit.

During the final years of the decade, a period of ongoing growth,
both the sector and the scale effects were diminishing. Due to new
sectoral shifts, less advantageous to SMEs, their position stabilized, as
did scale developments within sectors.

In terms of employment, scale developments were approaching the
limit of deconcentration. In terms of production, scales were
increasing rather than contracting with those latter years. A certain
parallel seems to exist with the recession of 1980–3: a negative scale
effect and a smaller sector effect than in periods of growth.

What conclusion should be drawn from these observations? Does
concentration occur in decreasing and stagnating growth periods
because of both sector and scale effects? Or are we, in fact, witnessing
the reversal of the scale-reduction process that began in the early
1970s – as described earlier in this chapter – into a continuation of
the long-term concentration trend from the 1950s and 1960s?

Some evidence is provided by the wave of mergers and take-overs
that took place in the second half of the 1980s. The increased
importance of national and international mergers and take-overs may

be considered as anticipating the further integration of the European economy, or may be closely tied to the phase of the business cycle.

To answer this question we need to address whether the concentration of business is initiated by the business cycle or by structural developments in the market, or whether these effects are cumulative.

MARKET DEVELOPMENTS IN THE PERIOD 1980–90

General remarks

The previous sections described the development of small and medium-sized enterprises in the long run as well as through different phases of the business cycle. As pointed out in the introduction, it is to be expected that SMEs and LSEs would evolve along different lines because they address different markets with different structures. The SME is oriented mostly to the domestic market, whilst larger firms sell much of their production abroad. We have observed how, after the recession of the early 1980s, the economy received alternate demand impulses from exports and private consumption.

This section considers how market developments have influenced the sales of smaller firms compared with larger ones. Sales are defined here as the difference between sold and purchased trade goods. In the trade sectors, the concept of sales is closely associated with that of gross margin. Sales data as defined above are always nominal, which means we cannot analyse how far prices and volumes develop differently in different markets.

In the 1980s, the sales of Dutch private companies increased by 218,400 million guilders. SMEs accounted for 47.5 per cent which is a higher share than in 1980. Indeed, in terms of sales, SMEs' market share increased from 44.1 per cent in 1980 to 45.3 per cent in 1990. This increase contrasts with the reduction of their share in production volume as already discussed, because of price effects. In short, prices which small firms were able to charge in the marketplace grew faster than those which large firms were able to charge.

The increase in the sales of all private enterprises (218,400 million guilders) was largely achieved on the domestic market, where a rise of 141,200 million guilders occurred, 65 per cent of total expansion. However, the share of foreign sales in total sales increased from 30 per cent in 1980 to 32 per cent in 1990.

SMEs benefited more from the domestic market than LSEs. They increased domestic sales by 76,600 million guilders, accounting for

Table 1.9 Sales increase 1980–90, by size class and submarket (billions of Dutch guilders)

	SMEs	LSEs	Total private enterprises
	%	%	%
Total sales	103.8 (47.5)	114.6 (52.5)	218.4 (100)
Domestic sales	76.6 (54.2)	64.6 (45.8)	141.2 (100)
Exports	27.2 (35.3)	50.0 (64.7)	77.2 (100)

Source: EIM

54.2 per cent of the domestic market increase. Thus, SMEs consolidated their position in that market: their share increasing from 52 per cent in 1980 to 54 in 1990.

On the foreign market the changes are different. Here, SMEs could 'only' claim 35.2 per cent the market increase. This is, however, far more than their share in total exports in 1980. Large firms benefited most from the expanding foreign market. Nevertheless, SMEs more than doubled their total exports: from 27,100 million guilders in 1980 to 54,300 million in 1990. Large firms increased their total sales abroad by about one-half to 151,400 million guilders in 1990. All this resulted eventually in a strengthened foreign-market position for SMEs. Their share of 21 per cent in 1980 had increased to 26 per cent by 1990.

The market and the phases of the business cycle

The fluctuations observed in production were reflected in sales, except that total nominal sales showed no decline during the second recession and continued to rise. SME sales showed persistent growth after 1983, virtually repeating the pattern of production growth.

It can be seen that the domestic market declined during the recession while the foreign market grew, albeit slowly. The second decrease of production growth (1985–7) was mostly due to falling sales growth on the foreign market where large firms performed less well.

Except for the last three years of the study period, SMEs saw their growth on the domestic market steadily increase, and between 1985 and 1987 they managed to escape or slow down the decline of the economy by maintaining high growth in the domestic market and by

Table 1.10 Percentage increase in sales volume by submarket, size class and cyclical phase, 1980–90

	1980–3 recession	1983–5 upswing	1985–7 slowdown	1987–90 continued upswing
Sales: total	−1.1	3.2	4.2	4.6
SMEs	−2.6	3.5	5.6	4.5
LSEs	0.2	3.0	3.2	4.7
Domestic sales: total	−2.0	2.0	4.0	3.8
SMEs	−3.7	3.3	5.3	4.0
LSEs	−0.2	0.6	2.6	3.5
Exports: total	1.2	5.7	4.6	6.3
SMEs	3.1	4.6	7.0	7.0
LSEs	0.6	6.0	3.9	6.0

Source: EIM

achieving a satisfactory 7 per cent growth on the foreign market. During the same period, LSEs were performing badly on both markets.

SMEs achieved a satisfactory growth in the export market of 3.1 per cent in the first downswing, much higher than larger firms. At that time, the depressed position of the United States adversely affected large firms. The depressed domestic market may also have played a role, forcing small entrepreneurs to enter foreign markets.

After an initial drop in domestic sales, from 1984 onwards, SMEs benefited from stronger domestic demand. This is the key for SMEs, which sell three-quarters of their output domestically. SMEs also benefited because during the period 1985–7 demand for final products increased more strongly than for basic products. At the same time, larger firms were faced both with a weak domestic market and only modest demand in its foreign markets. This meant lower sales and production growth among large companies and led to a declining business cycle.

To summarize: the export market caused the economy to recover in the periods 1983–5 and 1987–90, whereas the disappointing export growth in both recessions had a depressing effect on the economy. When the domestic market also slowed during the first downswing, this clearly led to recessionary conditions. Between 1985 and 1987 the domestic market continued growing even though there was a fall in exports. Hence, a major decline of the economy was avoided.

Understanding market developments is essential in charting the development of small and medium-sized enterprises. Because of its strong dependence on the domestic market, the position of the SME in the first recession period was difficult, with both domestic and foreign demand declining. With the subsequent recovery of domestic demand, SMEs flourished, and through exports even managed to compensate for the declining international trade in the period 1985-7.

Large companies, which are much more dependent on foreign demand, fluctuated in line with international trade, but managed to dampen the second slowdown because of a strong domestic market.

CONCLUSIONS

In the Netherlands, private enterprise has for a long time exhibited a deconcentration of employment. More and more labour is employed in small firms. This is partly because of a stronger growth of small-scale sectors and partly because of a deconcentration within sectors. In terms of production, however, the 1980s showed a concentration in favour of larger firms. Hence, the share of SMEs in production diminished, although their share in employment continued the increase which began in the 1970s.

Data on the development of SMEs and LSEs suggest the two groups follow very different patterns through the business cycle, and over time. Production and labour productivity in SMEs also vary greatly from one cyclical phase to another. SMEs were hit harder in recession, but in the upswing performed better than LSEs. Even when economic growth slackened off somewhat between 1985 and 1987, production in SMEs continued growing as before.

The better performance of SMEs is partly attributable to sectoral shifts that were favourable to small firms. Thus the sectors in which SMEs are well represented (wholesale trades, business services, transport) were ones which grew faster after the recession.

Concentration within sectors (the scale effect) occurred most notably during the recession, but also recurred to a lesser extent in the final stage of general economic upswing, but with slightly decreasing growth in SMEs.

More sophisticated econometric tests as well as a longer time series are necessary for a better understanding of the relationship between concentration and the business cycle. Nevertheless, some insights can be gleaned from the existing data. Sales markets seem an important element for understanding the different production growth of large and small firms. Indeed, in terms of sales, SMEs obtained an increased share in the domestic market in the years of growing domestic demand, that is, between 1983 and 1990. On the foreign market, too, SMEs acquired a greater share, except from 1983 to 1985 when a foreign trade was stimulated by demand in the United States, a market to which SMEs have only limited access.

We have observed that entrepreneurial behaviour as well as market developments influence the differential performance of SMEs and LSEs through the business cycle. In terms of employment, the growth of labour productivity among small firms dampens cyclical fluctuations. The growth of labour productivity slows when SMEs face declining production growth, and accelerates when production growth increases. There seems to be no such relationship for large firms.

Taking aspects of the market structure of SMEs and entrepreneurial behaviour into consideration, it suggests SMEs act as a 'built-in stabilizer' for employment for three reasons. First, SMEs are strongly linked to domestic markets; second, they export more in times of recession and third, they hoard labour during downturns.

APPENDIX

Table A1.1 Some macro-data of the Dutch economy (percentages of volume developments)

	Volume of world trade	Production of private sector	Export volume	Volume of private consumption	Growth investment of companies in fixed assets
1980	2.0	0.7	1.0	0.0	−1.6
1981	0.3	−1.1	0.6	−2.5	−11.5
1982	−2.5	−1.7	−0.5	−1.2	−3.5
1983	1.8	1.7	4.6	0.9	3.3
1984	8.5	3.7	7.6	1.0	5.0
1985	3.0	2.9	6.0	2.4	8.7
1986	4.0	2.2	3.9	2.7	9.0
1987	6.4	0.8	3.0	3.5	1.8
1988	9.0	3.2	8.2	1.3	10.1
1989	7.1	4.6	5.2	2.5	4.2
1990	5.3	3.7	5.5	3.7	4.3

Source: CPB

REFERENCES

Domowitz, I., Hubbard, R.G. and Peterson, B.S. (1986a) 'Business Cycles and the Relationship Between Concentration and Price Cost Margins', *Rand Journal of Economics* 17(1).
—— (1986b) 'The Intertemporal Stability of the Concentration–Margin–Relationship', *Journal of Industrial Economics* 35(1).
Prince, Y.M. and Thurik, A.R. (1992) 'Price Cost Margins in Dutch Manufacturing: Effects of Concentration, Business Cycle and International Trade', *De Economist* 140(3): 310–35.
Sengenberger, W., Loveman, G.W. and Piore, M.J. (1990) *The Regeneration of Small Enterprises: Industrial Restructuring in Industrialised Countries*, Geneva: ILO.
Taylor, J. (1974) *Unemployment and Wage Inflation*, Harlow: Longman.
Thurik, A.R. and Kleijweg, A. (1985) *Labour Productivity and Cyclical Effects in the Retail Industry*, Zoetermeer: EIM.

ACKNOWLEDGEMENTS

With thanks to Mr G. Elsendoorn, Mr W. Verhoeven and Mr A. Wennekers for their statisticai work and their useful comments on earlier drafts.

DISCUSSION

David B. Audretsch

Several important studies have identified a dramatic shift in economic activity away from large enterprises and towards small firms which took place during the 1970s and 1980s. Both Loveman and Sengenberger (1991) and Acs and Audretsch (1992) find that this shift occurred not just in a single country but in virtually every developed industrial nation. What are the factors underlying this shift? While Brock and Evans (1989) proposed five major hypotheses, only preliminary and anecdotal evidence has been available to date. An additional hypothesis is proposed – and tested – by Professor Vianen. He argues that the firm-size distribution is not neutral with respect to macro-economic fluctuations. Rather, the presence of small firms is hypothesized to be counter-cyclical. Small firms are expected to play a greater role in the economy during economic downturns and a lesser role during economic expansions.

Professor Vianen proposes a model where small firms essentially adjust prices more easily than their larger counterparts when confronted by demand fluctuations. This leads to the inference that sales fluctuate more for large companies than for small enterprises. Thus, over the business cycle, small firms can be characterized as having relatively flexible prices and constant output, while large companies tend to have relatively fixed prices and fluctuating output. This model leads to the prediction that small firms play a counter-cyclical role over the business cycle.

An alternative theory of the role of small firms was proposed by Mills and Schumann (1985), who built upon the arguments of Stigler (1939) and Marschak and Nelson (1962) that small firms serve a pro-cyclical function by absorbing fluctuations in demand. According to the theory of flexibility, increases in demand stimulate a wave of new-firm startups, while periods of recession and economic downturns are responsible for small-firm failures.

Professor Vianen finds evidence that during the 1980–3 recession the reduction in employment was greater in small firms than in large enterprises. And, while small-firm production fell, the output of large firms actually rose. Similarly, during the 1983–5 upswing, both small-firm employment and production rose more rapidly than was the case for large enterprises. Thus, the evidence is consistent with the pro-cyclical role of small firms predicted by the model of Mills and Schumann (1985) and inconsistent with the counter-cyclical role in the model proposed by Professor Vianen.

Thus, Professor Vianen appears to be correct in arguing that the firm-size distribution is not neutral with respect to the business cycle. Further, the pro-cyclical role of small enterprises over the business cycle may constitute one factor explaining the observed shift away from large enterprises and towards smaller firms. Virtually every developed nation experienced economic expansion between 1983 and 1990. An increased presence of small firms as a result of this prolonged expansion phase of the business cycle is certainly consistent with the findings of Professor Vianen as well as the theory proposed by Mills and Schumann (1985) and Stigler (1939). Since several of the leading industrial economies are now experiencing economic downturns, a decreased presence of small firms would be predicted. Future empirical research, along the lines undertaken by Professor Vianen, would make an important contribution either in verifying the generality of these findings, or else suggesting that they are specific to the special case of the 1980s.

REFERENCES

Acs, Z.J. and Audretsch, D.B. (eds) (1992) *Small Firms and Entrepreneurship: An East–West Perspective,* Cambridge: Cambridge University Press.

Brock, W.A. and Evans, D.S. (1989) 'Small Business Economics,' *Small Business Economics* 1(1) 7–20.

Loveman, G. and Sengenberger, W. (1991) 'The Re-emergence of Small-Scale Production: An International Perspective,' *Small Business Economics* 3(1): 1–38.

Marschak, T. and Nelson, R.R. (1962) 'Flexibility, Uncertainty and Economic Theory,' *Metroeconomica,* April–August–December 4 42–60.

Mills, D.E. and Schumann, L. (1985) 'Industry Structure with Fluctuating Demand,' *American Economic Review* September 75 758–67.

Stigler, G.J. (1939) 'Production and Distribution in the Short Run,' *Journal of Political Economy* June 47 305–27.

2   New-firm formation activity in US manufacturing

David Audretsch

INTRODUCTION

David Storey (1991) recently pointed out that a dichotomy exists in the literature that attempts to explain the determinants of new-firm formation. One approach has focused on the organization of the industry and examined the effect that market structure exerts on the ability of firms to enter an industry. A particular emphasis of the industrial organization approach has been on identifying those characteristics of market structure that either impede or facilitate entry.[1]

The alternative approach focuses on economic conditions in the macro-economic labour market.[2] Of particular interest to the labour market approach is the relative importance of push and pull factors in determining the aggregate amount of formation activity. That is, several studies (Evans and Leighton 1990; Meager 1992) have identified unemployed workers as having a greater propensity for becoming self-employed than do employed workers. This would support the push thesis that new-firm formation is especially influenced by a large supply of unemployed workers. However, it is precisely during high periods of cyclical unemployment where the pull factors – that is, the demand for additional goods and services – are at their weakest. The recent work by Storey (1991) and Meager (1992) demonstrates that a heated debate is emerging within the labour literature regarding the relative importance of these push and pull factors.

As Storey (1991) observes, the cross-section empirical model generally used in the industrial organization approach is unable to capture the impact that macro-economic fluctuations exert on entry. In addition, Storey correctly points out that the bulk of studies in industrial organization do not, in fact, examine new-firm formation, or gross entry by new firms, but rather focus on what is known as net entry, or the difference in the number of firms existing in a given industry over a certain time period. It is quite conceivable that an industry could have a negative amount of net entry, even if the number of new-firm startups was high, as long as the number of enterprises exiting in the market was even higher. Only a handful of studies have distinguished gross entry from net entry (Dunne, Roberts and Samuelson 1988; Acs and Audretsch 1989b; Baldwin and Gorecki 1991 and Siegfried and Evans 1992) and even fewer (Audretsch 1991; Revelli and Tenga 1989; and Johnson 1989) have been able to differentiate new-firm startups from all new entrants (which includes diversified entry by existing enterprises).

On the other hand, as Storey (1991) also makes clear, by aggregating new-firm formation at the macro-economic level and examining the impact of the business cycle on start-up activity, the labour market approach generally ignores the role that industry-specific characteristics play in facilitating and deterring entry. Only Yamawaki (1991) has been able to incorporate both the labour market and industrial organization approaches by using a pooled, cross-section, time series estimation model, but he was limited to focusing on net entry in Japan, and due to data limitations was unable to shed any light on either gross entry or, more importantly, on new-firm formation.[3]

The purpose of this chapter is to provide the first study examining new-firm formation that combines both the industrial organization and labour market approaches. By doing so, I am able to shed considerable light not only on the push–pull debate within the labour market literature, but also on identifying the role that technology and scale economies play in shaping the extent of new-firm formation within an industry. A model relating new-firm formation to both the macro-economic and micro-economic environments is introduced in the second section. In the third section the method used to measure new-firm formation is explained. Empirical results are provided in the fourth section and a summary and conclusion are made in the final one. The empirical evidence suggests that the pull factors exert a stronger influence on new-firm formation in US manufacturing than do the push factors. Macro-economic expansion apparently serves as a greater catalyst for new-firm formation than does the greater supply of unemployed workers during an economic downturn. While scale economies and a high capital intensity clearly deter new-firm startups, the effect of the technological environment is somewhat more ambiguous. Industries which are highly innovative are not generally hospitable to new-firm startups. However, new-firm activity seems to be promoted in those markets where small enterprises are particularly innovative.

A MODEL OF NEW-FIRM FORMATION

Each agent in the economy is assumed to confront a decision between employment with an existing firm, in which case (s)he receives a wage, or starting his or her own new firm. As Evans and Jovanovic (1989), Evans and Leighton (1989) and Blanchflower and Oswald (1990) argue, this entrepreneurial choice is essentially made by comparing the expected profits accruing from the new startup, P, with the wage earned from employment, W. The likelihood of starting a new firm, pr(E), is a monotonic function of the gap between P and W.

$$pr(E) = f(P - W) \tag{1}$$

There are essentially two ways for a new startup to operate. The first is to replicate the product and production technology currently used by the incumbent firms in the market. The alternative is to innovate, either by offering a new product or else by producing the existing product using a new production technology. In the first case, the difference between P and W should be directly influenced by the business cycle. During periods of expansion both P and W will rise, but as the peak approaches, W may rise less rapidly, reflecting a decline in the marginal product of labour as the incumbent enterprises approach full capacity. Conversely, it is a well-established stylized fact that during an economic downturn, wages tend to be more rigid than prices (Freeman 1989). That is, the gap between P and W will tend to narrow during a recession. Thus, there is a smaller likelihood that any given agent will opt for the entrepreneurial decision while demand is falling than when it is growing.

However, due to labour market rigidities, the growing number of unemployed during a recession face limited or even no wage opportunities. The gap between expected profits and wages, which are effectively substituted by any public support that can be obtained, may actually be at its greatest for unemployed workers confronting dismal employment prospects. In this case, new-firm startups may be triggered by a large army of unemployed workers.

These two influences represent the pull and push determinants of new-firm formation. Notice that the pull determinants are essentially pro-cyclical, whereas the push determinants are counter-cyclical.

In the second case, an agent has an idea for a potential innovation. The inventor of the idea can choose between remaining at or joining an incumbent enterprise, or else starting up a new firm. The inventor appraises the economic value of the potential innovation for the incumbent enterprise, $V(i)$, to be the difference between firm profitability if the innovation is realized, $R(i)$, and profitability in the absence of implementing the innovation, R

$$V(i) = R(i) - R \qquad (2)$$

The inventor would therefore expect the wage from the firm to approach $V(i)$. While the inventor appraises the potential innovation to have a market value of $V(i)$, the decision maker of the incumbent enterprise may have a different valuation. Because of either imperfect or asymmetric information combined with a positive economic cost of transacting information, the firm decision maker may evaluate the profitability gained by the firm from the innovation differently from that evaluated by the innovator, say $R(i+\theta)$. Notice that θ represents a wedge in the appraisal of the economic value of the innovation between the inventor and the firm decision maker.

Substituting into equation 2, the incumbent enterprise would presumably be willing to pay a wage to the innovator, $W(i)$, of

$$W(i) = R(i+\theta) - R = V(i+\theta) \qquad (3)$$

The likelihood of the inventor starting his/her own firm is therefore negatively related to the divergence between $W(i)$ and the expected value of the entrepreneurial startup

$$Pr(E) = f(P - V(i+\theta) - V(i)) \qquad (4)$$

P, or between $W(i)$ and the expected profits of the new firm the entrepreneur starts, which are based on the difference between output, q, times price, p, minus the average cost of producing q units of output, $c(q)$, times the amount of output produced, or

$$P = (p^*q) - (c(q)^*q) \qquad (5)$$

Assuming that the market price equals the average cost for firms that have attained the minimum efficient scale (MES) level of output, c^*

$$P = q(c^* - c(q)) \qquad (6)$$

One of the few stylized facts regarding new-firm startups is that they tend to be operate at a remarkably small scale of output. For example, in my 1991 study I found that about 95 per cent of the new-firm startups in US manufacturing in 1986 had fewer than fifty employees. One reason for this is undoubtedly the high cost of capital confronting new-firm startups compared to incumbent enterprises (Dunkelberg and Cooper 1990). If a relatively low start-up size, q, is assumed, then P will be particularly reduced by high values of c*. That is, the expected profitability of new firms will tend to be less in the presence of scale economies and other factors elevating the MES level of output.

This model suggests that the inventor is confronted with the choice of essentially trading the potential innovation to an existing firm for a wage, or else starting his/her own firm. If the technological conditions are such that the decision maker of the firm will tend to have a substantially different evaluation of the market value of the potential innovation than does the innovator, and if scale economies do not play a particularly important role in the industry, then the expected profitability from starting a new firm will appear to be more attractive than the wage alternative.

On the other hand, if the technological conditions are such that the appraisal of the economic value of the potential innovation converges between the inventor and the decision maker, and if substantial scale economies exist in the industry, then the wage alternative should be relatively attractive, resulting in less firm formation activity.

MEASUREMENT ISSUES

New-firm formation is measured using the Small Business Data Base (SBDB) compiled by the US Small Business Administration. The SBDB is derived from the Dun and Bradstreet market identifier file, which provides a virtual census on about 4.5 million US business establishments every other year between 1976 and 1986.[4] It should be emphasized that the SBDB has been adjusted from the original Dun and Bradstreet files.[5]

The dependent variable to be explained in this study is the number of new-firm startups in each four-digit standard industrial classification (SIC) industry for alternate years between 1976 and 1986. While there are over four hundred four-digit SIC industries, the annual number of new-firm startups is aggregated to major manufacturing sectors for presentation purposes and shown in Table 2.1. The share of the total number of enterprises in the sector accounted for by new-firm startups is listed in parentheses.

It is clear from Table 2.1 that, despite the relatively high degree of aggregation, firm formation activity clearly varies considerably across manufacturing sectors. Equally striking, firm formation activity varies

Table 2.1 New-firm startups by industrial sector[a]

	1976	1978	1980	1982	1984	1986
Food	474 (2.53)	481 (2.67)	374 (2.15)	209 (1.22)	480 (2.79)	535 (3.09)
Textiles and apparel	1,172 (4.03)	1,254 (4.20)	854 (2.95)	491 (1.69)	1,026 (3.41)	992 (3.34)
Lumber and furniture	1,325 (3.71)	1,375 (3.70)	868 (2.28)	425 (1.12)	1,060 (2.75)	1,106 (2.79)
Paper	126 (2.97)	191 (4.24)	101 (2.20)	50 (1.11)	149 (3.19)	152 (3.15)
Chemicals	322 (2.95)	390 (3.52)	284 (2.54)	164 (1.45)	332 (2.85)	335 (2.83)
Industrial	91 (3.62)	99 (3.76)	98 (3.69)	41 (1.55)	85 (3.12)	84 (3.09)
Drugs and medicinals	34 (2.75)	54 (4.47)	22 (1.82)	26 (2.11)	48 (3.60)	49 (3.50)
Other	123 (2.39)	154 (3.00)	116 (2.24)	65 (1.23)	130 (2.42)	138 (2.52)
Petroleum	41 (3.21)	42 (3.16)	57 (4.01)	11 (0.76)	43 (3.02)	46 (3.17)
Rubber	430 (4.72)	469 (4.78)	312 (2.97)	158 (1.44)	382 (3.26)	385 (3.18)
Stone, clay and glass	545 (3.86)	493 (3.41)	292 (2.00)	133 (0.93)	337 (2.41)	358 (2.58)
Primary metals	168 (2.97)	179 (3.07)	141 (2.36)	79 (1.32)	195 (3.22)	201 (3.25)
Ferrous metals	85 (3.21)	90 (3.28)	61 (2.24)	45 (1.67)	102 (3.70)	110 (3.80)
Non-ferrous metals	83 (2.76)	89 (2.89)	80 (2.47)	34 (1.04)	93 (2.82)	91 (2.76)
Fabricated metal products	962 (3.19)	1,042 (3.30)	782 (2.37)	362 (1.07)	913 (2.65)	877 (2.52)
Machinery	1,519 (3.14)	1,731 (3.38)	1,407 (2.60)	586 (1.02)	1,433 (2.43)	1,314 (2.22)
Office and computers	50 (4.73)	66 (5.27)	62 (4.14)	43 (2.21)	118 (4.58)	100 (3.64)
Other machinery, non-electrical	1,469 (3.10)	1,665 (3.34)	1,345 (2.56)	543 (0.98)	1,315 (2.33)	1,2.14 (2.15)
Electrical equipment	635 (4.41)	620 (3.98)	461 (2.88)	274 (1.62)	665 (3.63)	606 (3.21)

Table 2.1 continued

	1976	1978	1980	1982	1984	1986
Radio and TV equipment	79 (5.02)	82 (4.63)	53 (3.00)	21 (1.15)	43 (2.38)	49 (2.73)
Communications equipment	128 (5.27)	94 (3.59)	74 (2.77)	48 (1.62)	168 (5.02)	119 (3.40)
Electronic components	193 (4.83)	204 (4.64)	163 (3.40)	110 (2.10)	233 (3.98)	211 (3.46)
Other	235 (3.67)	240 (3.54)	171 (2.52)	95 (1.39)	221 (3.03)	227 (3.04)
Motor vehicles	147 (4.55)	149 (4.31)	116 (3.11)	57 (1.49)	147 (3.62)	148 (3.33)
Other transport equipment	247 (5.31)	250 (5.23)	142 (3.17)	76 (1.76)	191 (4.30)	127 (2.99)
Aircraft and missiles	26 (2.50)	36 (3.24)	26 (2.09)	13 (0.94)	33 (2.19)	42 (2.68)
Instruments	312 (3.94)	323 (3.72)	226 (2.41)	160 (1.60)	308 (2.79)	353 (3.01)
Scientific and measuring	130 (4.56)	120 (3.63)	104 (2.76)	66 (1.55)	145 (2.99)	141 (2.72)
Optical, surgical and photographic	182 (3.59)	203 (3.78)	122 (2.18)	94 (1.63)	163 (2.63)	212 (3.24)
Other manufacturing	2,703 (3.62)	2,703 (3.48)	2,082 (2.67)	1,081 (1.35)	2,361 (2.81)	2,435 (2.82)
Total manufacturing	11,154 (3.56)	11,728 (3.60)	8,525 (2.56)	4,329 (1.27)	10,055 (2.86)	10,012 (2.80)

Note: [a]The share (percentage) of the total number of firms accounted for by new-firm startups is indicated in parentheses.

substantially from year to year. While there were over 11,000 new-firm startups in all of US manufacturing in 1976, there was nearly 25 per cent less, around 8,500, in 1980. In 1982, a recession year, new-firm startups fell to just over 4,000 before rebounding to about 10,000 in 1984 and 1986. That firm formation activity is influenced strongly by macro-economic fluctuations is evidenced by Table 2.1.

In fact, no major industrial sector in the United States is immune from the impact of the business cycle.

According to the model introduced in the previous section, firm formation should be lower in industries where scale economies play an important role, but greater in rapidly growing markets. New-firm formation should be greater in industries where asymmetric conditions regarding innovation-generating information prevail. In addition, formation activity should be greater during the expansion phase of the business cycle but, holding the state of the business cycle constant, negatively related to the cost of obtaining financial capital. And, according to the push hypothesis, a high rate of unemployment should induce a larger number of new-firm startups.

The importance of scale economies is measured in two ways. The first is the Comanor–Wilson (1967) proxy measure of the MES, which is defined as the mean size of the plants accounting for the largest fifty per cent of industry value-of-shipments. In addition, the 1977 capital-labour ratio should reflect the degree to which scale economies exist in an industry. According to the model in the previous section, both should deter new-firm formation activity in industries where scale economies play an important role.

Industries characterized by asymmetric innovation-inducing information conditions are likely to be reflected by a high degree of small-firm innovation activity relative to the total amount of innovative activity in the industry. The total innovation rate is measured as the total number of 1982 innovations divided by industry employment. The small-firm innovation rate is measured as the number of innovations in 1982 made by firms with fewer than 500 employees divided by small-firm employment. These measures are explained and analysed in considerable detail in Acs and Audretsch (1988 and 1990). New-firm formation activity should be deterred where small firms do not contribute very much to the innovative activity of the industry and facilitated in those industries where small firms tend to have the innovative advantage.

It should be noted that all four of the above variables are measured at just one point in time. Presumably these structural variables remain fairly stable over a relatively short period of time. The industry-specific observations are then repeated throughout each of the time periods. By contrast, the industry growth rate, measured as the annual percentage change in value of shipments, has observations that are both industry- and time-specific. The industry growth rate should be positively related to new-firm formation activity.

The macro-economic variables are specific to each year but not to individual industries. Therefore, the values of each macro-economic variable are repeated across each four-digit industry in every year. Macro-economic growth is measured by the annual percentage change in real gross national product (GNP). The cost of capital is measured by the average three-month interest rate paid on US Treasury Bills. The unemployment rate, along with the growth rate of real GNP, is expected to be a catalyst for new-firm startups, while the interest rate should exert a negative influence on formation activity.

As was observed in Table 2.1, comparing new-firm formation activity across sectors or industries is confounded by the fact that industry size is clearly not homogeneous. This implies that, *ceteris paribus*, the larger the industry, the greater will be the number of new-firm startups. To control for industry size the value of shipments for each industry in each year is included. Although industry shipments should be positively related to new-firm formation, there is no particular economic content embodied in this measure other than as a variable controlling for industry size. All variable sources are provided in the data appendix.

EMPIRICAL RESULTS

Combining the 407 four-digit SIC industries for which compatible industry-specific characteristics exists with the six time periods available, results in a pooled cross-section regression estimated by 2,442 observations. Using the number of new-firm formations as the dependent variable in this model, the results can be found in Table 2.2. In order to distinguish the cross-section influences from the time series effects, the subscript $_i$ indicates that the variable varies across industries but is constant over time, the subscript $_t$ indicates that the variable varies over time but is constant across industries, and the subscript $_{it}$ indicates that the variable varies across both industries and time.

The negative and statistically significant (at the 95 per cent level of confidence) coefficients of the measures of scale economies and capital intensity suggest that new-firm formation is deterred in industries where scale economies play an important role. The negative coefficient of the total innovation rate combined with the positive coefficient of the small-firm innovation rate implies that new-firm startups are facilitated in industries where small enterprises have the innovative advantage. By contrast, in industries which are highly innovative, but where small firms contribute little to innovative activity, new-firm formation is relatively low.

Table 2.2 Regression results for new-firm formation activity[a]

	1	2
Scale economies$_i$	−0.043	0.004
	(−5.27)**	(0.39)
Capital intensity$_i$	−0.245	−0.243
	(−5.83)**	(−5.63)**
Total innovation rate$_i$	−0.094	−0.98
	(−2.27)**	(1.86)*
Small-firm innovation rate$_i$	6.002	4.263
	(2.45)**	(1.86)*
Industry growth$_{it}$	0.496	0.750
	(0.46)	(0.70)
Macro-economic growth$_t$	0.576	0.573
	(5.59)**	(5.43)*
Interest rate$_t$	−0.437	−0.432
	(−2.88)**	(−2.77)**
Unemployment$_t$	−1.626	−1.655
	(−5.24)**	(−5.20)**
Industry sales$_{it}$	0.147	–
	(10.57)**	
R^2	0.121	0.081
F	37.027**	26.702**
Sample size	2,442	2,442

Notes: [a] *t*-statistics listed in parentheses
*Statistically significant at the 90 per cent level of confidence for a two-tailed test
**Statistically significant at the 95 per cent level of confidence for a two-tailed test

Although the coefficient of the industry growth rate is positive, the *t*-statistic is sufficiently low as to preclude any inference about its having a significant impact on firm formation activity. The explanation is that the industry growth effect is probably overwhelmed by the overall macro-economic growth effect. That is, all boats are lifted by a rising tide.

The negative coefficient of the interest rate suggests that new-firm formation is sensitive to the cost of capital. Although the interest rate is pro-cyclical, and new-firm formation activity is also pro-cyclical, after controlling for the macro-economic growth rate, the interest rate is found to exert a negative influence on startup activity. The unemployment rate is apparently negatively related to firm formation activity. While this is consistent with the overall pro-cyclical tendency of new-firm startups, it contradicts the push hypothesis in the labour economics literature.[6]

As expected, the coefficient of industry value of shipments is positive, reflecting the tendency for new-firm formation activity to be positively related to industry size. It should be noted that, when this variable is omitted from the regression model in equation 2, the results remain virtually unchanged. The only major difference is that the measure of scale economies no longer has a significant impact on formation activity, but this most likely reflects the bias from omitting a variable which belongs in the model.

CONCLUSIONS

The industrial organization and labour market approaches to explaining new-firm formation have been combined in this chapter by utilizing a panel data set consisting of industry-specific observations for new-firm startups between 1976 and 1986. An important finding is that both market structure characteristics, particularly the extent of scale economies in an industry as well as the underlying technological conditions, and the macro-economic environment, shape the extent of new-firm formation activity.

In view of the growing number of studies relating unemployment to entrepreneurship (Storey 1991; Meager 1992), the result that new-firm formation activity is negatively and not positively related to the unemployment rate may seem surprising. However, there are several important qualifications which must be made with respect to this finding. First, most of the previous studies linking unemployment to firm formation have focused on either self-employment or else on the change in self-employment in all sectors of the economy, whereas this chapter is restricted to the manufacturing sector. The distinction is not trivial. Not only does manufacturing represent a small share of the total self-employed, at least in the United States, but there is no reason to think that the underlying behavioural relationships are consistent across the very different sectors of an economy. That is, when unemployment is prevalent, self-employment may rise in, say, the retailing sector, while not being particularly affected in manu-facturing. While this is only a conjecture here, it clearly remains within the province of future research to reconcile these different results.

Second, the negative coefficient may reflect the existence of a simultaneous relationship. To the extent that new firms are founded by previously employed workers, the unemployment rate will tend to fall as firm formation activity rises. Only a simultaneous estimation model could appropriately disentangle the joint endogeneity between unemployment and firm formation activity. Third, the few time period observations available may be inadequate accurately to capture the macro-economic influences on start-up activity. This might be particularly important if new-firm formation activity responds more to lagged than to contemporaneous unemployment. Unfortunately, six time period observations are simply too few to test for the existence of any such lagged relationships.

APPENDIX

The USEEM file of the US Small Business Administration's Small Business Data Base is used to measure new-firm formation activity between 1976 and 1986. Additional detailed description of the data base can be found in Phillips and Kirchhoff (1989), Acs and Audretsch (1990, ch. 2), Boden and Phillips (1985), and US Small Business Administration (1987). The innovation data for the number of total innovations and small-firm innovations, which are used to construct the innovation rates, come from the US Small Business Innovation Data Base. These data are explained in detail in Acs and Audretsch (1988).

The measures of MES, the capital-labour ratio, and the value of shipments come from the US Department of Commerce, Bureau of the Census, *Census of Manufactures*, 1977, Washington, DC, US Government Printing Office. The measure of growth is derived from the value of shipment data from the US Department of Commerce, Bureau of the Census, *Annual Survey of Manufactures: Industry Profiles*, Washington, DC, US Government Printing Office, various years between 1975 and 1986.

NOTES

1   The most recent work in this area can be found in the individual chapters contained in Geroski and Schwalbach (1991) and Acs and Audretsch (1989a).
2   For examples of recent work done using the labour market approach, see Storey and Jones (1987), Hamilton (1989) and Vivarelli (1991).
3   Highfield and Smiley (1987) do examine new-firm formation for the US based on both the industrial organization and labour market approaches, but due to data constraints are forced to do this using two completely independent data sets and estimation models. Then, based on a totally different data set, they identify those market structure characteristics impeding and facilitating entry, using a cross-section empirical model.
4   The raw data in the Dun & Bradstreet files have come under considerable criticism. In order to correct for at least some of the deficiencies inherent in the raw files, the Brookings Institution in conjunction with the US Small Business Administration and the National Science Foundation restructured, edited and supplemented the original Dun & Bradstreet records with data from other sources when compiling the SBDB. For

explanations and clarification concerning the editing of the SBDB, see Harris (1983), US Small Business Administration (1986 and 1987) and Brown and Phillips (1989).

5   Several important studies have compared the SBDB data with analogous measures from the establishment data of the US Census of Manufactures (Boden and Phillips, 1985; Acs and Audretsch, 1990, ch. 2), and from the establishment and employment records of the Bureau of Labor and Statistics data (Brown and Phillips 1989). Such comparisons have generally concluded that the SBDB data are remarkably consistent with these other major data bases providing observations on establishments and enterprises.

6   One possible explanation for the negative coefficient of the unemployment rate is the existence of a simultaneous relationship between unemployment and new-firm formation activity. That is, *ceteris paribus*, as the number of new-firm startups increases, the unemployment rate decreases, assuming no new entry into the labour force. Unfortunately, incorporating this into the empirical model is way beyond the scope of this chapter.

REFERENCES

Acs, Z.J. and Audretsch, D.B. (1988) 'Innovation in Large and Small Firms: An Empirical Analysis', *American Economic Review* September 78(4): 678–90.

—— (1989a) 'Small-Firm Entry in U.S. Manufacturing', *Economica* May 56(2): 255–65.

—— (1989b) 'Births and Firm Size', *Southern Economic Journal* October 56(2): 467–75.

—— (1990) *Innovation and Small Firms*, Cambridge, MA: MIT Press.

Audretsch, D.B. (1991) 'New-Firm Survival and the Technological Regime', *Review of Economics and Statistics* August 60(3): 441–50.

Baldwin, J. and Gorecki, P. 'Entry and Productivity Growth', in P. Geroski and J. Schwalbach, eds. (1990) *Entry and Market Contestability: An International Comparison*, Oxford: Basil Blackwell.

Blanchflower, D. and Oswald, A. (1990) 'What Makes an Entrepreneur?', NBER Working Paper 3252, September.

Boden, R. and Phillips, B.D. (1985) 'Uses and Limitations of USEEM/ USELM Data', Office of Advocacy, US Small Business Administration, Washington, DC, November.

Brown, H.S. and Phillips, B.D. (1989) 'Comparison Between Small Business Data Base (USEEM) and Bureau of Labor Statistics (BLS) Employment Data: 1978–1986', *Small Business Economics* 1(4): 273–84.

Comanor, W.S. and Wilson, T.A. (1967) 'Advertising, Market Structure, and Performance', *Review of Economics and Statistics* November 49: 423–40.

Dunkelberg, W.C. and Cooper, A.C. (1990) 'Investment and Capital Diversity in the Small Enterprise' in Z.J. Acs and D.B. Audretsch (eds) *The Economics of Small Firms*, Boston: Kluwer Academic Publishers: 119–34.

Dunne, T., Roberts, M.J. and Samuelson, L. (1988) 'Patterns of Firm Entry and Exit in U.S. Manufacturing Industries', *Rand Journal of Economics* Winter: 495–515.

Evans, D.S. and Jovanovic, B. (1989) 'Estimates of a Model of Entrepreneurial Choice under Liquidity Constraints', *Journal of Political Economy* August 95: 657–74.

Evans, D.S. and Leighton, L.S. (1989) 'The Determinants of Changes in U.S. Self-Employment, 1968–1987', *Small Business Economics* 1(2): 319–30.

—— (1990) 'Small Business Formation by Unemployed and Employed Workers', *Small Business Economics* 2(4): 319–30.

Freeman, R. (1989) *Labour Markets in Action: Essays in Empirical Economics*, London: Harvester Wheatsheaf.

Geroski, P.A. and Schwalbach (eds) (1991) *Entry and Market Contestability*, Oxford: Basil Blackwell.

Hamilton, R.T. (1989) 'Unemployment and Business Formation Rates: Reconciling Time Series and Cross Section Evidence', *Environment and Planning* 21: 249–55.

Harris, C.S. (1983) *U.S. Establishment and Enterprise Microdata (USEEM): A Data Base Description.* Business Microdata Project, The Brookings Institution, June.

Highfield, R. and Smiley, R. (1987) 'New Business Starts and Economic Activity: An Empirical Investigation', *International Journal of Industrial Organization* March 5(1): 51–66.

Johnson, P. (1989) 'Employment Change in the Small Business Sector: Evidence From Five Manufacturing Industries', *Small Business Economics* 1(4): 315–24.

Meager, N. (1992) 'Does Unemployment Lead to Self-Employment?', *Small Business Economics* June 4(2): 87–104.

Phillips, B.D. and Kirchhoff, B.A. (1989) 'Formation, Growth and Survival: Small Firm Dynamics in the U.S. Economy', *Small Business Economics* 1(1): 65–74.

Revelli, R. and Tenga, S. (1989) 'The Determinants of New Firm Formation in Italian Manufacturing', *Small Business Economics* 1(3): 181–92.

Siegfried, J.J. and Evans, L.B. (1992) 'Entry and Exit in U.S. Manufacturing Industries from 1977 to 1982', in D.B. Audretsch and J.J. Siegfried (eds) *Empirical Studies in Industrial Organization: Essays in Honor of Leonard W. Weiss*, Boston: Kluwer Academic Publishers: 237–52.

Storey, D.J. (1991) 'The Birth of New Firms – Does Unemployment Matter? A Review of Evidence', *Small Business Economics* September 3(3).

Storey, D.J. and Jones, A.M. (1987) 'New Firm Formation – Labor Market Approach to Industry Entry', *Scottish Journal of Political Economy* 34 (February): 37–51.

U.S. Small Business Administration (1986) *The Small Business Data Base: A User's Guide.* Washington, DC, July.

U.S. Small Business Administration, Office of Advocacy (1987) *Linked 1976–1984 USEEM User's Guide*, July Washington, DC.

Vivarelli, M. (1991) 'The Birth of New Enterprise', *Small Business Economics* August 3(3): 215–24.

Yamawaki, H. (1991) 'The Effects of Business Conditions on Net Entry: Evidence from Japan', in P. Geroski and J. Schwalback (eds) *Entry and Market Contestability: An International Comparison*, Oxford: Basil Blackwell 168–86.

P 40;

US

54-56   L11 L1

L60 J?

DISCUSSION

Robert Watson

This chapter is an interesting attempt to combine market structure and labour market approaches to the examination of new-firm formation in US manufacturing industries. Simply put, do new firms come into being primarily to exploit perceived market opportunities (so-called 'pull' factors such as favourable macro-economic and product market conditions) or primarily because of a lack of suitable employment opportunities in the labour market (i.e., 'push' factors such as actual or anticipated unemployment, poor promotion prospects, etc.)?

Audretsch seeks to explain the relative number of new firms entering 407 4-digit SIC manufacturing industry groups on a biannual basis over the period 1976 to 1986. The empirical analysis consists of a multiple regression model with the number of new entrants in each industry as the dependent variable and the following independent variables:

1   Scale economies$_i$ (the (1967?) mean size of the plants accounting for the largest 50 per cent of industry outputs by value);
2   Capital intensity$_i$ (the 1977 capital/labour ratio);
3   Total innovation rate$_i$ (number of 1982 innovations divided by industry employment;
4   Small firm innovation rate$_i$ (number of 1982 innovations by firms with <500 employees divided by small firm employment);
5   Industry growth$_{it}$ (annual percentage change in value of industry output);
6   Macro growth$_t$ (annual percentage change in GNP);
7   Interest rate$_t$ (average 3-month US Treasury Bill rate);
8   Unemployment$_t$ (average rate?, as at month j?);
9   Industry sales$_{it}$ (value of industry output).

The results (based on a 407 × 6 pooled data set) indicate that for industries where large scale economies exist, where capital intensity and innovation rates are greatest (but where the proportion of the innovations accounted for by small firms is low), new entrants will be relatively less frequent. The results also indicate that when unemployment and interest rates are low but macro-economic growth is high, relatively more new firms will be formed. The author suggests that these results indicate that, at least for the US manufacturing sectors examined, pull factors are of most importance in explaining the relative numbers of new entrants in each industry.

I have only a few (and relatively minor) comments to make and most of them refer to limitations in the available data about which the author is unlikely to be able to do much.

The dependent variable

Given the focus upon the push/pull hypotheses, the coverage of the dependent variable, the number of new firms entering industry i in time t, will be crucial because there may be systematic differences between the two types of new entrants. For instance, push entrants are likely to be smaller on average than pull entrants and, therefore, it would be helpful to know the coverage of the dependent variable. Does it, for example, include only incorporated businesses or only businesses above a certain size? If coverage is less than complete, particularly if the very smallest firms are excluded, then the results are likely to be biased against the push hypothesis.

Moreover, due to the vastly differing sizes of the various industries covered, a more appropriate specification of the dependent variable (and one that is less likely to cause statistical problems such as heteroscedastic residuals may be the number of new firms as a percentage of all firms in the industry. Though the author incorporates the industry sales variable to mitigate this problem, it may not adequately control for differences in industry size because it will not be perfectly correlated with the number of firms in the industry.

The lag structure

The empirical model does not include any lag structure. The dependent variable and the macro-economic variables which are presumed to influence new firm formation rates are observed contemporaneously. However, the decision to start up a new firm is unlikely to occur or be implemented and recorded immediately by the official statistics. Moreover, the speed and ease of entry are likely to differ across industries. However, because the author only has biannual data available, it may be impossible to incorporate a realistic lag structure into the model. Even so, some mention of this problem ought to be included in a footnote.

The unemployment variable

The unemployment variable is probably an inadequate method by which to capture labour market effects. Whether unemployment is rising or falling, not merely the level of unemployment, is likely to make a big difference in regard to new firm startup decisions. Perhaps recent changes in unemployment should be included in the model.

Alternatively, the sample could be partitioned into two groups depending on whether unemployment is rising or falling. The push hypothesis suggests that the estimated relationship between new-firm formation and unemployment will be positive for the time period(s) with rising unemployment and negative in periods of falling unemployment. A further consideration is that the model as it currently stands assumes that the direction and magnitude of the relationship between new-firm formation and unemployment is identical across all industries (and time periods). This is unlikely to be the case in practice.

The control variables

Since an eleven-year period is covered by the analysis, the variables that are measured at only one point in time must be assumed to be very stable indeed. What evidence is there that this is indeed the case?

3   The evolution of workers' cooperatives in southern Europe: a comparative perspective

Will Bartlett

Introduction

Since the mid-1970s there has been a rapid development in the cooperative sector in Italy and Spain, and to a lesser extent in Portugal. Within a decade the number of workers' cooperatives had grown to over 20,000 in Italy and over 10,000 in Spain, while in Portugal cooperatives developed mainly outside industry in the agricultural and services sectors. In Spain and Portugal these cooperatives were developed almost entirely during the period of democratic renewal which followed the end of the long period under authoritarian right-wing regimes. These had, for the most part, been opposed to the development of an autonomous, competitive and democratic cooperative sector. The Italian cooperative sector has had a longer period in which to emerge, but even there, the rate of new cooperative formations quickened after 1973.

In other European countries, with the possible exception of France, however, cooperative enterprises have remained only marginal. This marginality has enabled economists trained in the neoclassical tradition, particularly economists of the 'property rights' school, to argue that cooperatives must be inherently inefficient organizations since they have failed to emerge as viable institutions in market economies. The southern European experience, particularly in Spain and Italy, casts doubt on this simple approach.

Cooperative enterprises are characterized by being organizations within which membership and the associated voting rights derive not from the extent of financial equity holding, but from the employment relationship. In particular, it is normal for a 'one person one vote' rule to apply in the decision-making structure of the firm. Thus cooperative enterprises can be regarded as firms within which the rule that 'labour hires capital' reverses the rule that 'capital hires labour' which is characteristic of privately owned capitalist firms. Within this broad framework, the precise institutional arrangements which govern the financial, contractual and decision-making structure of the firm are rather variable. Whilst a variety of cooperative constitutions can often be observed within a country, variation of institutional arrangements between countries forms a convenient focus for comparative analysis. Typical dimensions of variation in institutional arrangements concern the position of hired non-member workers, the form of employee financial participation (whether in individual or collective ownership), and the general regulatory environment within which cooperatives operate.

Economic theorists have contentionally taken the position that cooperative enterprises can be modelled as firms whose objective is the maximization of income per member, rather than profit (Bartlett and Uvalic (1986). This model of the labour-managed firm gives rise to a variety of predictions which distinguish the behaviour of cooperative enterprises quite starkly from that predicted for their capitalist counterparts. Perhaps the strongest of these predictions concerns the so-called 'degeneration' thesis, which asserts that co-operative enterprises will evolve counter-cyclically over the business cycle, both in terms of the evolution at a sectoral level (entry and exit), and in their internal structure (of employment and member-ship). Ben-Ner (1988a, 1988b) provides the clearest analyses of the economic theory which underlies this prediction that cooperative development takes place in a counter-cyclical fashion.

In this chapter, that part of the theory which deals with the sectoral evolution of cooperative enterprises (the 'birth' process) is assessed in the light of the available empirical evidence from the southern European examples, including evidence from publicly available time series sources.

Briefly stated, the argument runs as follows. During a downswing in economic activity the rate of formation of new cooperatives is likely to rise for two related reasons. First, newly unemployed workers seek to protect their incomes by establishing new cooperative firms; and second, firms which are closing down may be rescued by employee buy-outs or takeovers. As emphasized by Paton (1989), worker takeovers of private firms may occur where there is an asymmetry of information between employees and capital owners, and where as a result the underlying long-run viability of a bankrupt firm is visible to the insider employees but not to potential outsider purchasers. Also, during the downswing, the asset values of firms decline and the costs of job search and relocation rise, so that it may be less costly for employees to buy the firm's assets than to quit the firm and seek employment elsewhere (Ben-Ner 1988b). At the same time the increase in unemployment which takes place during a downswing may induce the formation of new cooperative enterprises by workers who prefer to pool their savings to create new jobs in a collective enterprise rather than to remain unemployed for an uncertain period until new jobs in private firms emerge in the economic upswing. This part of the theory is similar to some so-called 'push' explanations of the formation of small private firms (Storey 1991), except that the effect might be expected to be even stronger in the case of cooperatives (and equally in the case of self-employed individual firms and simple labour partnerships) where it is un-employed workers, rather than capital owners, who provide the entrepreneurial motivation to the establishment of a new enterprise. The effect of unemployment on the formation of new cooperatives may be further reinforced by explicit government job creation programmes to support the development of cooperative enterprises. Finally, in a later phase of the business cycle as the economy picks up, the rate of cooperative formations will slow down, and existing cooperatives will be wound up as their workers take on higher paid jobs in the expanding capitalist sector. Thus the cooperative sector as a whole is expected to contract, at least in relation to the rest of the economy, during the upswing.

Ben-Ner, in a detailed review of the degeneration theory and of the experience of cooperative development in Western Europe, concludes that '(worker-owned firms') birth and demise rates follow a fairly counter-cyclical pattern relative to the cycles of the market economy and to the cycles of formation and demise of (capitalist firms)' (Ben-Ner 1988a: 21). However, this conclusion, in so far as it reflects the empirical evidence, is based on sparse and incomplete data. In this chapter I consider whether the theory, as it applies to the pattern of cooperative formations, is borne out by evidence available from new time series data on cooperative formations in Italy, Spain and Portugal, where relatively large numbers of cooperative enter-prises can be observed. In the next section I describe the institutional framework within which these types of firms are established.[1] In the third section evidence on the rate of change of the cooperative sector over the business cycle is presented, and the final section presents some conclusions.

THE INSTITUTIONAL BACKGROUND

Italy

After the war the cooperative principle was enshrined in the Italian Constitution, and a special branch of the Banco Nazionale del Lavoro established a fund for the development of the sector. In addition the existence of national federations of cooperatives has given a focus to the development of the cooperative sector, especially in terms of political leadership and influence. The main federations are the *Lega* and the *Confederazione* which have links with the Communist and Christian Democratic Parties respectively. After World War II other associations emerged, the *Associazione*, and the *Unione*, although these have remained relatively small groupings.

Italian cooperatives may be founded by no less than nine members, which defines the minimum legally permitted membership. Each member has the right to a single vote, irrespective of the extent of capital shareholding, and has the right to participate in the management of the enterprise, to inspect the books of the enterprise and to a share in profits. Non-member workers may be employed, but members must form a majority in the cooperative's workforce. In practice, members normally form a large majority of the workforce. For example, in a recent survey of 100 cooperatives affiliated to the *Lega*, amongst 29,794 employees, 28,183, or 95 per cent, were members (Petrucci 1984). There also appears to be considerable variation in the proportion of worker-members employed according to sector. For example, in 1978 the proportion of worker members in producer cooperatives affiliated to the *Lega* varied from 96.6 per cent in glass production to only 65 per cent in construction (Zevi 1982).

Alongside regulation on the side of employment there are also a number of regulations concerning the capital and financial structure of the cooperative enterprise. In particular, and in contrast to cooperative enterprises in the UK, for example, cooperative members in Italy may hold (non-tradeable) capital shares in their enterprises, although only up to a maximum limit, which since 1983 has been set at 20 million lire: about £10,000 (30 million lire in the case of industrial cooperatives). These capital shares, known as 'social capital', provide a basis for the distribution of part of the profits as dividends, and are reimbursed at their paid-up value when a member leaves the enterprise.

The distribution of profits is subject to some limitations: at least 20 per cent must be placed in reserve funds, and the part which is distributed as dividends on shareholding must not exceed 50 per cent of total profits (*utile nette*). In addition, profits distributed in the form of dividends to members' capital should be paid at a rate which does not exceed that paid on members' loans to the cooperative, which itself may be no more than 2.5 per cent above that available on post-office savings accounts (Cotronei 1987). The remaining profits may be distributed as a simple profit-share, proportional to each member's salary; or to insurance, mutual or training funds.

A further important consideration as regards the legal position of the cooperatives concerns the various types of subsidies to which they are entitled. Normally, an enterprise would pay company income tax at a rate of 36 per cent of profits, plus a local tax at 15 per cent. However, cooperatives are exempt from these taxes so long as members' remuneration is more than 60 per cent of value added (if it should lie between 60 per cent and 40 per cent of value added, the tax liability is only reduced by 50 per cent). Cooperatives also benefit from subsidized interest rates on credit obtained from the special fund for cooperative development managed by the Banco Nazionale del Lavoro (100 billion lire in 1981 plus a further 50 billion lire managed by the Istituto di Credito delle Casse di Risparmio Italiane and the Istituto Centrale delle Banche Popolari Italiane).

Spain

In common with Italy, Spain has a long historical tradition behind its cooperative movement. The early development of the cooperative sector began in the middle of the nineteenth century, followed by gradual sectoral and territorial expansion well into the present century. The military defeat of the left in the Civil War in the 1930s, and the subsequent establishment of an authoritarian system under Franco, represented a reversal of this development, and there was a marked reduction in the number of cooperatives with many dissolved or their property confiscated. However, cooperatives were not banned outright, but came under tight government control with the law of 1942 which remained in force until 1974, although there was some growth in the number of cooperatives as an outcome of the economic growth of the 1960s.

The transition to democracy in Spain after 1975 opened up new opportunities for cooperative development. Most of all, the new Constitution of 1978 recognized the promotion of the cooperative sector as an important instrument of public policy towards employee participation within companies (article 129). Eventually, legislation was implemented both on a national basis – with the general law on cooperatives of 1987 – and a separate regional basis. The regional emphasis arose from the establishment of 'autonomous communities' throughout the country which enjoy considerable freedom of action in formulating their own economic policies. This decentralization of political authority brought about a need for special regional laws to regulate cooperative institutions in each area, and such laws were passed in the Basque Country (1982), Catalonia (1983), Andalusia (1985) and Valencia (1985). The laws were supplemented by the emergence of a number of regional policy initiatives to promote the development of the cooperative sector. In Catalonia, for example, the regional government established an agency to provide training and support for workers' cooperatives in the local economy. Grass roots associations of cooperatives, such as the Catalan Federation (FCTAC), were also developed to represent the interests of cooperatives to the policy-making bodies. In this favourable policy climate, recent estimates suggest that as many as 9,000 workers' cooperatives had been established in Spain by 1986 (Vidal-Alonso and Hernandez 1990).

Broadly, the history of Spanish cooperatives has its roots in the various political and cultural traditions which have developed in Spain including anarchism, socialism and social Catholicism. For example, in the Basque region, the Mondragon system of industrial cooperatives, which originated in 1956 and comprised as many as sixty cooperatives by the time of Franco's death in 1975, had roots in the Roman Catholic tradition of social harmony and drew strength from the Basque sense of community (which had no sympathy at all or the Franco regime). By 1990 the Mondragon group had grown to include some ninety-seven industrial and service sector cooperatives, employing over 22,000 workers, and there are a further 300 cooperatives in the region outside the Mondragon group. In contrast, the more recent parallel developments in Catalonia have roots which reach back to the local political traditions of the anarchist movement. There, the cooperative sector has grown rapidly throughout the 1980s, increasing from around 950 active worker cooperatives in 1985 to a peak of 1,800 in 1989, falling to around 1,500 by 1991.

Portugal

The basis for the recent development of the cooperative sector in Portugal is set out in the 'Cooperative Code' (*Codigo Cooperativo*) of 1980, which is the legal framework under which Portuguese cooperatives operate. The *Codigo Cooperativo* established the basic principle of democratic management, i.e., each member must have one vote on the key decision-making body, the General Assembly. As in Italy, the minimum number of members needed to form a cooperative is rather large, and is set at ten workers.

Each member must buy at least three shares, and must subscribe a minimum amount of investment capital to the cooperative on taking up membership. However, this is not a very large amount, and is currently set at 5,000 escudos (about two pounds sterling). This minimum initial investment can take the form either of an individual subscription to an internal capital account, or of a contribution to collective reserves. At the same time, liability for debts is limited to the subscribed collective reserves. Unlike the practice in other countries, non-members may buy non-voting shares, and receive interest free of tax – but at a limited rate. Limitations are placed on the rewards to private shareholding, and members' shares can be remunerated up to a global limit of only 30 per cent of operating surplus after allocations have been made to collective reserves.

When cooperatives form, they may choose to register with INSCOOP, the state cooperative support agency, established in 1976 with assistance from the Swedish International Development Authority and, from 1978, with the support of the United Nations Development Programme. INSCOOP is a government agency within the Ministry of Planning, and its employees are civil servants. It provides training services to cooperatives in conjunction with the Ministry of Education and through programmes which have been organized in conjunction with the European Social Fund of the EC and the ILO, although in recent years its activities have been sharply curtailed.

The advantage for newly established cooperatives in registering with INSCOOP is that the credentials obtained can be used as an introduction to the Ministry of Planning and other government ministries in applications for financial support. However, in order to receive state subsidies such as exemption from corporate income tax, at least 75 per cent of the cooperative's workers must be members in the enterprise, and all the members must work in the cooperatives.[2] This restriction implies that there is much less flexibility for the Portuguese cooperatives to employ hired non-member workers than is the case for cooperative firms in Italy or Spain.

EVOLUTION OF THE COOPERATIVE SECTOR

Italy

The rapid growth of the Italian cooperative sector in the 1970s and 1980s is documented in a number of sources of varying reliability. By 1989, the Ministry of Labour had over 160,000 cooperatives of all types (including consumer as well as producer cooperatives), on its central register (*Archivio Anagrafico*) in Rome. However, this figure is generally recognized to be an overestimate, as the ministry does not monitor cooperative failures.

Another source of information is the four cooperative associations (or 'centrals' – *centrali*: the *Lega, Confederazione, Associazione*, and *Unione*). The figures provided by the associations are likely to be fairly accurate as they are the base upon which their revenues depend,[3] although they are likely to provide an underestimate of the numbers of cooperatives overall, since not all cooperatives are affiliated to the associations. In 1989, the number of cooperatives affiliated to the *Confederazione* was 24,261. This compares to the 17,451 affiliated to the *Lega*, the 5,105 affiliated to the *Associazione* and the 2,779 affiliated to the *Unione*. Of these, industrial sector cooperatives accounted for 4,118, 4,725, 1,111 and 491 respectively, indicating that a little more than half of the industrial cooperatives identified in the prefectural registers adhere to the associations.

The largest number of cooperatives were affiliated to the *Confederazione*, with the *Associazione* and the *Unione* being relatively small organizations. However, considering industrial cooperatives alone, it is the *Lega* which represents a larger number of cooperative enterprises. In any case, it is clear that the *Lega* and the *Confederazione* are the two largest representative associations. As for growth, between 1979 and 1984, the *Lega* has increased the number of its industrial cooperatives 36 per cent whilst the *Confederazione* has increased its industrial cooperative membership by only 6 per cent. Thus, in the field of industrial cooperatives, the *Lega* was the most dynamic and influential of the cooperative federations in the early 1980s. In recent years this position has been reversed. Between 1984 and 1989 the *Confederazione* increased its membership among industrial cooperatives by 45.6 per cent, whilst the *Lega* increased membership by a comparatively modest 25.9 per cent.

In particular sectors, such as construction, ceramics and wood products, cooperative firms account for a large share of the market,

Table 3.1 Growth of workers' cooperatives in Italy

Year	A	B %	C %	D %	E %	F %
1964	4,694	−1.80	2.80	4.00	−0.60	1.20
1965	4,669	−0.53	3.30	5.00	−1.70	4.60
1966	4,719	1.07	6.00	5.40	−1.50	11.40
1967	4,208	−10.83	7.20	5.00	1.10	8.20
1968	4,256	1.14	6.50	5.30	0.00	6.50
1969	4,384	3.01	6.10	5.30	0.50	3.70
1970	4,370	−0.32	5.30	5.10	0.00	6.40
1971	4,626	5.86	1.60	5.10	−0.10	−0.50
1972	4,139	−10.53	2.70	6.00	−0.60	5.00
1973	4,420	6.79	7.10	5.90	2.20	9.70
1974	4,860	9.95	5.40	5.00	2.00	3.90
1975	5,377	10.64	−2.70	5.50	0.10	−8.80
1976	5,893	9.60	6.60	6.20	1.50	11.60
1977	6,696	13.63	3.40	6.70	1.00	0.00
1978	7,854	17.29	3.70	6.70	0.50	2.10
1979	9,055	15.29	6.00	7.20	1.50	6.70
1980	10,140	11.98	4.20	7.10	1.90	5.10
1981	11,203	10.48	1.00	7.40	0.00	−2.20
1982	12,536	11.90	0.30	8.00	0.60	−3.10
1983	13,716	9.41	1.10	8.80	0.60	−2.40
1984	14,563	6.18	3.00	9.50	0.40	3.20
1985	15,633	7.35	2.60	9.40	0.90	1.40
1986	17,270	10.47	2.50	10.40	0.80	4.10
1987	18,628	7.86	3.00	10.20	0.60	2.60
1988	20,071	7.75	3.90	10.80	1.40	6.90
1989	21,199	5.62	3.20	10.80	0.20	3.90

Source: *Schedario Generale* derived from *Ministero del Lavoro Statistiche delle Cooperazione*, various issues; European Economy 1991
Notes: A Industrial producer cooperatives registered
  B Rate of change of registered cooperatives (DCOOPS)
  C Rate of growth of GDP (GDP)
  D Unemployment rate (UR)
  E Employment growth rate (ER)
  F Growth of Industrial Output (IR)

and in some sectors, notably construction, quite large cooperatives can be found. In Emilia-Romagna, for example, there are ten construction cooperatives with more than 500 worker-members. However, this is exceptional and the average size of producer cooperatives is around twenty members, so that they are for the most part small firms.

Table 3.2 Regression relationships between proportionate change in registration rate of cooperatives in Italy (DCOOPS) and various macro-economic indicators, 1966–89

	Coefficient	t-stat	DW
GDP	−0.25	(0.5)	2.35
GDP(−1)	0.26	(0.5)	2.18
IR	−0.19	(0.82)	2.36
IR(−1)	0.06	(0.24)	2.15
ER	3.17	(2.36)	1.34
ER(−1)	4.01	(3.24)	1.74
DUR	−0.06	(0.4)	2.40
DUR(−1)	0.06	(0.40)	2.20

Note: The 5 per cent bounds for the Durbin–Watson (DW) statistic are: $d_l = 1.26$, $d_u = 1.44$. Regressions on GDP, IR and DUR and lagged values use the Cochrane–Orcutt correction for the presence of first-order serial correlation of the residuals.

However, the data available from the associations are only partial, and the most reliable alternative source of time series data which provide information on the global rate of change of the cooperative sector in Italy, both for affiliated cooperatives and for those outside the main associations, is that available from provincial prefectures' general register (*Schedario generale*). These data show a total number of 105,000 cooperative associations of all types in existence in 1989. Cooperatives need to be registered on this list in order to benefit from public subsidies, and tax breaks. Earle (1986) has criticized these data on account of the inadequate sectoral breakdown between industrial cooperatives (*cooperative di produzione e lavoro*) (of which there were 21,199 in 1989) and service cooperatives (*cooperative miste*) (14,086 in 1989). He has emphasized that this sectoral breakdown is not very precisely defined. Nevertheless, taking the annual changes in these numbers provides the most reliable available picture of the gross rate of formation of cooperatives over time.

The rate of formation of industrial cooperatives (*produzione e lavoro*) derived in this way for the period 1964–89 is shown in column B of Table 3.1. Alongside it are shown various business cycle indicators including data for GDP growth (C), unemployment rate (D), employment growth (E), and the growth of industrial output (F).

These time series data provide no immediately obvious evidence of counter-cyclical behaviour of the cooperative formation rate. Casual inspection suggests that there may be some more systematic relationship between the series, in particular, peaks of the business cycle which appear in 1967, 1975, 1978, 1982 and 1986 appear to be associated with troughs in the rate of cooperative formations in 1967, 1975, 1977, 1982 and 1986. However, more systematic investigation of the inter-correlations between the time series relating to the rate of cooperative formations, and the time series of business cycle indicators are required to establish the statistical significance of such relationships. As a preliminary approach, Table 3.2 presents some results of simple bivariate regressions between the two classes of time series. The table presents information about the relevant regression coefficients, associated t-statistics, and the Durbin-Watson statistic (DW). The regression methodology (either OLS or Cochrane-Orcut) has been selected with a view to reducing biases resulting from the presence of first-order serial correlation of the residuals.[4]

The simple bivariate regressions reported in Table 3.2 show that there is no consistent relationship between the net birth rate of cooperative enterprises and the GDP growth rate, the growth rate of industrial output or the rate of change of the unemployment rate, or their lagged values. On the other hand, there does appear to be a consistent significant positive relationship between the cooperative birth rate and the rate of employment growth (ER) and its lagged value. These regressions provide tentative evidence that the hypothesis that cooperative birth rates follow a counter-cyclical pattern should be rejected. Rather, a determining influence appears to be the rate of employment growth, with birth rates being high when employment growth is high. Specifically, a one percentage point increase in the employment growth rate leads to a three percentage point increase in the net birth rate of cooperatives in the current year, and a four percentage point increase in the following year (equivalently for decreases in employment growth). One possible explanation for this apparently strong impact of employment growth upon the birth rate of cooperatives is that periods of rapid employment growth are associated with reductions in the riskiness of establishing new enterprises of all types. Since the costs of job search are relatively low during times of rapid job growth, the costs of failure of a cooperative venture would not impose high search costs upon cooperative members. This explanation highlights the close links between workers' decisions to establish cooperatives and labour market conditions. An additional explanation is that much job growth over the period in question has taken place in light manufacturing. And the expansion of this sector provides relatively greater opportunities for cooperatives to be established due to the lower capital requirements for establishing cooperatives in that sector.

Spain

After Italy, Spain is the country with the largest number of producer cooperatives. According to official figures for 1985, these amounted to as many as 12,000 in the country as a whole, although as with the Italian data this is probably an overestimate, with a more reliable figure for the number of active cooperatives being around 9,000. The cooperatives are typically found in sectors such as construction, footwear and ready-made clothing trades, also metalworking, wood and furniture (Monzon Campos 1987: 24–6).

More detailed data are available on a regional basis. The main concentrations of cooperatives are found in Andalucia (30 per cent), Catalonia (16.4 per cent) and the Basque country (12 per cent) (Martinez 1987: Table 20). In Catalonia the number of cooperatives registered rose from 251 in 1971 to 1,520 in 1984, a sixfold increase; while in Barcelona the increase was eightfold in the same period (Generalitat de Catalunya 1986). The Catalan cooperatives, although centred around Barcelona where there are over 600 cooperatives, are widely distributed throughout the region. Particular concentrations are also found in Baix Llobregat (159) and Valles Oriental (198).

A survey carried out by the Catalan Ministry of Labour in 1985 found that nearly half of the cooperatives were in the industrial sector (47.6 per cent), over a third were in the services sector (35.5 per cent) and the rest were in construction (15.6 per cent) and agriculture (1.3 per cent) (Generalitat de Catalunya 1986, Table 6). In terms of employment, the orientation towards the industrial sector was even more pronounced with 65.5 per cent of employment in cooperatives in that sector, and only 23.1 per cent in services, 10 per cent in construction and 1.3 per cent in agriculture (Generalitat de Catalunya 1986, Table 9). This is associated with a larger size for the industrial sector cooperatives, at around twenty-three members in each, compared to an average size of eleven members in each of the services and construction sectors. The cooperatives are predominantly small enterprises, with 97 per cent employing fewer than 100 workers, although the larger cooperatives account for a significant share of total employment, with 28.7 per cent of employment in firms with over 100 member-workers (Generalitat de Catalunya 1986). Moreover, a significant proportion (22.6 per cent) of the cooperatives have the minimum permitted number of member-workers (five), and a further 45.4 per cent have only between six and ten members.

The survey also revealed that nearly half (45.4 per cent) of the cooperatives formed in the first half of the 1980s, when growth of real GDP was sluggish, and unemployment rose rapidly to 20 per cent by 1984, were the outcome of previously existing enterprises being transformed into cooperatives (Generalitat de Catalunya 1986). Thus, a major factor behind the rapid development of the cooperative sector in Catalonia was the takeover by workers of failed or bankrupt enterprises. On the other hand, after 1985, when economic growth resumed and unemployment rates began to fall, it appears that worker takeovers were a less important source of new cooperative formations, with proportionately more cooperatives being established from scratch (Vidal-Alonso and Hernandez 1990).

State subsidies for cooperatives include financial support to reduce interest costs on loans for fixed capital investments and technical assistance; grants for subsistence income; and exceptional support for newly established workers' cooperatives. These subsidies are available from the Ministry of Labour and Social Security. In addition, there is provision for training. Since 1983, the directorate-general for cooperatives and workers' companies has brought in a training scheme for cooperatives. And from 1986 programmes for the management and administration of cooperatives have been added. There are also other agencies such as the solidarity fund and a programme for generating employment in cooperatives, involving, for example, technical assistance and financing educational meetings (Fundación para el Desarrollo del Cooperativismo 1985).

Data on the rate of formation of cooperatives in Spain is presented in Table 3.3. The table shows the number of worker cooperatives (ALCs) registered in each year from 1971 to 1987 (column A). Column B shows the cumulative registrations and column C the derived gross birth rate of Spanish cooperatives over the period. These data will be biased downwards over time since they fail to adjust the computed stock figures for deregistrations. The table also shows the changes in employment growth, the unemployment rate, GDP growth and industrial output growth in Spain over the period. As in the Italian case there was a steady increase in the unemployment rate in Spain, especially following entry into the EEC in 1976. There was a simultaneous increase in the numbers of cooperatives being established. However, since there is a common time trend this does not establish that unemployment growth caused the increase in cooperative formations.

In Table 3.3 the results of regressions relate the proportionate rate of cooperative registrations (DCOOPS) to the various business cycle indicators. Since the stock variable used to construct DCOOPS is, as explained above, downward biased over time, the estimated regres-

Table 3.3 Growth of cooperatives in Spain

Year	A	B	C %	D %	E %	F %	G %
1971	121	121	0.0	0.5	3.4	4.6	3.2
1972	206	327	1.70	0.3	2.9	8.0	15.8
1973	146	473	0.45	2.0	2.6	7.7	15.2
1974	183	656	0.39	0.7	3.1	5.3	9.3
1975	203	859	0.31	−1.6	4.5	0.5	−6.6
1976	352	1,211	0.41	−1.1	4.9	3.3	5.1
1977	412	1,623	0.34	−0.7	5.3	3.0	5.2
1978	617	2,240	0.38	−1.7	7.1	1.4	2.4
1979	438	2,678	0.20	−1.7	8.8	−0.1	0.7
1980	1,325	4,003	0.49	−3.0	11.6	1.2	1.3
1981	1,506	5,509	0.38	−2.6	14.4	−0.2	−1.0
1982	1,535	7,044	0.28	−0.9	16.3	1.2	−1.1
1983	1,556	8,600	0.22	−0.5	17.8	1.8	2.7
1984	1,492	10,092	0.17	−2.4	20.6	1.8	0.8
1985	1,406	11,498	0.14	−1.3	21.8	2.3	2.0
1986	2,119	13,617	0.18	2.3	21.0	3.3	3.1
1987	1,639	15,256	0.12	5.4	20.4	5.5	4.6

Source: Vidal-Alonso, A. L. and Hernandez, A.
'Labour Co-operatives, other Associative Production', *International Cooperative Review* 1990, Vol. 83: 60–6
Note: A ALCs registered
   B Cumulative registrations
   C Rate of registration against lagged stock (DCOOPS)
   D Employment growth (ER)
   E Unemployment rate (UR)
   F GDP growth (GDP)
   G Industrial output growth rate (IR)

sion equations include a time trend. In addition, structural stability tests indicated that the first few years' observations should be dropped, since the implied growth rates are dominated by the relatively low cumulated stock figures at the beginning of the time series. Table 3.4 therefore reports the results over the period 1975 to 1987, and although the standard post-regression tests for normality and functional form were satisfactory, it should be noted that these results are based on a much shorter time series than is available for the Italian case reported above.

These data show little observable systematic relation between the fluctuations of the business cycle and the rate of cooperative formations. Although the regression coefficients have the 'correct' signs they are uniformly insignificant. The only significant regressor is

Table 3.4 Relationship between proportionate change in registration rate of cooperatives in Spain (DCOOPS) and business cycle variables, 1975–87

	Coefficient	t-stat	DW
GDP	−0.00	(0.24)	2.18
GDP(−1)	−0.03	(2.10)	2.54
IR	−0.00	(0.50)	1.96
IR(−1)	−0.01	(1.17)	2.16
ER	−0.01	(0.09)	2.15
ER(−1)	−0.02	(1.25)	2.48
DUR	0.02	(1.14)	2.26
DUR(−1)	0.02	(0.72)	2.30

Note: The 5 per cent bounds for the Durbin–Watson (DW) statistic are: $d_l = 1.08$, $d_u = 1.36$. Regressions on lagged GDR, IR and DUR use the Cochrane–Orcutt correction for the presence of first-order serial correlation of the residuals. Reported coefficients are taken from regressions which include a constant term and a time trend.

the lagged GDP growth rate, which is significant at the 5 per cent level; it is negatively related to the cooperative birth rate. However, the negative relationship between GDP growth and cooperative formation rates is rather weak. A one percentage point increase in GDP growth leads to a reduction of 0.03 percentage points in the rate of cooperative formations with a one-year lag. As in the Italian case, the data reject any significant influence of the growth of industrial output or of the unemployment rate change upon the rate of cooperative formation. In addition, there is no significant inverse relationship to the employment growth rate. Nevertheless, the significant inverse relationship between lagged GDP growth and the rate of cooperative formations, suggests that the counter-cyclical model cannot be rejected as irrelevant to the Spanish case.

Portugal

Less adequate information is available for the Portuguese case, and it is not possible to carry out systematic time series analyses. We do know that after the 1974 coup a large number of cooperatives were established, and by 1976 it was estimated that there were about 3,000 cooperatives in Portugal, of which some 900 were workers' cooperatives. A statistical breakdown of the cooperative firms by type of formation, or sector, is not available for this period, although it is likely that most were established by conversion, with 'from scratch' cooperatives being established mainly in the construction and services sectors.

Bermeo (1983) estimates that the average size of cooperative firms in 1976 was around forty-five workers. Within the group of 'conversion' cooperatives, some 50 per cent had been previously abandoned by their owners following the turmoil of the coup and the ensuing sharp increase in wage rates. At first the cooperatives were organized centrally in a National Federation of Cooperatives, and along sectoral lines in consortia, a leading example being the textile cooperative COOPTEXTIL. However, many of the member cooperatives of the consortia had inherited obsolete equipment from their former owners; they were inefficient and faced financial difficulties. COOPTEXTIL and other consortia collapsed in 1979. Thereafter the cooperatives became suspicious of the centralized model, the National Federation became fragmented into sectoral organizations, and the cooperatives abandoned the idea of forming consortia in favour of a greater degree of independence.

By 1985, the average size of cooperatives in the manufacturing sector had fallen to thirty-nine, and in the services sector it was twenty-three permanent employees (INSCOOP 1987: Table 06).

A survey conducted by INSCOOP revealed that a large number of cooperatives which had been established in the aftermath of the coup have since failed. Since the data on the numbers of cooperatives prior to 1986 had not picked this up, it is not possible to evaluate the extent of the growth which has taken place in the past ten years.

The most recent survey indicates that in 1989 there were some 2,374 cooperatives operating in Portugal, of which only 167 were industrial cooperatives and 471 were in the services sector (INSCOOP 1990: Table 12). The sectoral distribution of the cooperatives is shown in Table 3.5.

The table reveals that the number of industrial sector cooperatives was falling in the late 1980s, whilst rapid growth was occurring among service sector cooperatives. This was a period of rapid rates of real GDP growth (1987: 5.3 per cent p.a.; 1988: 3.9 per cent; 1989: 5.4 per cent) and of declining unemployment rates (1987: 6.8 per cent; 1989: 5.0 per cent).

Data available from the national survey conducted by INSCOOP in 1986 shows that the service sector cooperatives performed somewhat better than the cooperatives in the industrial sector in terms of sales per worker, and wages per worker, and also in terms of profit and investment per firm (although it should be noted that no tests of statistical significance of these differences are available). The

Table 3.5 Cooperatives in Portugal, 1987 and 1989

Sector	1987	1989	% p.a. growth
Agriculture	1,118	1,114	−0.02
Artisan	30	48	30.00
Commerce	88	88	0.00
Culture	205	280	18.29
Teaching	145	160	5.17
Fishing	43	46	3.49
Industrial	178	167	−3.09
Services	359	471	15.60
Total	2,166	2,374	4.80

Source: *Annuario Comercial do Sector Cooperativo* 1990: 25, Table 12

service sector appears therefore to be more dynamic and successful than the manufacturing sector.

This is borne out by observations on the trends of new cooperative formations: 86 per cent of industrial sector cooperatives but only 56 per cent of service sector cooperatives were formed between 1974 and 1979; whilst only 10 per cent of the industrial cooperatives, compared to 31 per cent of service cooperatives, were formed since 1980 (INSCOOP 1987: Table 01).

Macroeconomic evidence from Portugal is thus both sparse and mixed. Industrial sector cooperatives have declined during a period of economic boom, yet in the service sector, simultaneously, some expansion in the entry rate of cooperatives can be observed.

CONCLUSIONS

This paper has presented new evidence on the evolution of the workers' cooperatives in southern Europe where large numbers of such firms can be observed. The conventional economic theory of cooperative enterprises suggests that their rate of formation will change over time in a systematic relationship with the business cycle. During the downswing, the rate of cooperative formations is expected to increase, as workers find it relatively less costly to buy up a failing firm than to quit to search for a new job from a diminishing pool of hobs on the labour market. Simultaneously, lengthening dole queues and the increase in job search costs induce workers to pool their savings to establish cooperative enterprises. During the upswing, cooperatives begin to employ hired labour and start a process of transformation ('degeneration') into private capitalist firms; or skilled workers leave the egalitarian cooperatives in search of higher paying jobs in the inegalitarian private sector and the cooperatives collapse and close down. According to these arguments, the rate at which new cooperatives are formed in a market economy should proceed counter-cyclically, increasing with increases in some negative business cycle indicators such as the unemployment rate, and decreasing with other positive business cycle indicators such as the rate of growth of GDP, the rate of growth of industrial output and the employment growth rate.

This chapter has considered the evolution of the cooperative sectors in Italy, Portugal and Spain in the light of these theories. In the cases of Italy and Spain, in particular, it has been possible to make direct tests of the predictions of the theory on the basis of time series data available on the birth of new cooperative enterprises in each country. The results indicate conflicting support for the theory.

In the Italian case, the rate of cooperative formations was found to be strongly influenced by the rate of employment growth, indicating a positive impact of improving economic conditions on the desire to establish collective work organizations. Related to this is the effect of reduced costs of job search during a period of rapid employment growth, which reduces the potential cost to workers of the failure of a newly established cooperative. Given the favourable cultural, legal and policy disposition towards cooperative enterprises in the Italian case, the link between expanding employment opportunities and the growth of the cooperative sector can be readily understood.

In Spain, on the other hand, the rate of cooperative formations was found to be most strongly influenced by the fluctuations in GDP. There, increases in the cooperative birth rate appear to be inversely associated with this business cycle indicator. It seems likely that the dominating influence in the Spanish case has been the defensive reaction of workers in failing enterprises which experienced difficulties adjusting to the new economic conditions emerging in the years immediately following Spanish accession to the EEC. This impression is reinforced by the findings of studies undertaken by the Catalan regional government which show that a large proportion of cooperative enterprises in that region at least had been formed as a result of worker takeover rather than as wholly new enterprises. In addition, although there is a cultural tradition of cooperative development in Spain, this tradition is regionally fragmented and has been subject to a long period of relative inactivity in the years prior to the recent transition to democracy. Similar effects can be observed in

Portugal, but there, even more so than in Spain, the evidence on which to base firm conclusions is fragmentary.

Overall, it would seem that the determinants of the evolution of workers' cooperatives differ from one national setting to another. The evidence indicates that where cooperatives have established a legitimate role as a widely recognized form of industrial organization, as in Italy, then the long-term evolution of the sector may follow the positive movement of the business cycle, increasing more quickly when economic conditions, especially conditions on the labour market, are improving. Elsewhere, where the cooperative form of enterprise is less well established and regionally fragmented, as in Spain and Portugal, the influences described by the economic ('degeneration') theory would appear to play a significant role in the evolution of the cooperative sector, and a counter-cyclical pattern of evolution may emerge.

NOTES

1   For a more detailed account see Bartlett and Pridham (1991).
2   Tax Exemption Law number 456/80.
3   The League, for example, charges a membership fee which amounts to 4.5 per cent of each cooperative's gross revenue.
4   The regressions have been produced using the Microfit econometrics programme.

REFERENCES

Bartlett, W. and Pridham, G. (1991) 'Cooperative Enterprises in Italy, Portugal and Spain: History, Development and Prospects', *Journal of Interdisciplinary Economics* 4(1): 33–60.

Bartlett, W. and Uvalic, M. (1986) 'Labour-Managed Firms, Employee Participation and Profit-Sharing: Theoretical Perspectives and European Experience', *Management Bibliographies and Reviews* (Special Issue) 12(4): 1–66.

Ben-Ner, A. (1988a) 'Comparative Empirical Observations on Worker-Owned and Capitalist Firms', *International Journal of Industrial Economics* 6.

—— (1988b) 'The Life Cycle of Worker-Owned Firms in Market Economies: A Theoretical Analysis', *Journal of Economic Behaviour and Organization* 10: 287–313.

Bermeo, N.G. (1983) 'Worker-Management in Industry: Reconciling Representative Government and Industrial Democracy in a Polarized Society' in S.G. Lawrence and D.L. Wheeler (eds), *In Search of Modern Portugal: the Revolution and its Consequences*, Madison: University of Madison Press.

Cotronei, G. (1987) *Societa cooperative: manuale giuridico-fiscalecon formiulario e giurisprudenza*, Roma: Buffetti.

Earle, J. (1986) *The Italian Cooperative Movement*, London: Allen & Unwin.

Fundación para el Desarrollo del Cooperativismo (1985) *Programas de Ayudas Oficiales al Fomento del Empleo*, Documentos de Economía Social (1).

Generalitat de Catalunya (1986) *El Cooperativisme de Treball Associat a Catalunya*, Barcelona.

Holmstrom, M. (1989) *Industrial Democracy in Italy: Workers Co-ops and the Self-management debate*, Aldershot: Avebury.

INSCOOP (1987) *Inquerito Nacional ao Sector Cooperativo*, Ministerio do Planeamento e da Administracao do Territorio, Instituto Antonio Sergio do Sector Cooperativo, Direccao de Servicos de Fomento e Coordinacao, Divisao de Estatistica, June.

INSCOOP (1988) *O Sector Cooperativo em 1987, Vol 1*, Ministerio do Planeamento e da Administracao do Territorio, Instituto Antonio Sergio do Sector Cooperativo, Direccao de Servicos de Fomento e Coordinacao, Divisao de Estatistica, March.

INSCOOP (1990) *Anuario Comercial do Sector Cooperativo 1990*, Lisboa: Instituto Antonio Sergio do Sector Cooperativo.

ISFOL (1989) *Fattori di successo delle imprese cooperative: economia e modelli socio-organizzativi nelle aziende autogestite* (Research conducted by Teresa Farnetti), Milano: Angeli.

Lega Cooperative Emilia Romagna (n.d.) *Il movimento, il sistema. la rete: un decennio di cambiamenti nelle imprese cooperative*, Bolgona: Editrice Emilia-Romagna.

Martinez, I.V. (1987) *Crisis Economica y Transformaciones en el Mercado de Trabajo*, Barcelona: Diputación de Barcelona.

Monzon Campos, J. (1987) 'L'economie sociale et cooperative en Espagne', *Annals of Public and Cooperative Economy* 58(1): 23–30.

Paton, R. (1989) *Reluctant Entrepreneurs: the Extent, Achievements and Significance of Worker Takeovers in Europe*, Milton Keynes: Open University Press.

Petrucci, P. (ed.) (1984) *La struttura di bilancio di 482 cooperative, 1981–1982*, Roma: Editrice Cooperativa.

Storey, D. (1991) 'The Birth of New Firms: Does Unemployment Matter? A Review of the Evidence', *Small Business Economics*, 3: 167–78.

Vidal-Alonso, A.L. and Hernandez, A. (1990) 'Labour Co-Operatives, Other Associative Production', *International Cooperative Review*: 60–6.

Zevi, A. (1982) 'The Performance of Italian Producer Cooperatives', in D. Jones and J. Svejnar (eds) *Participatory and Self-managed firms: Evaluating Economic Performance*, Lexington: Lexington Books.

ITALY, PORTUGAL
SPAIN. J54
p 57:)

DISCUSSION

77~b

Mette Mønsted

This chapter is based on an ongoing research project in Italy, Spain and Portugal. Its perspective is both to discuss cooperatives in economic theory, and to work on the registration of cooperatives in the three countries.

In economic theory, cooperatives are seen not only as marginal to economic growth, but also as inefficient organizations. The author discusses the 'degeneration' thesis, arguing that cooperative enterprises will evolve counter-cyclically over the business cycle, both in terms of the evolution of the sector and of their internal structure. Bartlett discusses the key assumption that the efficiency of hired labour is equal to member's labour If these two forms of labour are not identical then the conclusion that cooperatives are inefficient may not hold.

One of the problems in a discussion of registration is the clear discrepancy between marketing cooperatives and labour cooperatives. Bartlett focus on labour cooperatives, but it is important to be clear on this matter since the objectives of the different types of cooperatives will differ.

There is always an important cultural dimension in any comparison of enterprises in different countries. The cultural setting of the cooperative enterprise is particularly important, and this should be dealt with carefully in an analysis of the registration data. The motivation to register also depends totally on the benefits obtained from registration, e.g. will there be certain tax benefits, financial resources, or other benefits of registration and acceptance as a cooperative? Access to financial resources will usually be very different for labour cooperatives and marketing cooperatives.

Registration data are used as a comparison with private firm formation rates. The results suggest a counter-cyclical relationship with formation being high when the cycle is at a low point, except perhaps in Spain. Such correlations, however, need more specification of possible explanations, e.g. is this related to certain areas? And what are the traditions for forming cooperatives in the regions?

The instability of cooperatives is viewed in economic theory as reflecting inefficiency. But what is the comparative basis for this? Surely all firms change over time and according to changes in market conditions: the leadership structure changes, and this is not seen as a negative change process. If cooperatives are forming a supplementary organization, leading firms through a crisis, and keeping people employed, they may be an efficient form of organization. It may be under another paradigm than that of economic growth, but the evidence to prove that cooperatives are less efficient than private firms does not seem very strong.

4 Regional characteristics affecting business volatility in the United States, 1980–4[1]

Paul D. Reynolds,[2] *Brenda Miller*[3] *and*
Wilbur R. Maki[4]

INTRODUCTION

There is little question that economic growth and the founding of firms are closely related (Birch 1981; Kirchhoff and Phillips 1988). Recent analysis has found strong evidence that firm births, as a component of volatility or turbulence among business establishments, have a causal impact on subsequent economic growth (Reynolds and Maki 1990b). The major question that remains, however, is to determine which features of an economic system will lead to higher rates of firm births.

This chapter will report on a preliminary analysis of fifteen features of 382 labour market or journey-to-work areas of the US and their impact on births and deaths of autonomous firms and branches. This is a preliminary analysis covering only two time periods. Predictions based on data for 1978–80 (a period of national economic stability) are made for business volatility in 1980–2 (during a major national recession). Predictions based on data for 1980–2 (during the recession) are made for business volatility in 1982–4 (the beginning of a national recovery).

The presentation begins with a review of fifteen start-up processes for which data was available. This is followed by a discussion of the geographic unit of analysis (labour market areas) and the data assembled as multi-item indicators of each of the processes. Factor analyses were completed for the two data sets to determine the extent to which the fifteen aspects of these labour market areas could be represented by a smaller set of more general dimensions. The result was a partial success. The major analysis focuses on linear regression models that provide evidence of the relative causal impact of these fifteen processes on five measures of changes in the population of business establishments: autonomous firm births and deaths, branch births and deaths, and an index of business volatility. The concluding discussion looks at the major policy implications. The success of the analysis should encourage those completing similar projects on other countries.

FOUNDING PROCESSES

New businesses are clearly a critical element in job growth. The processes that lead to the founding of a new business establishment are less clear. Attention to variations in business births can be organized around two questions: What is responsible for differences across regions at the same time? What is responsible for differences over time in the same region?

A number of processes or mechanisms have been proposed as explanations for new formations. The specific propositions are often presented in sets, as part of a more general statement or argument. For example, the business climate argument – that an appropriate business climate will lead to higher firm births – often has a number of components, including lower costs, reduced taxes, and a responsive government administration. For the following discussion, each process will be treated singly, not as a feature of a more elaborate model of a fertile region.

Autonomous firms

This section presents fifteen hypotheses or postulates regarding causes of new firm births. They are summarized, in relation to the two issues above, in Table 4.1.[5]

Unemployment, desperation[6]

It is often assumed that desperate individuals, unable to pursue careers in established organizations, will start new firms. If accurate, regions with higher unemployment should have increased levels of new-firm birth rates. A recent review of several time series analyses of the United Kingdom, where this is often called 'recession-push', suggests there is systematic empirical support for this process under certain conditions.[7]

Career opportunities[8]

Complementing the unemployment hypothesis, this perspective

Table 4.1 Firm birth start-up processes

	Differences among regions	*Differences over time*
Unemployment, desperation	More firm births where more unemployment	As unemployment increases, so do firm births
Career opportunity	More firm births where mid-career, experienced adults reside	As proportion of mid-career experienced adults grows, so will firm births
Volatile industries	More firm births where volatile industries more prevalent	As proportion of volatile industries increases, so will firm births
Factors of production costs	More firm births where input costs are lower	As input costs are reduced, firm births will rise
Factors of production access	More firm births where factors of production are accessible	As factors of production become available, more firm births
Efficient public infrastructure	More firm births where public infrastructure better	As public infrastructure improves, more firm births
Access to customers, clients	More firm births where access is more convenient	As access improves, more firm births
Information, R&D base	More firm births where better access to R&D information, innovation	As access to R&D, information, innovation, increases, more firm births
Greater personal wealth	More firm births where greater personal wealth is present	As personal wealth increases, more firm births
Ethnic–cultural diversity	More firm births where there is greater ethnic–cultural diversity	As ethnic–cultural diversity increases, more firm births
Population growth	More firm births in regions with more population growth	As population increases, firm births increase
Economic system size	Higher firm birth rates in larger economic systems	As size of economic system grows, birth rates will grow faster
Economic diversity	Higher firm birth rates in more diverse economic systems	As economic system becomes more diverse, firm birth rates will increase
National transportation access	Higher firm birth rates where access to national transportation is convenient	As access to national transportation improves, firm births will rise
Employment policy flexibility	More firm births in contexts with greater employment flexibility	As employment flexibility increases, firm births increase

assumes that individuals start new firms to achieve personal career goals that cannot be achieved in the context of existing organizations. This implies that regions with well educated individuals in mid-career (25–45 years old) with positions that provide experience valuable for successful entrepreneurial activity (managerial and administrative experience) should have higher rates of new-firm births, when compared to regions with an absence of potential entrepreneurs.

Volatile industries[9]

There is some evidence that the turnover of businesses is higher in some industries than others. Consumer services, construction and retail have higher birth and death rates than manufacturing or distributive services. Hence, it is to be expected that, overall, new-firm birth rates would reflect the industry mix. The higher the proportion of more volatile industries, the higher the new-firm birth rates.

Factors of production costs[10]

It is argued that if prices and the demand for products are stable, and there is no change in the nature of the product, that the only factor that can encourage a new-firm formation is lower input costs. Without lower input costs, there will be no competitive advantage. Hence, relatively lower business costs – land, capital, labour, equipment, taxes – are assumed to encourage new firm startups. A low cost region might encourage entrepreneurial in-migration, as entrepreneurs seek a low cost context in which to start new firms.

Factors of production access[11]

A somewhat different issue is the availability of factors of production. It is argued that new firms often require a number of inputs, specialized parts or subassemblies, workers or consultants with unique skills, or access to other firms with distinctive competencies. The cost of acquiring information and assembling these inputs – measured in the time and energy of the start-up team – is reduced when access is convenient. As a new firm will not provide the sales volume that will encourage factors of production (suppliers, workers, capital) to move near it, new firms are more likely to be initiated where factors of production are established.

Efficient public infrastructure[12]

A number of factors are necessary for smoothly functioning businesses: transportation, communication (electronic and hard copy), education, health care, police and fire protection, sanitation and utilities. While not always provided by government organizations, most are provided under the supervision of governments and often paid for with public funds. It is argued that as more of these elements are provided in a form appropriate for businesses, they enhance the capacity to start a new firm by reducing the costs or complications of startup. For example, an educated workforce means that trained, skilled employees are available. The presence of reliable energy (gas, electricity) and suitable transportation systems can expedite the implementation of a new firm.

Access to customers, clients[13]

Customers and clients, either private citizens or other businesses, are a critical constituency for new businesses. The easier the access to those who will buy the goods or services, the greater the opportunity to fulfil their needs. In addition, most new firms have competition, and the best way to be informed of competitor's actions (new products, level of service provided, prices) is to have ready access to their customers.

Access to research and development, information, innovation[14]

The causal relationship between the presence of innovation and new and small firms is not clear, but they seem to be highly associated. It is argued that where information is readily available and innovation and creativity flourish, the formation rate of new firms is enhanced.

Personal wealth[15]

Those with higher personal incomes may seek greater diversity in their personal consumption (housing, clothing, food, recreation, etc.). This, in turn, provides more opportunities for small specialized firms. This could be reflected in more new firms.

Ethnic-cultural diversity[16]

Complementing the arguments associated with diversity in personal income are arguments related to ethnic-cultural diversity. As this diversity increases, there is a wider range of demand for goods and services and, in turn, more diverse opportunities for new and small firms.

Population growth[17]

Population growth should provide an increase in demand, certainly for goods and services sought by individuals and, in turn, opportunities for new firms to be profitable. This should lead to new-firm formations.

Economic system size[18]

This argument assumes that a larger socio-economic system will, by virtue of its size, have substantially higher birth rates. Conceptually, it is important to distinguish size from other attributes highly associated with it, such as diversity, complexity and the density of economic activity. All are considered to improve the climate for new firm development.

Economic diversity[19]

Distinct from the size of an economic system is the diversity. It is assumed that diversity in productive activities as well as diversity in skills and occupations will provide more opportunities to develop markets or clientele for new firms. Further, it is assumed this will enhance the capacity to identify suitable suppliers and human talent. All should encourage new-firm births.

National transportation access[20]

For new firms oriented towards a national market, convenient access to the entire nation is a major issue. While overnight delivery services and modern communications provide timely exchanges of major messages and material, direct face-to-face contact remains critical for maintaining effective relationships with suppliers and customers. Hence, those areas convenient for national transportation, such as access to major airline hubs, provide an advantage not available in more remote areas.

Employment policy flexibility[21]

The rate of change in economic activity appears to be increasing. There is an accelerated introduction of new products and new production methods. Managers and workers are a major aspect of most economic production, and the ability to respond quickly and efficiently to changes by adjusting the workforce or its duties is considered by many to be a major asset. New firms are often introduced in the most volatile of industry contexts. It is suggested that a capacity for flexible employment relationships reduces some of the risks and complications associated with initiating a new firm. Hence, the greater the employment policy flexibility, the higher the rate of new-firm formation.

Branches

Multi-establishment firms exist in a wide range of industries. Branches may be utilized in at least two distinct ways. First, branches may be a unique source of intermediate or final products (productive branches). Second, branches may have a major role in the distribution and delivery of the firm's output to the final customer (sales branches).

Each productive branch may provide a unique contribution to the final output of a multi-branch firm. The headquarters establishment is considered responsible for coordinating branch plant output to ensure a useful final product. For example, a firm producing trucks may produce transmissions in one plant, diesel engines in a second, and the bodies and final assembly in a third. Properly coordinated, the output from each branch will be of the appropriate type and volume to provide a balanced, timely flow of the final product.

The second function of branches is as outlets for products destined for the final user, either consumers or other businesses. In some cases, the product may be assembled at the sales branch, as with fast food products, or provided by a producing branch or another firm.

For the purposes of this analysis the processes leading to the establishment of each type of branch may be quite different. For example, founding a productive branch may give substantial consideration to the costs and availability of inputs, an efficient public infrastructure (roads, communications), the presence of responsive governments providing subsidies, and, should the productive branch be discontinued, low exit costs. Equally important may be accessibility to other productive branches associated with the same firm.[22]

In contrast, the establishment of a sales branch would emphasize access to customers and clients, the extent to which the potential clients are interested in the products or services (based on their wealth or cultural predilections), potential growth in customers, and the presence of competitors.

In short, the founding of different types of branches is likely to reflect quite different processes or factors. These may differ from those having an impact on autonomous new firms. In the following analysis branch births and deaths are used as a basis for comparisons with autonomous firms. It is not possible to separate the different types of branches. It is expected that the ability to predict branch births based on features of the immediate region will be, compared to predictions for autonomous firm births, less successful.

SOURCES OF DATA AND MEASURES OF PROCESSES

Several definitions are critical for the analysis strategy: the geographical unit of analysis, classification of region type, the measurement of establishment birth and death rates, and the sources of the indicators reflecting the processes leading to establishment formations.

Labour market (travel-to-work) areas

Labour market areas (LMAs) are the geographical unit of analysis. They are aggregations of the 3,124 US counties into 382 travel-to-work areas identified in cluster analyses using the 1980 census of population data (Tolbert and Killian 1987). A map of US labour market areas is provided in Figure 4.1. It appears unfamiliar because one-third of these LMAs involve counties from two or more states. A consideration of the industry of employment, using 1980 census data, leads to a topology based on variations from the national averages in industry mix: the eighty-one 'metropolitan' LMAs are those with a slight emphasis, when compared to the average for all 382 LMAs, on business and distributive services and include most of the major metropolitan areas.[23] The 160 'transitional rural' LMAs are those with a moderate manufacturing or an extreme emphasis on manufacturing and most are not metropolitan.[24] 'Traditional rural' are those 103 in rural areas which have a diversity of emphasis, including twenty-nine with a heavy emphasis on agriculture. The 'other' category includes thirty-eight with a diversity of emphases such as government employment, health or education services, or consumer services (resort areas).

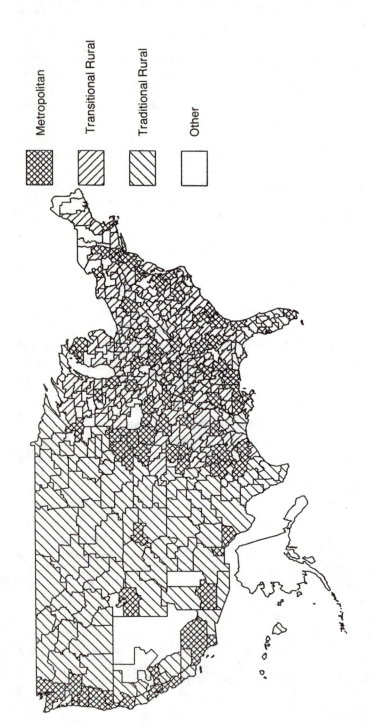

Metropolitan

Transitional Rural

Traditional Rural

Other

Figure 4.1 US labour market (journey-to-work) areas, 1980

Source: Based on analysis reported in Tolbert and Killian 1987.

Business births and deaths

Data on establishments and their formations originates with the files of the Dun and Bradstreet and the Dun's Market Identifier files. The complete national file has been leased by the US Small Business Administration in December of every even year since 1976 (US Small Business Administration 1988). Comparisons of two consecutive files are used to identify new or deceased establishments. Establishments present only in the second period file are considered births; those present only in the first period file are considered deaths. 'Autonomous firms' (or just firms) are those which are a single establishment firm, a headquarters establishment, or a branch with a headquarters in the same county. 'Branches' include all establishments owned by a headquarters outside the county. This analysis, therefore, includes all types of establishments. For each labour market area, data are available on the total number of new autonomous firm and branch establishments that appear or disappear during two-year periods starting in 1976 (1976–8, 1978–80, 1980–2, 1982–4, 1984–6, 1986–8). All industries (except agricultural production, which is not included in the data assembled by Dun and Bradstreet) are included in the analysis. This differs from many analyses that focus only on manufacturing. In this analysis, manufacturing firms or employment represent less than 20 per cent of total economic activity.

Birth rates and death rates are computed as the annual number of establishment (autonomous firm or branch) births or deaths per 10,000 population in the labour market area. A business volatility index was created by taking the average of the standardized Z-scores (mean of zero, standard deviation of 1.0) for the four measures. All five distributions are normal for the two time periods involved in this analysis.

Multi-item indicators of birth processes

All other data on the characteristics of the regions are taken from a diversity of federal data sources, most represented in the County-Statistics 3 file provided by the US Census or information derived from the 1980 Census of Population. They are assembled in terms of their absolute value at the county level and then aggregated into LMAs. This places some restrictions on the precision of some data. For example, industry by employment is available only at the one-digit standard industrial code (SIC) level at county level. Some data

Table 4.2 Multi-item measures: labour market area characteristics

Process represented	Items	Variable name	1980 reliability if item deleted[25]	1980 reliability total scale[26]	1982 reliability if item deleted	1982 reliability total scale
Unemployment	Unemployment	GUExxP	N/A		N/A	
	Transfer payments[27] as percentage of total personal income	MWFIN80P	N/A	0.67	N/A	0.74
Career opportunity	Per cent population age 35–44	GPO44xxP	0.90		0.70	
	Per cent some college	FPOSCxxP	0.87		0.75	
	Per cent college degree	FPOCOxxP	0.85		0.64	
	Per cent managers	FEMMAxxP	0.87		0.64	
	Per cent professionals	FEMPRxxP	0.86		0.64	
	Per cent technical occupations	FEMTLxxP	0.87	0.89	0.66	0.85
Industry mix	Pct workforce: construction	GEMCNxxP	0.41		0.40	
	Pct workforce: retail	GEMRTxxP	0.37		0.15	
	Pct workforce: consumer services	TEMPLxxP	0.34		–	
	Pct workforce: services	GEMSCxxP	–		0.26	
	Pct establishments: construction	ESCNxxP	0.59		0.34	
	Pct establishments: consumer serv.	ZESCSxxP	0.42	0.64	0.26	0.61
Costs of factors of production	Business tax/worker	KBUTXxxJ	0.59		0.68	
	Local government revenue/capita	TLGTXxxC	0.54		0.65	
	Local government debt/capita	TLGGDxxC	0.55		0.62	
	Earned income/worker	EARNxxJ	0.43	0.69	0.54	0.69

Category	Indicator	Code				
Availability of production factors	Per capita demand deposits	TDMDPxxC	0.91		0.91	
	Per capita savings deposits	TSADPxxC	0.93		0.90	
	Per cent with HS Diploma only	FPOHS80P	0.92		0.90	
	Per cent adults age 15–64	C1564xxP	0.91	0.90	0.89	0.89
	Sales workers per square mile	SEMSL80M	0.87		0.85	
	Clerical workers per square mile	SEMCL80M	0.87		0.85	
	Service workers per square mile	SEMSV80M	0.87		–	
	Skilled craftsmen per square mile	SEMCF80M	0.88		0.85	
	Machine operators per square mile	SEMOP80M	0.88		0.86	
	Transport operators per square mile	SMETO80M	0.88		0.85	
	Labourers per square mile	SEMLB80M	0.88		0.85	
Efficient public infrastructure	Per capita govt exp: education	GEDEXxxC	0.40		0.52	
	Per capita govt exp: highways	GHIEXxxC	0.44	0.67	0.66	0.70
	Per capita govt exp: welfare	TPWEXxxC	0.57		0.66	
	Per capita govt exp: police	TCPEXxxC	0.44		0.66	
Access to customers, clients	Population/square mile	TPOxxM	N/A	0.99	N/A	0.99
	Establishments/square mile	ZESxxM	N/A		N/A	
Knowledge, R&D base	Post-college/1,000 sq miles	SPOGDxxM	0.87		0.98	
	Professionals and technical employees/ 1,000 square miles	SPRTLxxM	0.88	0.99	–	0.98
	Patents granted/1,000 square miles	ZPATxxM	0.89		0.98	
	Doctorates granted/1,000 sq miles	ZGDxxM	0.87		0.97	
Personal wealth	Personal income per capita	GPIxxC	0.77		0.71	
	Income per household	GPIOHxx	0.82	0.87	0.84	0.89
	Dividend, interest, + rent per capita	DIRxxC	0.85		0.97	

Table 4.2 continued

Process represented	Items	Variable name	1980 reliability if item deleted[25]	total scale[26]	1982 reliability if item deleted	total scale
Social status diversity	Educational diversity index (a)	FEDxxV	N/A		N/A(b)	
	Household income diversity index (a)	FINESxxV	N/A	0.72	N/A(b)	0.72
Population growth	Ten year population change	MPO70xxP	0.55		N/A	
	Per cent living in same country five years earlier	JPOCY75P	0.77		N/A	
	Per cent in migration	JPOMG75P	0.78	0.79	–	0.77
Size of economic base	Total population	TRESPOxx	0.99		0.99	
	Total labour force	ZRIESExx	0.99		0.99	
	Total establishments	ZSBAESxx	1.00	0.99	1.00	0.99
Economic diversity	Establishment/employees	MEMESxx	N/A		N/A	
	Occupational diversity index (a)	TEMxxV	N/A	0.58	N/A	0.65
National transportation access	Distance to closest hub airport	HAPDS1	N/A		N/A(b)	
	Difference in distance to closest and second closest hub airports	HAPDS12	N/A	0.79	N/A(b)	0.79
Flexible employment policies	Labour force, per cent unionized	ZNRTWxxP	N/A		N/A	
	Per cent employees without state right-to-work laws[28]	ZMLUxxP	N/A	0.88	N/A	0.88

Business volatility (for 1982–4 and 1984–6)

Autonomous firm births per 10,000 population	TBRPOxx	0.86	0.87
Branch/subsidiary births per 10,000 population	BBPROxx	0.88	0.86
Autonomous firm deaths per 10,000 population	TDTPOxx	0.90	0.87
Branch/subsidiary deaths per 10,000 population	BDTPOxx	0.88	0.86
		0.91	0.89

Note: (a) Diversity index computed the M5 formula discussed in Gibbs and Poston (1975)
(b) Because of lack of data, same values used for both 1980–2 and 1982–4 data-sets

(such as the number of union members or patents approved) was only available at state level. In these cases the absolute counts were distributed across all counties in proportion to some county level characteristic, such as the number of workers for union membership, prior to aggregation to the labour market area.

Multi-item indices were developed for the fifteen processes for the two time periods represented by the independent variables (1980–2; 1982–4). They are presented in Table 4.2. This presents the items included in each index and also the estimated reliability (Chronbach's alpha) for each index. The effect on the overall reliability from deleting each item is also noted for indices with three or more items.

The reliabilities are, for most indices, quite high. Of the thirty indices to be used in the analysis, reliabilities are in excess of 0.80 for 46 per cent and in excess of 0.70 for 73 per cent. For three indices – access to customers, clients; availability of R&D and information; and size of the economic base – reliabilities are essentially 1.00.

The reliability of the business volatility index (provided at the bottom of Table 4.2) is approximately 0.90 for both predictive time periods (1980–2; 1982–4).

No issue in this analysis is more important than the capacity for inferences about causality. Hence, all independent measures are for the period immediately prior to the periods for which business volatility is measured. For the first data set independent variables are measured for 1980 and dependent for 1980–2; for the second data set the independent are measured for 1982 and the dependent for 1982–4. For two independent variables, measures of social-cultural diversity and national transportation access, the same indices are used for both data sets.

Determining common dimensions: factor analysis results

A factor analysis was completed on both sets of independent variables to determine the extent to which these fifteen dimensions might be representing a smaller set of differences among the 382 US labour market areas. A five factor solution was forced with each data set as it provided the most stability across the two analyses. The results are presented in Table 4.3. Twelve indices appear to have a stable structure across the two time periods. Three indices tended to shift factors across the two time periods: measures of career opportunity; efficient public infrastructure; and economic diversity. The last, economic diversity, is of particular significance because of its major, pervasive impact in the linear regression models, discussed in

Table 4.3 Process dimensions: factor weighting for 1980 and 1982

Factor analysis 80	82		Variable name	Factor loadings 1980 I	II	III	IV	V	Factor loadings 1982 I	II	III	IV	V
		Factor 1 – Agglomerative/access											
I	I	Availability of factors of production	PFAVLxx	0.93					0.95				
I	I	Access to customers, clients	ACCSSxx	0.95					0.96				
I	I	Knowledge, **R&D** base	TECHxx	0.95					0.95				
I	I	Size of economic base	BASExx	0.80					0.80				
II	I	Career opportunity	CARERxx		0.52				0.58				
		Factor 2 – Wealth/costs/variety											
II	II	Unemployment/desperation	DESPxx		−0.77					−0.86			
II	II	Costs of factors of production	PFCSTxx		0.81					0.75			
II	II	Personal wealth	WELTHxx		0.80					0.75			
II	II	Social status diversity	SOCxxV		0.77					0.70			
II	IV	Public infrastructure expenditures	INFEFxx		0.71							0.73	
III	II	Economic diversity	ECONxxV			0.64				0.71			
		Factor 3 – Growth/volatile industries											
III	III	Industry mix (volatile industries)	ESMIXxx			0.86					0.68		
III	III	Population growth	POPxxD			0.83					0.88		
		Factor 4 – Employment rigidities											
IV	IV	Flexible employment policies (lack of)	LUxx				0.88					0.84	
		Factor 5 – National transportation difficulties											
V	V	Lack of national transportation access	AIRPxx					0.88					0.92

Note: The factor analysis procedure in SPSS-PC V3.1 was utilized, standard defaults including varimax rotation. For the 1980–2 factor analysis, 84.4 per cent of the cumulative variance was accounted for by five factors, the fourth eigenvalue was 1.13, and the fifth factor eigenvalue was 0.73. For the 1982–4 factor analysis, 83.5 per cent of the cumulative variance was accounted for by five factors, the fourth eigenvalue was 1.15, and the fifth factor eigenvalue was 0.68.

the following section. Because of the instability in the factor solutions, no attempt was made to develop a smaller set of five mega-indices to represent the fifteen processes indicators.

There is, however, some stability in the two factor analyses. Four indices: availability of factors of production; access to customers or clients; knowledge, R&D base; and the size of the economic base, form a major cluster, labelled agglomerative/access. Four other factors: unemployment/desperation with negative loadings; costs of factors of production; personal wealth; and social status diversity, are consistently associated in a second major cluster, labelled wealth/costs/variety. Two items (industry mix or volatile industries; population growth) are consistently associated in a third factor labelled growth/volatile industries. One factor incorporates one item in the first analysis (lack of flexible employment policies) and two in the second (efficient public infrastructure is added). A fifth factor consists of a single item in both analyses – lack of national transportation access.

Many analyses of causes of variation in new-firm birth rates tend to emphasize 'models' of fertile regions. Such models tend to incorporate collections of different founding processes. For this reason, the analysis of the temporal relationship between founding processes and measures of business volatility will be organized around these 'pseudo' factors.

LINEAR MODEL RESULTS AND INTERPRETATIONS

Three analyses are presented. Correlations of indicators of all fifteen start-up processes with the five measures of business volatility are presented for both time periods in Table 4.4. This is followed by two sets of linear regression model results. The first linear regression models for the five measures of business volatility for the two time periods is presented in Table 4.5; models of the processes affecting the business volatility index for the three types of regions for the two time periods are presented in Table 4.6.

Inspection of the correlations between the process indicators and the measures of business volatility in Table 4.4 indicates little difference across the two time periods. There are, however, substantial differences in the correlations across the various start-up processes. For example, most correlations associated with pseudo-factor I, agglomerative/access, are extremely low, very close to zero. In contrast, those associated with pseudo-factor II, wealth/costs/variety, and pseudo-factor III, growth/volatile industries, are

Table 4.4 Correlations between process indicators and measures of business volatility, 1980–2 and 1982–4

Factor analysis 80	82		Variable name	Business volatility index 80–82	82–84	Birth rates Auton. firms 80–82	82–84	Branches 80–82	82–84	Death rates Auton. firms 80–82	82–84	Branches 80–82	82–84
			Factor 1 – Agglomerative/access										
I	I	Availability of factors of production	PFAVLxx	-0.04	0.11	-0.09	0.17	0.05	0.09	-0.11	-0.04	-0.01	0.14
I	I	Access to customers, clients	ACCSSxx	-0.01	0.00	-0.06	0.07	0.10	0.02	-0.11	-0.14	0.02	0.05
I	I	Knowledge, R&D base	TECHxx	0.02	-0.05	0.00	0.04	0.12	-0.04	-0.08	-0.17	0.03	0.00
I	I	Size of economic base	BASExx	0.38	0.39	0.36	0.44	0.40	0.34	0.25	0.22	0.33	0.38
II	I	Career opportunity	CARERxx	0.49	0.33	0.52	0.47	0.45	0.28	0.40	0.18	0.36	0.24
			Factor 2 – Wealth/costs/variety										
II	II	Unemployment/desperation	DESPxx	-0.55	-0.58	-0.52	-0.42	-0.51	-0.60	-0.39	-0.47	-0.52	-0.54
II	II	Costs of factors of production	PFCSTxx	0.61	0.51	0.58	0.45	0.49	0.38	0.50	0.46	0.60	0.49
II	II	Personal wealth	WELTHxx	0.60	0.56	0.56	0.52	0.48	0.43	0.56	0.46	0.51	0.54
II	II	Social status diversity	SOCxxV	0.56	0.54	0.54	0.57	0.48	0.45	0.47	0.40	0.48	0.46
II	IV	Public infrastructure expenditures	INFEFxx	0.43	0.30	0.43	0.32	0.25	0.14	0.51	0.35	0.33	0.22
III	II	Economic diversity	ECONxxV	0.74	0.74	0.69	0.58	0.57	0.62	0.74	0.71	0.60	0.67
			Factor 3 – Growth/volatile industries										
III	III	Industry mix (volatile industries)	ESMIXxx	0.47	0.48	0.51	0.54	0.38	0.36	0.46	0.44	0.31	0.33
III	III	Population growth	POPxxD	0.53	0.43	0.58	0.51	0.48	0.33	0.44	0.33	0.39	0.31
			Factor 4 – Employment rigidities										
IV	IV	Flexible employment policies (lack of)	LUxx	-0.12	-0.16	-0.19	-0.10	-0.23	-0.35	0.06	-0.03	-0.06	-0.11
			Factor 5 – National transportation difficulties										
V	V	Lack of national transportation access	AIRPxx	0.29	0.30	0.30	0.26	0.18	0.23	0.29	0.31	0.26	0.24

Note: All variables transformed to approximately normal distributions, skewdness between +1.00 and −1.00
As the entire population is included in the analysis, the correlations represent the true relationship and statistical significance is not relevant

consistently in the medium range, from 0.3 to 0.6. Consistently the highest correlations, generally above 0.60, are associated with the economic diversity index. With many correlations in excess of 0.70, economic diversity alone would account for half of the variation in the measures of business volatility. Correlations associated with the remaining two pseudo-factors, related to rigidity of employment relationships and lack of national transportation access, are consistent and in the low range, from about 0.10 to 0.30.

The major issue in any multivariate analysis is, of course, the extent to which the different independent variables are making distinctive contributions to the variation of the dependent variables. This was completed with the standard stepwise regression procedure from SPSS-PC V3.1. The factor analysis indicates that many of the independent variables are associated with each other. High levels of multi-collinearity among the independent variables could be expected. Hence, the tolerance was set at 0.10, rather than the SPSS-PC V3.1 default of 0.01. In other words, if 10 per cent or more of the variation in a candidate for inclusion in the model could be predicted by the variables already in the equation, the new candidate is not included. Note that the tolerances for all variables in the equation are recomputed after each new variable is added. Those with new tolerances that fall below these criteria are excluded (Norusis 1988; B-221-3).

Ten linear regression models are presented in Table 4.5, one model for each of the five indicators of business volatility for each of two time periods. The body of the table presents the standardized beta weights for indices which made a statistically significant contribution to the fit of the model. The overall success of the models is indicated by the explained variance in the last row. This varies from a low of 0.59 to a high of 0.78.[29] The explained variances are highest for predictions of business volatility; almost as high for most models related to autonomous firm births and deaths; and somewhat lower for branch births and deaths. The relatively loser success at predicting branch births and deaths based on the immediate regional context is consistent with the expectations discussion above. Decisions about branch formations and dissolutions are expected, in many cases, to reflect the branch's role in the total organization and not just the regional context.

Linear regression models for predictions of the business volatility index for the three types of labour market areas – metropolitan, transitional rural, and traditional rural – are presented in Table 4.6. These models tend to be quite successful, with explained variances of about 0.75, for both the metropolitan and traditional rural labour

Table 4.5 Linear regression models predicting business volatility, 1980–2 and 1982–4

Factor analysis 80	82		Variable name	Business volatility index 80–2	82–4	Birth rates — Auton. firms 80–2	82–4	Birth rates — Branches 80–2	82–4	Death rates — Auton. firms 80–2	82–4	Death rates — Branches 80–2	82–4
		Factor 1 – Agglomerative/access											
I	I	Availability of factors of production	PFAVLxx					0.25				0.04	0.04
I	I	Access to customers, clients	ACCSSxx										
I	I	Knowledge, R&D base	TECHxx		0.08					−0.10	−0.09		
I	I	Size of economic base	BASExx						0.09			0.09	
II	I	Career opportunity	CARERxx		−0.08	0.07	0.19					−0.30	−0.19
		Factor 2 – Wealth/costs/variety											
II	II	Unemployment/desperation	DESPxx	−0.21	−0.24	−0.09		−0.26	−0.25	−0.11	−0.22	−0.25	−0.18
II	II	Costs of factors of production	PFCSTxx	0.12		0.11	−0.10	0.09				0.24	
II	II	Personal wealth	WELTHxx	0.20	0.20	0.26	0.34			0.22	0.24		0.33
II	II	Social status diversity	SOCxxV						0.12			0.21	
II	IV	Public infrastructure expenditures	INFEFxx							0.16			−0.07
III	II	Economic diversity	ECONxxV	0.52	0.44	0.38	0.30	0.42	0.38	0.59	0.46	0.46	0.43
		Factor 3 – Growth/volatile industries											
III	III	Industry mix (volatile industries)	ESMIXxx	−0.09	0.07		0.11			−0.10	0.09	−0.14	
III	III	Population growth	POPxxD	0.28	0.33	0.26	0.40	0.26	0.19	0.20	0.26	0.25	0.25
		Factor 4 – Employment rigidities											
IV	IV	Flexible employment policies (lack of)	LUxx	−0.08		−0.20	−0.11	−0.18	−0.24		0.16		
		Factor 5 – National transportation difficulties											
V	V	Lack of national transportation access	AIRPxx	−0.06						−0.08			
		Adjusted explained variance (R**2)		0.78	0.75	0.74	0.66	0.59	0.61	0.67	0.63	0.60	0.61

Note: All analysis completed with SPSS-PC V3.1 regression, stepwise procedure, standard defaults except that tolerences set to 0.10. Independent variables transformed to normal distribution and standardized, residuals normally distributed for all models

Table 4.6 Linear regression models predicting business volatility by type of region, 1980–2 and 1982–4

Factor analysis		Description	Variable name	Business volatility index							
80	82			All regions (n=382)		Metropolitan (n=81)		Transitional rural (n=160)		Traditional rural (n=103)	
				80–82	82–84	80–82	82–84	80–82	82–84	80–82	82–84
		Factor 1 – Agglomerative/access									
I	I	Availability of factors of production	PFAVLxx								
I	I	Access to customers, clients	ACCSSxx						0.16		
I	I	Knowledge, R&D base	TECHxx								
I	I	Size of economic base	BASExx		0.08				0.15		
I	II	Career opportunity	CARERxx		−0.08				−0.21		
		Factor 2 – Wealth/costs/variety									
II	II	Unemployment/desperation	DESPxx	−0.21	−0.24	−0.27	−0.38		−0.35	−0.41	−0.16
II	II	Costs of production	PFCSTxx	0.12		0.15					
II	II	Personal wealth	WELTHxx	0.20	0.20	0.28					0.35
II	II	Social status diversity	SOCxxV					0.67			
II	IV	Public infrastructure expenditures	INFEFxx			−0.17				0.14	
III	II	Economic diversity	ECONxxV	0.52	0.44	0.42	0.48	0.55	0.54	0.54	0.40
		Factor 3 – Growth/volatile industries									
III	III	Industry mix (volatile industries)	ESMIXxx	−0.09	0.07			−0.12			0.30
III	III	Population growth	POPxxD	0.28	0.33	0.36	0.46	0.25	0.28	0.25	0.21
		Factor 4 – Employment rigidities									
IV	IV	Flexible employment policies (lack of)	LUxx	−0.08			0.18	−0.34			
		Factor 5 – National transportation difficulties									
V	V	Lack of national transportation access	AIRPxx	−0.06					0.12	−0.15	
		Adjusted explained variance (R**2)		0.78	0.75	0.75	0.73	0.63	0.66	0.74	0.74

Note: All analysis completed with SPSS-PC V3.1 regression, stepwise procedure, standard defaults except that tolerences set to 0.10. Independent variables transformed to normal distribution and standardized, residuals normally distribute for all models market areas. These models are, however, somewhat less complex, with a slightly reduced set of independent variables. Models for the transitional rural areas are not quite as successful, with an explained variance of about 0.65, and more differences between the two time periods. This probably reflects greater heterogeneity and instability in economic structures among the transitional rural areas. Perhaps most significant, the models for the different types of labour market areas are basically quite similar to those for all 382 labour market areas. The four most significant start-up processes – unemployment/desperation; personal wealth; economic diversity; and population growth – have major impacts in models for all types of regions.

Impact of start-up processes

The impact of the various start-up processes in the models presented in Table 4.5 are varied and, in some cases, completely unexpected. The levels of impact fall into three categories. First, are four processes that have a consistent and major presence in almost all linear models predicting business volatility. Second, are six processes that have a moderate, occasionally inconsistent impact on business volatility linear models. Finally, there are five processes that have little or no impact in any of the linear models. A summary of the influences, based on Table 4.5, is presented in Table 4.7.

Major influences

Economic diversity: the most significant factor affecting future business births, deaths, and volatility was economic diversity, represented by an index based on the density of establishments and diversity of occupations present in the workforce. By itself, this process would account for half of the variance in business volatility. There is little question that it has an impact independent from other aspects of the region, such as size and growth. If business volatility is a source of diversity, there is no question that diversity breeds diversity.

Population growth: a major predictive contribution, independent of diversity, is provided by population growth. The index was based on the percentage population growth in the previous ten years as well as the percentage of residents in the county five years previously and a measure of in-migration. While it is not surprising that expansion of the socio-economic system would lead to more business births, it was also a significant factor predicting business deaths and, consequently, business volatility.

Table 4.7 Summary of influences of major processes

	Differences among regions	Summary of impact	
Economic diversity	Higher firm birth rates in more diverse economic systems	Major	Consistent for all models
Population growth	More firm births in regions with more population growth	Strong	Consistent for all models
Greater personal wealth	More firm births where greater personal wealth is present	Strong	Consistent for firm births
Unemployment, desperation	More firm births where more unemployment	Strong *Direction reversed*	Consistent, particularly for branches
Employment policy flexibility	More firm births in contexts with greater employment flexibility	Strong	Consistent impact on births
		Small	Little impact on deaths
Factors of production costs	More firm births where input costs are lower	Small, reversed	Direction reversed 80–82
		Small, consistent	For 82–84 firm births
Economic system size	Higher firm birth rates in larger economic systems	Small, consistent	Consistent for 82–84 branches
		Small, reversed	Reversed for 80–82 firm deaths
Career opportunity	More firm births where more mid-career, experienced adults reside	Small, consistent	Firm births
		Small, reversed	Branch deaths
Volatile industries	More firm births where volatile industries more prevalent	Small, reversed	For 80–82 deaths
		Small, consistent	For 82–84 firms
National transportation access	Higher firm birth rates where access to national transportation is convenient	Very small	Present only for 80–82 firm deaths
Factors of production access	More firm births where factors of production are accessible	Very small	

Access to customers, clients	More firm births where access is more convenient	Very small
Efficient public infrastructure	More firm births where public infrastructure better	Very small
Social status diversity	More firm births where there is greater social status diversity	Very small
Information, R&D base	More firm births where better access to R&D, information, innovation	None

Personal wealth: relatively higher personal wealth is measured by an index that reflects personal income per capita, income per household, and the total of dividend, interest, and rental income per capita. The fact that it has its major impact on autonomous firm volatility, birth *and* death rates, is support for the argument that greater personal wealth leads to diversity in personal consumption with a stronger impact on businesses oriented towards local markets. Subsequent analysis will indicate the extent to which personal wealth has an impact on retail branches equivalent to that on retail autonomous firms.

Unemployment, desperation: there is no question that the extent of unemployment and desperation has an impact on firm and branch births, as it makes a statistically significant contribution in nine out of ten models. However, the direction of causality is reversed from the usual interpretation. Higher levels of this index, a combination of the unemployment rate and the percentage of household income represented by transfer (welfare) payments, are associated with a depression in business volatility; business births and deaths are reduced. It seems reasonable to assume that in the United States higher levels of unemployment occur in stagnant regions where there is little economic change or business volatility.

Moderate influences

Employment policy flexibility: the lack of employment policy flexibility is indicated by the percentage of the workforce that is unionized and the extent to which workers are required by state law to join a union at their place of work. This index is consistently included in all models predicting firm and branch births. The less flexible the employment policies, the lower the birth rates of firms and branches. It is, however, absent from three of the four models of death rates, having a positive impact on autonomous firm deaths for 1984–6. This process seems to have a small, consistent impact depressing firm and branch births.

Factors of production costs: the factors of production cost index is a combination of measures of business taxes per worker, local government revenue per capita, local government debt per capita, and earned income per worker. The first three are measures of the cost of government and the fourth would reflect wages and salaries. This measure is included in five of the linear models but for four it is positive. Higher costs of production were associated with higher firm and branch births in 1980–2, but also higher branch death rates in 1980–2. Higher costs of production were associated with lower firm birth rates only for 1982–4. If this is considered the major indicator of business climate, it is clear that its effect is by no means equivocal and predictable. This is consistent with a host of other research on the impact of government taxation on economic growth; there is little evidence of a major association between variations in taxation and regional economic well-being (Newman and Sullivan 1988).

Economic system size: the index of economic system size is based on total human population, total labour force, and total establishment count. It had a reliability as close to perfect as can be obtained in social science. For the United States, the range was quite extreme, from labour market areas with a population of 100,000 to those of about 12,000,000. It is difficult to imagine a better test of the impact of this process. Yet the results make clear that size, in and of itself, is of marginal significance. It has a small independent effect. In fact, greater size is related to increases in branch births in 1982–4, a decrease in firm deaths in 1980–2 and an increase in branch deaths in 1980–2. Its major impact appears to be on volatility in transitional rural areas in 1982–4 (Table 4.6).

Career opportunities: the career opportunity index is a combination of six indicators reflecting the percentage of young adults with post-high school education and the percentage of employment in occupations from which entrepreneurs are likely to emerge (managers, professionals and technical workers). As expected, it does have a small, consistent, positive impact on the birth of autonomous firms. The presence of this pool of potential entrepreneurs seems to have a more significant impact in depressing branch deaths. Perhaps their presence reduces deaths of retail branches of national firms. In short, this process seems to have some influence on specific birth and death processes, rather than on business volatility *per se.*

Volatile industries: the index of volatile industries reflects the proportion of a region's workforce or establishments in retail, consumer service or construction. A higher index is associated with greater autonomous firm births and deaths in 1982–4, and a reduction of firm and branch deaths in 1980–2. Its largest standardized beta weight was for business volatility in traditional rural areas in 1982–4. Clearly this process could have a significant impact under certain conditions. Establishing those conditions will take some additional research.

National transportation access: indicated by the average distance from a labour market area to a national transportation hub and the distance between the closest and second closest hub airports. This seems to have almost no impact on business births and deaths. The evidence from comparisons of region types in Table 4.6 is inconsistent. Travel distances are greatest for transitional rural and traditional rural regions, yet this measure of travel distance has small and inconsistent effects. Greater average travel distance actually enhanced business volatility in transitional rural regions in 1982–4 and depressed same in traditional rural regions in 1980–2. It would not appear to be a major short term factor. Access to national markets may be equally convenient, or inconvenient, across all US labour market areas despite the differences in geographical distances from major hub airports in the early 1980s.

Minimal effect

Factors of production access: eleven indicators representing the availability of demand and checking bank deposits, potential workers, high school graduates, and personnel in seven occupational categories (sales, clerical, service, skilled workmen, machine operators, transport operatives, and labourers) are used to create this very reliable index of access to factors of production. It is not included in any of the linear models predicting business volatility. It is included, as a significant positive influence, in the models predicting branch births for 1980–2. It also had a smaller positive impact on branch deaths for the same period. This may reflect the heavy emphasis in the index on worker availability.

Access to customers, clients: an index based on the density of population and establishments per square mile is used to indicate convenient access to customers. Greater access to customers seemed to reduce firm deaths for 1982–4 and overall business volatility in transitional rural areas in 1982–4. Compared to other factors, it is not a major influence on business volatility.

Efficient public infrastructure: the index for this variable is computed in reverse, so to speak, as it is a combination of per capita spending for education, highways, welfare, and police services. A higher index represents more expenditures. Higher expenditures are associated with higher firm death rates in 1980–2 and lower branch death rates in 1982–4. Higher public expenditures tended to reduce business volatility in metropolitan regions in 1980–2 but increased business volatility in traditional rural areas in the same period. As this index correlates about 0.5 with the measure of costs of factors of production, which largely reflects the costs of government, it is remarkable it would have any independent effect.

Socio-cultural diversity: measured by an index that reflects diversity in household income and educational attainment, this can be considered an indicator of socio-cultural heterogeneity. It does not, however, incorporate variation in ethnic composition. It seemed to have a small impact in increasing branch birth rates in 1982–4 and branch death rates in 1980–2. It is not incorporated in any model predicting the business volatility index.

Access to research and development, information, innovation: among the most difficult to construct, the index of the potential for more innovation involves measures of the density (per square mile) of those with post-college educational attainment, of professional and technical employees, patents granted, and doctorates granted.[30] The last component is considered to be a measure of the presence of major research-oriented educational institutions. Index reliabilities were 0.99 and 0.98. Yet this was the only process not included in any model for any dependent variable. Even the correlations between this index and the measures of business volatility, presented in Table 4.4, ranged around zero. Either this index is a poor reflection of differences in sophisticated technical information and research and development, there is much less variation across the United States than generally expected, or this process has no effect on new-firm births. Perhaps it will be significant in models related to industry-specific measures of business volatility.

This analysis has been a very stringent test of the impact of many of these processes. The measures of business births, deaths, and volatility have represented virtually all industry sectors, where almost half of all establishments and employment are in retail, construction, and consumer services. Most models or theories of entrepreneurship have been developed with either an explicit or implicit emphasis on manufacturing The next analysis in the research programme will emphasize industry-specific predictions. It may well be that some of these processes with little or no weight in predictions of all industry birth and death rates will have a more substantial rôle in industry specific predictions.

IMPLICATIONS

An analysis has been completed predicting business births and deaths for 382 labour market areas of the United States for 1980-2 and 1982-4. The factors having a major impact on firm births (one aspect of business volatility) are: the presence of economic diversity,[31] population growth, greater personal wealth, and lower unemployment. Greater flexibility in employment relations seemed to promote firm and branch births and the presence of potential entrepreneurs seemed to have a positive impact on firm births. Few other processes had more than a marginal impact on predictions of firm births, deaths or general business volatility. Of particular note was the complete absence of any impact from variation in the presence of research and development and sophisticated knowledge bases.

The potential for policy intervention seems quite limited, for the major factors are difficult to influence through public policy. Certainly efforts to enhance diversity – a reduction in the average establishment size (branch or firm) and the widest possible range of occupations – are to be recommended, but how to accomplish this is not clear. Both population growth and enhanced personal wealth are positive features, but they are major indicators of economic well-being. Reductions in unemployment are at the top of virtually every public policy agenda, and are also a reflection of economic well-being.

Two other processes with consistent impact are the presence of a large pool of potential entrepreneurs and flexible employment relationships. The first may not be easy to enhance through public policy, other than to further 'quality of life' to attract and retain potential entrepreneurs in a region.[32] The second, flexible employment relationships, is consistent with other research which suggests that if small firms have special advantages in financing, regulations, and employment relationships, it will encourage the founding of new firms when production expands, rather than the expansion of existing firms.[33] This is one area – legal standards regarding the status of new and small firms – where public policy can have a direct impact. How much this would increase firm births is difficult to say at this time.

Cross-national comparisons

The results of this endeavour should encourage cross-national comparisons. First, it is based on indices of the independent effects (the various start-up processes). While it is unlikely that the same indicators would be available in other nations, comparable indices might be developed to represent the start-up processes and almost any measure of business volatility might be seen as suitable. Second, the most influential processes had clear and consistent impacts. The linear models for business births, deaths and volatility were quite similar, even across different types of labour market areas. This suggests that these influences may be easy to discern in other countries. Cross-region analysis in the United States has one major advantage, the great diversity across the 382 labour market areas. Such diversity may not be present in most other countries, especially in Europe. Third, the major success of this analysis was related to measures of business volatility, rather than restricted to firm births. This suggests that a range of volatility measures might be satisfactory for analysis in other countries. Fourth, the high level of explained variance – reflecting a good fit of the models – suggests that the major processes affecting business volatility have been incorporated in this analysis. This may help guide scholars pursuing analysis in other countries as they select processes and indicators for inclusion in their data sets.

Similar analyses in other countries may be useful to pursue and the general results – the relative impact of different start-up processes – may be compared with the findings related to the United States. There is a very real potential for cross-national comparisons of major entrepreneurial phenomena.

APPENDIX

Table A4.1 Correlation matrix: 1980 data-set

Correlations:	PFAVL80	ACCSS80	TECH80	BASE80	CARER80	DESP80	PFCST80	WELTH80	SOC80V	INFEF80	ECON80V
PFAVL80	1.000										
ACCSS80	0.9663**	1.0000									
TECH80	0.9705**	0.9820**	1.0000								
BASE80	0.6975**	0.7171**	0.7235**	1.0000							
CARER80	0.3485**	0.3122**	0.3950**	0.6127**	1.0000						
DESP80	−0.0672	−0.0538	−0.0642	−0.3296**	−0.4360**	1.0000					
PFCST80	0.1585*	0.1311*	0.1645**	0.4535**	0.5222**	−0.5399**	1.0000				
WELTH80	0.4439**	0.3793**	0.4382**	0.6161**	0.5841**	−0.5644**	0.6596**	1.0000			
SOC80V	0.4083**	0.3369**	0.4234**	0.6527**	0.8757**	−0.6005**	0.6836**	0.8015**	1.0000		
INFEF80	−0.0626	−0.1301*	−0.0403	0.1731**	0.4020**	−0.2915**	0.5477**	0.5808**	0.5420**	1.0000	
ECON80V	−0.2423**	−0.1960**	−0.1957**	0.2151**	0.3360**	−0.2313**	0.4722**	0.3993**	0.3201**	0.4105**	1.0000
ESMIX80	−0.3265**	−0.3336**	−0.2961**	−0.0493	0.3303**	−0.1234*	0.2681**	0.1859**	0.2261**	0.3693**	0.5789**
POP80D	−0.2079**	−0.1723**	−0.1632**	0.0983	0.3418**	−0.1492*	0.2192*	0.1524*	0.2046**	0.1460*	0.4145**
LU80	0.3567**	0.2201**	0.3036**	0.1618**	0.1072	0.2951**	0.1077	0.3204**	0.2390**	0.2855**	−0.0115
AIRP80	−0.3566**	−0.3592**	−0.3282**	0.0584	0.2544**	−0.1639**	0.2529**	0.1616**	0.2625**	0.3957**	0.4056**

Correlations:	ESMIX80	POP80D	LU80	AIRP80
ESMIX80	1.0000			
POP80D	0.6105**	1.0000		
LU80	−0.1831**	−0.2546**	1.0000	
AIRP80	0.2721**	0.2811**	0.0258	1.0000

Minimum number of cases: 370   1-tailed Signif: * −0.01 ** −0.001

Table A4.2 Correlation matrix: 1982 data-set

Correlations:	PFAVL82	ACCSS82	TECH82	BASE82	CARER82	DESP82	PFCST82	WELTH82	SOC80V	INFEF82	ECON82V
PFAVL82	1.000										
ACCSS82	0.9531**	1.0000									
TECH82	0.9522**	0.9791**	1.0000								
BASE82	0.7785**	0.7194**	0.6980**	1.0000							
CARER82	0.5981**	0.4391**	0.4843**	0.6608**	1.0000						
DESP82	−0.2252**	−0.0785	−0.0471	−0.3517**	−0.3817**	1.0000					
PFCST82	0.3870**	0.2398**	0.2344**	0.5288**	0.5330**	−0.4887**	1.0000				
WELTH82	0.6455**	0.4699**	0.4917**	0.6985**	0.6546**	−0.6370**	0.7436**	1.0000			
SOC80V	0.5465**	0.3499**	0.3911**	0.6624**	0.8705**	−0.5688**	0.6840**	0.8277**	1.0000		
INFEF82	0.1056	−0.0230	0.0662	0.2255**	0.3933**	−0.1666**	0.4799**	0.4992**	0.5443**	1.0000	
ECON82V	−0.0476	−0.1412*	−0.1859**	0.2700**	0.2059**	−0.4737**	0.5003**	0.4285**	0.3753**	0.2966**	1.0000
ESMIX82	−0.0783	−0.1598**	−0.1384*	0.1618**	0.4299**	−0.2056**	0.3233**	0.2710**	0.4338**	0.4133**	0.4748**
POP82D	−0.1198*	−0.0717	−0.0991	0.0584	0.0474	0.0178	0.0333	−0.0298	0.0947	−0.0009	0.1774**
LU82	0.2945**	0.2129**	0.3233**	0.1414*	0.2581**	0.2968**	0.1302*	0.2257**	0.2231**	0.3915**	−0.1045
AIRP82	−0.2804**	−0.3512**	−0.3431**	0.0583	0.1805*	−0.1503*	0.1940**	0.1145	0.2683**	0.3463**	0.3839**

Correlations:	ESMIX80	POP80D	LU80	AIRP80
ESMIX82	1.0000			
POP82D	0.3395**	1.0000		
LU82	−0.0011	−0.2176**	1.0000	
AIRP82	0.3037**	0.1465*	0.0213	1.0000

Minimum number of cases: 380   1-tailed Signif: *−0.01 **−0.001

NOTES

1 The analysis reported is based on data provided by the US Small Business Administration to Regional Economic Development Associates Incorporated (Edina, Minnesota) in fulfilment of Contract SBA 3067-0A-88 and financial support provided through the University of Minnesota by the Rural Poverty and Resources Program of the Ford Foundation (Grant No. 900-013) and administered by the Aspen Institute. None of the sponsors are responsible for the analysis or the interpretations.

2 Currently Coleman/Fannie May Candies Chairholder in Entrepreneurship at Marquette University, Milwaukee, Wisconsin 53233, USA.

3 Currently Research Consultant, Center for the Study of Entrepreneurship, Marquette University, Milwaukee, Wisconsin 53233, USA.

4 Currently with the Department of Agricultural and Applied Economics, University of Minnesota, Minneapolis, Minnesota.

5 The numbers used to provide unique identifiers reflect the development of a more extensive analysis of 31 start-up processes that is part of the major report to the project sponsor, the Ford Foundation (Reynolds and Maki 1991).

6 In various forms, this is among the most popular of processes (Creedy and Johnson 1983: 178–9; Hamilton 1986: 1401–4; Hamilton 1989; Harrison and Hart 1984: 1406; Highfield and Smiley 1986: 53; Hudson 1989: 72; Johnson 1986: 120; Mason 1989: 332; Moyes and Westhead 1990: 124; Storey 1990: and Whittington 1984: 255).

7 Time series analysis provides substantial support for this process in the United Kingdom (Storey 1990). Time series analysis of the entire United States economy has not provided strong support (Highfield and Smiley 1986). Further, there is very modest support in cross-regional analysis; there have been some attempts to reconcile the discrepancy (Hamilton 1989).

8 Measures have included the proportion of college graduates (Bartik 1989: 1016); presence of managers and skilled craftspersons (Johnson 1986: 110); employees with strong technical knowledge and customer contact (Mason 1991: 99); occupational experience and education (Moyes and Westhead 1990: 124); rates of entrepreneurship for post-high school males (O'Farrell and Pickles 1989: 323); individual drive for economic leadership (Schumpeter 1934: 93); occupational experience as managers and educational attainment (Storey 1982: 185); and the absence of manual workers in a region (Whittington 1984: 255).

9 Measures that have been proposed include intra-industry mobility (turnover) or turbulence differences (Beesley and Hamilton 1984: 221); loss of employment in various industries, percentage employment in various industries, or age investment in various industries (younger industries have more new investments) (Moyes and Westhead 1990: 124); industry variation in proportion of men starting new firms (O'Farrell and Pickles 1989: 325); and percentage of workforce in low entry barrier industries (Storey 1982: 185).

10 There is a wide range of specific costs associated with this argument, including the cost of capital, labour, premises, local taxes, land, energy, transportation, living, insurance and so forth (Bartik 1989: 1015–16;

Creedy and Johnson 1983: 180; Highfield and Smiley 1986: 53; Hudson 1989: 72; Morky 1988: 20; Moyes and Westhead 1990: 124; Pennings 1982a: 128).

11 This has included a wide range of measures, including diversity in social contacts or networks (Aldrich and Zimmer 1986: Birley 1985); presence of state-wide rather than unit banking (Bartik 1989: 1016); access to capital, skilled specialists, universities, supporting services, distance to suppliers, availability of premises, skilled specialists, and so on (Brusco 1982: 173; Johnson 1986: 110; Mason 1991: 99; Morky 1988: 20; Moyes and Westhead 1990: 124; Oakey 1984: 146; Pennings 1982a: 127; Schumpeter 1934: 72; and Storey 1982: 185).

12 Public infrastructure expenditures may be considered in terms of the spending per capita on fire protection, local schools, highways and roads, police services, welfare services (Bartik 1989: 1015) or on services not privately provided that enhance regional economic efficiency, such as child care or low cost housing and commercial space (Brusco 1982: 182).

13 This has received less explicit attention, although it is part of the general incubator analysis (Oakey 1984: 146; Hoover and Vernon 1959).

14 A number of writers have emphasized the importance of a 'high information' ambiance (Brusco 1982: 179; Mason 1991: 99; Oakey 1984: 146; Sabel and Zeitlan 1985: 144; Schumpeter 1934: 66).

15 A number of discussions present this view (Brusco 1982: 171; Hudson 1989: 72; Johnson 1986: 110; Mason 1991: 99; Whittington 1984: 255; and Storey 1982: 185).

16 Morky 1988: 19.

17 Morky 1988: 19.

18 Two opposite processes are included in this discussion. Some emphasize he size of the population: larger regions are expected to have higher birth rates (Bartik 1989: 1013; Morky 1988: 19; Pennings 1982a: 127). Others expect a reverse relationship, with higher birth rates in more rural areas (Johnson 1986: 115; Moyes and Westhead 1990: 124; O'Farrell and Crouchley 1984: 233; and O'Farrell and Pickles 1989: 318). Higher rural areas' birth rates may reflect differences in industry structure, with a greater presence of more volatile industries (construction, retail, consumer services) in rural areas.

19 This is treated as a separate issue in a number of discussions (Chinitz 1961: 288; Morky 1988: 19; Pennings 1982b: 126; Whittington 1984: 255).

20 This is a more subtle issue, often related to dominance associated with the restructuring of the relationships among urban areas (Pennings 1982a: 124, 125). Major causal effects of airline hubs on urban economic dominance have been suggested (Irwin and Kasarda 1991).

21 This may be indicated by the presence of 'right to work laws', which allow employees to work in a plant with collective bargaining and not be dues-paying members of the bargaining unit as well as the percentage of all workers that are members of unions (Plaut and Pluta 1983). In Italy, firms with more than fifteen employees have a more difficult time releasing workers for any reason (Brusco 1982).

22 This latter factor would be specific to the individual firm and not amenable to analysis based on data reflecting geographic regions.

23 The emphasis in business and distributive services tends to include some non-metropolitan LMAs in the central part of the US that serve as major distribution centres.

24 Several major metropolitan areas with extremely high emphasis on manufacturing, such as Detroit, Michigan, are included in this category. They are, however, a minority.

25 Estimate of Chronbach's alpha without the item from SPSS-PC V3.1 'reliability' procedure. Provides an estimate of the contribution of the item to overall scale reliability. A negative value indicates serious departures from linearity in the inter-item relationships. Can only be computed if at least three items are candidates for an index.

26 Chronbach's alpha as estimated by SPSS-PC V3.1. Estimate of the extent to which errors of measurement are reduced by an index that gives equal weight to the constituent items.

27 Transfer payments are mostly welfare and retirement benefits payments.

28 In about two-fifths of the states of the United States, workers have the right to a job in an establishment with a collective bargaining agreement without being a dues-paying member of the union. Such states are referred to as 'right-to-work' states.

29 Explained variances in excess of 0.80 or 0.90 can be achieved when all of the indicators, over sixty are included in the regression model. When this is done for more than one period or dependent variable the results are difficult to interpret, as different indicators of the various processes become incorporated in the different models. The use of the fifteen multi-item indicators of the various processes results in acceptable levels of explained variance and more consistent models across time periods, measures of volatility, and types of labour market areas.

30 Doctorates granted and patents granted were only available at the state level. These counts were then distributed across counties, based on the number of persons aged 25 and older. These counts were then aggregated into the labour market areas.

31 This is consistent with the basic focus developed by Jane Jacobs (1984) regarding the importance of cities, and their diversity, as a source of national wealth.

32 At least one analysis indicates there is no systematic relationship between measures of quality of life and the presence of entrepreneurship among major metropolitan regions of the US (Pennings 1982b).

33 This is one of the major conclusions of Weiss (1988) based on her analysis of contemporary Italy.

REFERENCES

Aldrich, H.E. and Waldinger, R. (1990) 'Ethnicity and Entrepreneurship', *Annual Review of Sociology* 16: 111–35.

Aldrich, H.E. and Zimmer, C. (1986) 'Entrepreneurship Through Social Networks', in D. Sexton and R. Smilor (eds.) *The Art and Science of Entrepreneurship*, Cambridge, MA: Ballinger, 3–24.

Amin, A., Johnson, S. and Storey, D. (1986) 'Small Firms and the Process of Economic Development', *Journal of Regional Policy* 4: 493–517.

Averitt, R. (1968) *The Dual Economy*, New York: Norton.
Bain, J.S. (1962) *Barriers to New Competition*, Cambridge, MA: Harvard University Press.
Bartik, T.J. (1989) 'Small Business Start-Ups in the United States: Estimates of the Effects of Characteristics of States', *Southern Economic Journal* 55: 1005–18.
Beesley, M.E. and Hamilton, R.T. (1984) 'Small Firms' Seedbed Role and the Concept of Turbulence', *Journal of Industrial Economics* 33(2): 217–31.
Berger, S. and Piore, M.J. (1980) *Dualism and Discontinuity in Industrial Societies*, Cambridge: Cambridge University Press.
Birch, D.L. (1981). 'Who Creates Jobs?' *The Public Interest* 65: 3–14.
Birley, S. (1985) 'The Role of Networks in the Entrepreneurial Process', in J.A. Hornaday, *et al.* (eds) *Frontiers of Entrepreneurial Research: 1985*, Wellesley, MA: Babson College, Center for Entrepreneurial Studies, 325–337.
Booth, D.E. (1986–7) 'Long Waves and Uneven Regional Growth', *Southern Economic Journal* 53: 448–60.
Brown, C., Hamilton, J. and Medoff, J. (1990) *Employers: Large and Small*, Cambridge, MA: Harvard University Press.
Brusco, S. (1982) 'The Emilian Model: Productive Decentralization and Social Integration', *Cambridge Journal of Economics* 6: 167–84.
Cable, J. and Schwalbach, J. (Forthcoming) 'International Comparisons of Entry and Exit', in P.A. Geroski and J. Schwalbach (eds) *Entry and Market Contestability: An International Comparison*, London: Basil Blackwell.
Carroll, G.R., Delacroix, J. and Goodstein, J. (1988) 'The Political Environment of Organizations: An Ecological View', *Research in Organizational Behavior* 10: 359–92.
Chinitz, B. (1961) 'Contrasts in Agglomeration: New York and Pittsburgh', *American Economic Review* 51(2): 279–89.
Corporation for Enterprise Development (1991) *The 1991 Development Report Card for the States*, Washington, DC: The Corporation for Enterprise Development.
Creedy, J. and Johnson, P.S. (1983) 'Firm Formation in the Manufacturing Industry', *Applied Economics* 15: 177–85.
Davis, S.J. (1990) 'Size Distribution Statistics from County Business Pattern Data', Chicago, IL: University of Chicago, Graduate School of Business, unpublished report.
Del Monte, A. and de Luzenberger, R. (1989) 'The Effect of Regional Policy on New Firm Formation in Southern Italy', *Regional Studies* 23(3): 219–30.
de Soto, H. (1989) *The Other Path: The Invisible Revolution in the Third World*, (trans by June Abbott) New York: Harper Row.
Fratoe, F. (1986) 'A Sociological Analysis of Minority Business', *Review of Black Political Economy* 15(2): 5–30.
Gartner, W.T. (1989) '"Who is an Entrepreneur?" Is the Wrong Question', *Entrepreneurship Theory and Practice* 13(4): 47–68.
Gibbs, J.P. and Poston, D.L. Jr. (1975) 'The Division of Labor: Conceptualization and Related Measures', *Social Forces* 53(3): 468–76.
Goode, F.M. (1989) 'Rural Industrial Location Versus Rural Industrial Growth', *The Annals of Regional Science* 23: 59–68.

Granovetter, M. (1985) 'Economic Action and Social Structure: The Problem of Embeddedness', *American Journal of Sociology* 91(3): 481–510.

Hamilton, R.T. (1986) 'The Influence of Unemployment on the Level and Rate of Company Formation in Scotland, 1950–84', *Environment and Planning A* 18: 1401–4.

—— (1989) 'Unemployment and Business Formation Rates: Reconciling Time-Series and Cross-sectional Evidence', *Environment and Planning A* 21: 249–55.

Hannan, M.T. and Freeman, J. (1989) *Organizational Ecology*, Cambridge, MA: Harvard University Press.

Harrison, R.T. and Hart, M. (1983) 'Factors Influencing New-Business Formation: A Case Study of Northern Ireland', *Environment and Planning A* 15: 1395–412.

Highfield, R. and Smiley, R. (1986) 'New Business Starts and Economic Activity: An Empirical Investigation', *International Journal of Industrial Organization* 5: 51–66.

Hoover, E. and Vernon, R. (1959) *Anatomy of a Metropolis*. Cambridge, MA: Harvard University Press.

Hudson, J. (1989) 'The Birth and Death of Firms', *Quarterly Review of Economics and Business* 29(2): 68–6.

Irwin, M.D. and Kasarda, J.D. (1991) 'Air Passenger Linkages and Employment Growth Among US Metropolitan Areas', *American Sociological Review* 56(4): 524–37.

Jacobs, J. (1984) *Cities and the Wealth of Nations*, New York: Vintage Books.

Johnson, P. (1986) *New Firms: An Economic Perspective*, London: Allen & Unwin.

Keeble, D. (1990) 'New Firms and Regional Economic Development: Experience and Impacts in the 1980s', *Cambridge Regional Review* 1.

Kihlstrom, R.E. and Laffont, J–J (1979) 'A General Equilibrium Entrepreneurial Theory of Firm Formation Based on Risk Aversion', *Journal of Political Economy* 87(4): 719–48.

Kirchhoff, B. and Phillips, B. (1988) 'The Effect of Firm Formation and Growth on Job Creation in the United States', *Journal of Business Venturing* 3: 361–72.

Knudsen, K. and McTavish, D.G. (1988) 'Interest in Venturing in Minnesota', Duluth, MN: University of Minnesota-Duluth: Bureau of Business and Economic Research, Working Paper 88–19.

Leon, R.A. and Struyk, R. (1976) 'The Incubator Hypothesis: Evidence from Five SMSAs', *Urban Studies* 13: 325–31.

Loveman, G. and Sengenberger, W. (1991) 'The Re-emergence of Small-Scale Production: An International Comparison', *Small Business Economics* 3(1): 1–38.

Malecki, E.J. (1985) 'Industrial Location and Corporate Organization in High Technology Industries', *Economic Geography* 61(4): 345–69.

Markusen, A.R. (1985) *Profit Cycles, Oligopoly, and Regional Development*, Cambridge, MA: MIT Press.

Mason, C.M. (1989) 'Explaining Recent Trends in New Firm Formation in the U.K.: Some Evidence from South Hampshire', *Regional Studies* 25(4): 331–46.

Mason, C.M. (1991) 'Spacial Variations in Enterprise: The Geography of New Firm Formation', in R. Burrows (ed.) *Deciphering the Enterprise Culture*, New York: Routledge, 74–106.

Mokry, B.W. (1988) *Entrepreneurship and Public Policy*, New York: Quorum Books.

Moyes, A. and Westhead, P. (1990) 'Environments for New Firm Formation in Great Britain', *Regional Studies* 24(2): 123–6.

Newman, R.J. and Sullivan, D.H. (1988) 'Econometric Analysis of Business Tax Impacts on Industrial Location: What Do We Know and How Do We Know It?', *Journal of Urban Economics* 23: 215–34.

Norusis, M.J. (1988) *SPSS/PC+ V2.0: Base Manual*, Chicago, IL: SPSS Inc.

O'Farrell, P.N. and Crouchley, R. (1984) 'An Industrial and Spatial Analysis of New firm Formation in Ireland', *Regional Studies* 18(3): 221–36.

O'Farrell, P.N. and Pickles, A.R. (1989) 'Entrepreneurial Behavior Within Male Work Histories: A Sector-Specific Analysis', *Environment and Planning A* 21: 311–31.

Oakey, R. (1984) *High Technology Small Firms: Regional Development in Britain and the United States*, New York: St. Martin's Press.

Orr, D. (1974a) 'The Determinants of Entry: A study of the Canadian Manufacturing Industries', *Review of Economics and Statistics* 5: 58–66.

—— (1974b) 'An Index of Entry Barriers and Its Application to the Market Structure Performance Relationship', *Journal of Industrial Economics* 23(1): 39–49.

Pennings, J.M. (1982a) 'Organizational Birth Frequencies: An Empirical Investigation', *Administrative Science Quarterly* 27; 120–44.

—— (1982b) 'The Urban Quality of Life and Entrepreneurship', *Academy of Management Journal* 25(1): 63–79.

Piore, M. and Sabel, C.F. (1984) *The Second Industrial Divide: Possibilities for Prosperity*, New York: Basic Books.

Plaut, T.R. and Pluta, J.E. (1983) 'Business Climate, Taxes and Expenditures, and State Industrial Growth in the United States', *Southern Economic Journal* 50(1): 99–119.

Reynolds, P.D. (1991) 'Predicting New Firm Births: Interactions of Organizational and Human Populations', in D. Sexton and J. Kasarda (eds) *Entrepreneurship in the 1990s*, Boston, MA: PWS-Kent, in preparation.

Reynolds, P. and Maki, W. (1990a) 'U.S. Regional Characteristics, New Firms, and Economic Growth: Preliminary Overview of a Research Program', Presented at the Cross-National Workshop on the Role of Small, Medium Enterprises in Regional Economic Growth, University of Warwick, Coventry, UK, 28 March.

—— (1990b) *Business Volatility and Economic Growth*, Project Report prepared for the US Small Business Administration (Contract SBA 3067-0A-88).

—— (1991) *Regional Characteristics Affecting Business Growth: Assessing Strategies for Promoting Regional Economic Well-being*. Project report submitted to the Ford Foundation, Grant No. 900–013.

Sabel, C. and Zeitlin, J. (1985) 'Historical Alternatives to Mass Production: Politics, Markets and Technology in Nineteenth-Century Industrialization', *Past & Present* 108: 133–76.

Schmenner, R.W., Huber, J.C. and Cook, R.L. (1987) 'Geographic Differences and the Location of New Manufacturing Facilities', *Journal of Urban Economics* 21: 83–104.

Schumpeter, J.A. (1934) *The Theory of Economic Development*, Cambridge, MA: Harvard University Press.

Singh, J.V. and Lumsden, C.J. (1990) 'Theory and Research in Organizational Ecology', *Annual Review of Sociology* 16: 161–95.

Singelmann, J. (1978) *From Agriculture to Services: The Transformation of Industrial Employment.* Beverly Hills, CA: Sage Publications.

Storey, D.J. (1982) *Entrepreneurship and the New Firm*, London: Croom Helm.

—— (1990) 'The Birth of New Firms – Does Unemployment Matter?' Conference on *The Role of Small Firms and Entrepreneurship: A Comparison of East and West Countries*, Wissenschaftszentrum Berlin fur Sozialforschung [WZB], Berlin.

Suarez-Villa, L. (1989) *The Evolution of Regional Economies: Entrepreneurship and Macroeconomic Change*, New York: Praeger.

Tolbert, C.M. and Killian, M.S. (1987) *Labour Market Areas for the United States*, Agriculture and Rural Economy Division, Economic Research Service, US Department of Agriculture, Staff Report AGE870721, August.

Walker, R. and Greenstreet, D. (1990) 'The Effect of Government Incentives and Assistance on Location and Job Growth in Manufacturing', *Regional Studies* 25(1): 13–30.

Weber, M. (1930) *The Protestant Ethic and the Spirit of Capitalism*, (Trans. by A.M. Henderson) New York: Charles Scribner's Sons.

Weiss, L. (1987) 'Explaining the Underground Economy: State and Social Structure', *The British Journal of Sociology* 38(2): 216–34.

—— (1988) *Creating Capitalism: The State and Small Business Since 1945*, Oxford: Basil Blackwell.

Wheaton, W.C. (1983) 'Interstate Differences in the Level of Business Taxation', *National Tax Journal* 56(1): 83–94.

Whittington, R.C. (1984) 'Regional Bias in New Firm Formation in the UK,' *Regional Studies* 18(3): 253–6.

Wilken, P.H. (1979) *Entrepreneurship: A Comparative and Historical Study*, Norwood, NJ: Ablex.

P78.

DISCUSSION

115 - 16

Christer Olofsson

US L11 J23 R12

I feel in great sympathy with the basic model being used in this study. It may have to do with the fact that my colleagues and I have chosen to use the same basic model as a departure for a parallel project in Sweden.

A complex project like this one provides rich opportunities to discuss (and question) theory and modelling, measurements, and analysis. There are a lot of conceptual and definitional problems that have to do with the inherent complexity of the issues raised. Not only are business birth and business death problematic no establish in a precise way, the measurements over time are subject to a lot of difficulties.

To name just one of the problems, the coverage of the population of establishments. Even though the Dun and Bradstreet files are the best available in the US, the hypothesis is that a lot of the smallest establishments are not covered; and the coverage for certain industries like retailing might be weaker than for the rest of the population.

The project, however, has produced some very clear cut results from the analysis; for example, when it comes to the effects of economic diversity and some other variables on business volatility. One can't help but wonder what results an even better data-set would produce.

One of the fascinating problems to come back to must be the time order and time lag for different variables. Is the wealth an effect of the volatility or is it a cause? Or could the model include that variable as well as others both as causes and effects, given the over time perspective?

One of the interesting aspects to be discussed would be what policy implications follow from this study and other studies in the same area. I certainly look forward to future opportunities to compare the results from this US study with the European project now under way.

5 Designing supportive contexts for emerging enterprises

Bengt Johannisson

STATING THE PROBLEM

Sweden, like most industrialized countries, provided a broad repertoire for encouraging and supporting business venturing during the 1980s. Private financial institutions escalated their support for individual startups basically by reducing their demands on real security for loans provided. Public bodies, on the other hand, have in more general terms stimulated business venturing by offering, for example, start-up courses and advice to businesses in operation. The unreflected assumption on which these measures rest seems to be that entrepreneurs will be successful in the venturing process if they properly manage their internal resources. In Sweden it is implicitly assumed that, if the entrepreneur is knowledgeable and financial resources available, the venture will succeed. However, entrepreneurial competences are beyond formal training (*cf.* Johannisson 1991), and financial resources secondarily positioned against other kinds of internal and external resources (*cf.* Vesper 1990; Johannisson 1990a).

Equally unquestioned is the adoption of the individual growth-driven person and his or her firm as the unit of analysis in the majority of the contributions to entrepreneurship research. There is some debate about whether the focus should be on the person or the process (see Carland *et al.* 1988; Gartner 1989). Even the notion of 'emerging enterprises' is equivocal; it does not refer to new business alone but also the fact that ventures continuously change one by one and overlap and cluster into institutionalized structures, basically the firm or a set of firms associated with an entrepreneur. Ventures and firms become integrated by way of personal networks that make it possible to capitalize upon the tacit competences that experience accumulates (*cf.* Johannisson 1992).

The notion of entrepreneurship suggested here is that any statement concerning entrepreneurs' individual capabilities or formal ventures only reflects partial components of the entrepreneurial process. Here I specifically argue that the character of the context wherein the entrepreneurial career takes place has to be recognized in order first, to understand the conditions for new and habitual entrepreneurship and, second, to design ways of supporting entrepreneurs.

Context is here defined as the concrete and symbolic circumstances that surround the venturing process and make it intelligible to the entrepreneur (Johannisson 1988). The context may be functionally, spatially or culturally demarcated. Every business is linked to a business sector with its own logic and recipes. However, such primarily economic contexts are not appropriate for all small businessmen. As highlighted in research into ethnic-minority entrepreneurship, the businessman does not exist in a socio–economic vacuum but uses his or her personal community as a spring board in order to overcome entry barriers (see Light 1972; Ward 1987). Genuine entrepreneurs need self-confidence since, by definition, they question established orders such as the conventional way to meet customer demand. I have therefore hypothesized that the necessary contextual support with respect to entrepreneurs is more general, i.e. it includes socio–cultural factors in addition to those which are usually considered to be more instrumental to commercial success, e.g. material and financial resources. If the entrepreneur is focused as a complete human being, it becomes obvious that the individual way of life reflecting social background and habitat will define the type of support strategies feasible to help entrepreneurs make their venture viable.

My own research into the venturing process suggests that, at least in Sweden, the personal networks of the entrepreneur organizing the exchange between venture and context are spatially concentrated (see Johannisson 1990a and this chapter).

A contextual approach to entrepreneurship suggests, for a number of reasons, that support for the budding venture should explicitly consider the general characteristics of the context and not only the individual entrepreneur/venture. First, direct support contradicts the major motive for establishing one's own business: the need for independence. It would be paradoxical to expect entrepreneurs to accept obtrusive support structures. Second, starting a new firm often implies a career change which is rooted in the general way of life of the individual. Third, the venturing process starts long before the entrepreneur is visible in the marketplace. The incubation process includes building self-confidence and shaping a business concept. The entrepreneur must be able to deal with these venturing stages on his or her own. Fourth, previous research has stated that only an environment that makes venturing both feasible and desirable will foster new entrepreneurs (*cf.* Shapero and Sokol 1982). Fifth, for cultural and institutional reasons, local and regional community life is especially important in the Swedish setting. Swedish characteristics that are relevant here include a sparsely populated country and financially strong municipalities.

My point of departure is that it would be inconsistent to argue that supportive contexts can be designed and induced by a pro-active planning process with the objective of instrumentally strengthening emerging individual ventures. A relevant ambition would rather be to ensure that the context provides an 'arena' where the natural or organic processes – which entrepreneurs initiate as soon as they identify and activate opportunities offered by emerging market changes – can be facilitated and enforced. Induced contexts for entrepreneurship, e.g. science and industrial parks, have difficulties in meeting expectations (see, for example Monck *et al.* 1988; Stöhr 1990). The increasing research into corporate entrepreneurship – 'intrapreneurship' – also reports both great ambitions and numerous problems in designing a context for entrepreneurship within a formally demarcated and professionally managed organization (see Miller 1983; Kanter 1983).

Reasons why contexts cannot be designed and planned in the technical sense are to a great extent circumscribed by my notion of contexts as partially defined by history and saturated by tacit local knowledge, i.e., as much a symbolic space as an informational condensation and a variable resource bank. The making of a context for entrepreneurship calls for unique capabilities which only partially coincide with those of the market-oriented entrepreneur. We have introduced the notion of 'community entrepreneur' as the person who guides the creation of a local context (see Johannisson and Nilsson 1989).

In the following section I elaborate on the suggested model of entrepreneurship which implies that contextual networks are crucial for the creation and development of new ventures. In the third section alternative models for explaining differences between Swedish regions (counties) with respect to their potential as venture incubators are introduced. The presentation of the models states the basic assumptions and logic of these models which in turn define what support strategies will be adequate. In the fourth section tentative data from a study into regional differences in firm formation in Sweden during the second half of the 1980s are presented. In the fifth section, the Swedish small-business policy is confronted with the alternative models and alternative model implications are discussed. The final section provides some issues for further inquiry.

ORGANIZING THE *LEBENSRAUM* OF THE ENTREPRENEUR

The framework for entrepreneurship promoted here suggests that the existential arena for the operations of the emerging firm is circum-scribed by the personal network of the entrepreneur. It defines the community with which the entrepreneur identifies him- or herself and thus builds and maintains self-confidence and willpower. Since the personal network includes ties where social and business strands intertwine, the network provides a framework where both emotional/ cognitive, irrational/rational choice models can be considered. This means that theories of entrepreneurship which anchor the entre-preneurial career in positive or negative experiences in early years can be combined with the propositions that the career is defined by a random search for opportunities. Besides combining the contrasting assumptions that an entrepreneurial career is defined by both fate and individual will, the network metaphor links macro and micro approaches to entrepreneurship (Johannisson 1990b).

International comparative research covering Sweden suggests that entrepreneurial networking shares many characteristics cross-nation-ally (*cf.* Aldrich *et al.* 1987, 1989; Birley *et al.* 1989). The Swedish findings suggest that:

(a) Entrepreneurs who are about to launch a venture include more social ties in their networks and spend less time on maintaining networks than colleagues already in business;

(b) Entrepreneurs typically build local networks: eight out of ten personal contacts live within a distance of one hour's driving;

(c) In the personal networks of entrepreneurs, socially dominated ties are almost as frequent as professional/business linkages;

(d) Women entrepreneurs build more social networks, invest more time in maintaining networks and less time in developing new ties than their male counterparts;

(e) Cosmopolitan entrepreneurs invest relatively little time in network maintenance and relatively much more in developing new network linkages;

(f) Academic entrepreneurs invest above average time in network management but build networks which are average socially oriented;

(g) Among new entrepreneurs network resources and business success are not correlated.

Research into the existential setting of entrepreneurs as defined by their personal networks thus suggests that the spatial vicinity or context is pivotal, and that the context is organized by way of networking. The role of these networks is to create meaning for the entrepreneur throughout his/her career, as well as to add to business success. Characteristics of the region, then, must determine, first, the potential for an enterprise spirit and, second, which measures can be taken in order to create a new, or nurture an already established, spirit.

In Figure 5.1, context and network functions are summarized as they emerge over the venturing process. (The presentation is very

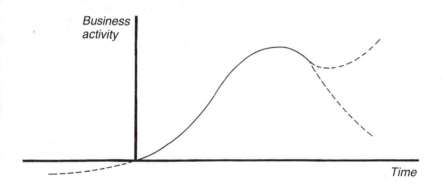

Venture phase	Venture concept	Start-up	Growth	Maturity	Rejuvenation/ decline
Role	Innovator	Artisan	Classical entrepreneur	Manager	Reconstructor/ 'undertaker'
Context support	Venture ideas	Social back-up	Operative resources	Social status	Venture ideas
Network focus	Local	Local	Local and global	Local and global	Global and local

Figure 5.1 The evolving business venture defining entrepreneurial roles and needed contextual support

simplistic in that it assumes that the venture cycle equals the entre-preneurial career.) The model suggests that the major functions of the context – to provide commercially valid ideas, to be a resource bank and to legitimate the entrepreneur – offer different combinations as the venturing process and the entrepreneurial career evolve. While the importance of contextual personal networks remains, the need for supplementary global networks increases as the venture cycle matures.

MODELLING CONTEXTUAL VARIATIONS IN FIRM FORMATION

Because of definitional problems, as stated above, and because public statistics lack network data, a contextual model focusing on networks as a means of organizing cannot directly be adopted for an investiga-tion of the impact of different spatial contexts on firm formation. Intervening models that reflect the assumed features of the context are therefore needed. Thanks to the emerging theoretical under-standing, several alternative models, or rather metaphors, can be introduced. Using different perspectives in parallel to frame a phenomenon such as firm formation is also in accordance with my basic paradigm, that of reality as a social construction. Thus, in specifying the impact of regional characteristics on firm formation, different explanations come to the fore:

(a) The established determinant of new-firm formation is a dynamic market where variability and change provide a flow of oppor-tunities in terms of niches with low entry barriers. The role of contextual networks is to provide information in this scanning process (Aguilar 1967).

(b) The making of a venture calls for resources, not just physical, financial and informational, or human in terms of knowledge, but also socio–cultural, e.g. regional identity. The role of the network then is to provide a business exchange structure that mobilizes resources (Johannisson 1990a).

(c) The creation of a genuinely new business must have its origin in a unique business concept; continued growth calls for a creative environment as well. Thus the social and cultural milieu will directly and indirectly – in terms of providing agreeable living conditions – influence firm formation. Such a milieu is expected to provide arenas where social exchange can be spontaneously initiated and cultivated.

(d) Entering the entrepreneurial career in most cases means career change. Such career transitions are more or less radical (see Driver 1988), and include both pull and push determinants. Pull factors include reaching a higher educational or motivational level, push factors include being made redundant; socio–biological explanations include both pull and push factors.

The proposed models do not, of course, exhaust the possible frameworks for interpreting regional variations in firm formation. Elsewhere we have also included a 'labour market model' based on unemployment data over a period of years (Johannisson and Bång 1992). Because of the simplicity and insignificant prediction capacity the model is excluded here (although unemployment figures are included in the 'career model', see p. 126). Considering only static unemployment figures there is a negative correlation between unemployment and business venturing formation. However, preliminary analysis indicates that, in Sweden, when unemployment is low in the national economy, there is a positive, although weak, correlation between relatively high unemployment and firm formation regionally. These findings are in accordance with those reported by Storey 1991.

Each one of the four proposed models is also incomplete in several respects. First, and obviously, as with any model details are omitted and these are not necessarily irrelevant. Second, the models could each be conceptually elaborated. Third, operationalization of the models should be made much more carefully than is possible here (see Appendix, pp. 139–40). These (indicators of) determinants of firm formation according to the different models are not integrated into a conceptual scheme within the scope of each model. In addition, because of these imperfections, among other things, the models presented here are neither conceptually nor empirically mutually exclusive. This may on one hand indicate lack of rigour in research procedures; on the other hand, more general models can be developed and the number of alternatives consequently reduced. The latter ambition is then more of an analytical exercise than something called for by my scientific standpoint.

My general argument thus is that contexts and not individual entrepreneurs/ventures should be the focus. Accordingly, the various models differ with respect to what support strategies are appropriate. Obviously the market and resource models are more consistent with induced strategies than the milieu and career models The two first mentioned models also have a logic that will produce results in the

Table 5.1 Firm formation – basic models and critical venturing issues

Basic model	Critical venturing issues
Market	Demand characteristics* Marketing systems Production networks
Resource	Local control over resources* Venture capital Economies of overview
Milieu	Socio–economic variability* Flexible specialization Investments in leisure and culture
Career	Volatile labour market* Availability of role models* Sociobiological and sociocultural factors

short run, while the milieu and career models will generate late but sustainable effects. This suggests that the models and associated measures could preferably be combined in industrial and regional policies. Since the needed conceptual framework is lacking, however, each model and the associated policies are here treated separately.

Although further research is needed in order to complete the making of models for interpreting regional variations in firm formation (in Sweden) and the available conceptual platform is fragile, I want to expand somewhat on the implications the different models may have on proper support measures and their implementation. In Table 5.1 I present the four models and associated 'critical venturing issues', i.e., the assumptions concerning successful firm formation which the models implicitly suggest. Obviously, proposed support strategies must consider these issues. The issues being empirically considered are marked with asterisks.

The 'market model' suggests that local market opportunities stimulate individuals to start their own business. There are various practical and psychological reasons for the decision to start to operate on the local market: its size, growth and accessibility to name a few. Within the market model accessibility is related to marketing management. Elaborate local production systems will facilitate market access. As the asterisks in Table 5.1 indicate and the Appendix expands upon, the empirical research reported here only encompasses (local) market characteristics.

The 'resource model' suggests that the business-venturing process needs different types of input resources: physical, financial, human and socio–cultural (*cf.* Coleman 1989; Johannisson 1990a). The socio–cultural resources include the personal network of the (would-be) entrepreneur. Local access to resources is crucial for the new entrepreneur in order to overcome cost and cultural barriers. Further critical resources include venture capital and management capabilities. The notion of 'economies of overview' (Schumacher 1975; Johannisson 1990b), suggests that the effort the entrepreneur puts into local networking pays off since it makes potential resource providers visible and the entrepreneur legitimate as a buyer.

The 'milieu model' originated in the 1980s when the debate on strategies for new-venture creation to a great extent concerned providing would-be entrepreneurs and new founders with favourable and creative living conditions. This model underlines the fact that entering an entrepreneurial career means taking social risks as well as financial ones. Thus, regions which provide both a favourable physical/social climate and a dynamic business climate will promote entrepreneurship by merging social and business concerns into trust building and general concern for cooperation. A context that is favourable to business will also provide a spontaneous flow of ideas for new businesses across community sectors, not least by way of personal networking. A region with great vitality in the fine arts may thus also flourish economically. In order to promote exchange of ideas and business experience, availability of arenas or meeting places for (would-be) entrepreneurs and other community members is crucial.

Internationally well-known regions where entrepreneurship is socially embedded, albeit for very different historical reasons, include, for example, Emilia Romagna in Italy, Silicon Valley in California, USA, and Västbo in Sweden (Marshall 1920; Johannisson 1983, 1988a; Piore and Sabel 1984; Lorenzoni and Ornati 1988; Zeitlin 1989; Porter 1990; Pyke *et al.* 1990). The socio–economic setting promotes intra- and interorganization production by way of flexible specialization.

The 'career model' suggests that taking on the role of the entrepreneur means a substantial change in a person's socio–economic status. In order to overcome barriers in this transition, a combination of pushing and pulling forces are usually needed. The need for restructuring is the concern of both the private and public sectors. In the late 1980s the need for reduction of Sweden's huge public sector was actively debated and the conservative–liberal victory in the 1991 general election will certainly make these speculations come true. Obviously, one way of achieving this is privatization. The perceived resistance towards these different imposed changes calls for support by, for example, the existence of role models for an alternative career as self-employed, i.e., living, active entrepreneurs. In addition to these external determinants in the venturing process, research indicates that individuals, depending on age and the way of life they acquire through birth and training, have different propensities to take up new careers, for example, that of an entrepreneur.

EMPIRICAL FINDINGS

The indicator of new-firm formation applied here is the creation of genuinely new firms in Sweden. With the focus on new firms in a local/regional context, estimated public regional start-up frequencies are related to the number of households in each of Sweden's twenty-four counties. The argument for using the household as the denominator is that most new firms are run as family businesses and that the household in turn is the natural economic unit. Thus, the dependent variable in the following statistical analyses of regional distributions is generally the average annual number of genuinely new firms 1985–9 per thousand households (N8589a). New firms in agriculture, forestry and fishing are not included. The methodology is elaborated in Johannisson and Bång 1992 where more detailed data are also reported.

In Figure 5.2 the regional distribution of firm formation in Sweden during the second half of the 1980s is reported. Obviously the metropolitan areas provide the highest frequencies, with Stockholm outstanding with an annual average of 6.8 new firms per thousand households as compared to the national average of 4.0. A more surprising finding is that the very sparsely populated northern county (approximately three inhabitants per thousand square kilometres) also seems to provide a favourable venturing context.

Each of the four proposed perspectives/models of firm formation are operationalized below and regression analyses are carried out accordingly. In the Appendix bivariate correlation coefficients are reported model by model.

The market model

As an indicator of the general potential of the market, total income per capita (20 years and older) 1985 (INC85) is used. Income growth

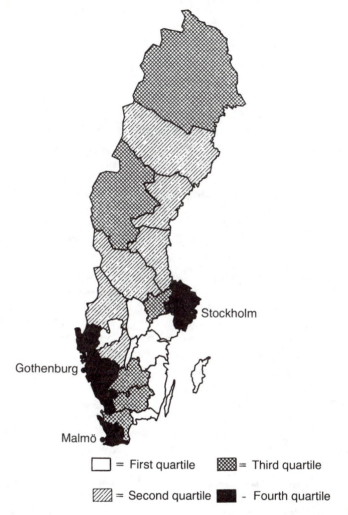

Figure 5.2 The regional distribution of firm formation in Sweden, 1985–9

over the period 1980–8 (INC8088) and increase in number of households over the period 1985–9 are both indicators of increase in market potential (H8589). Market accessibility is also reflected in two variables: population density (PD87) and the share of population that is economically active, i.e. aged 15–64 (P1564). The regression analysis shows that the combined explanatory power of the market model is considerable – 83.0 per cent.

$$N8589A = -2.346 + 0.010 \text{ PD87} + 0.346 \text{ H8589}$$
$$+ 0.053 \text{ INC8088}$$

Adjusted R Square: 0.830 $F = 38.5$

The resource model

Inexpensive and appropriate premises are usually considered to be a basic prerequisite for new-business operations. Within the resource model this is indicated by the portion of the families/households which either own their own homes or run farms (HOUSE). As a combined indicator of access to financial and human resources, the portion of the working population employed in banking and professional services (e.g. consulting) is used (FINPRO). The share of the population (aged 16–74) with a college education 1985 (CED85) is included as an indicator of human resources. The resources provided publicly are considered to include two variables; the public regional industry location support 1985–9 per thousand households 1987 (LOC87) and the public expenses for the regional development funds 1985 (per thousand inhabitants) (FUND85).

The findings according to the resource model indicate the turbulent character of the venture-creation process in Sweden. The move away from the industrial society, where new-business creation was usually associated with artisan operations in the home, means that access to premises (HOUSE) now correlates negatively with business startups! Service production either needs separate premises, e.g. catering, or can take place in an apartment or with only a briefcase, e.g. consulting. Instead, the resource model reports very strong positive correlations between start-up frequencies and, on one hand, the level of education (CED85), on the other, access to producer and associated services (FINPRO). A considerable share of startups in professional services is probably included in the dependent variable – in 1988 and 1989 25 per cent and 22 per cent of all new Swedish firms were set up by consultants. Level of education (CED85) alone provides 63.1 per cent (Adjusted R Square) of the explanation of the regional variations in business startups; additional independent variables do not increase that percentage significantly.

The milieu model

Five indicators of the creative potential of the context are adopted. First, the share of the population being employed in artistic professions 1980 (ART80). Second, the possible location of a full university provides a dummy variable (UNI). Third, since Sweden for historical reasons is (still) a very homogeneous country, immigrants are supposed to play an important role in the vitalization of the Swedish culture. The share of foreign citizens (FCIT), ranging from 1 to 9 per cent over the twenty-four regions, is therefore included in the model. The fourth indicator used is the municipal budget for spending on culture 1988 (per capita) (MCB88). In Sweden, voluntary associations contribute significantly to social cohesiveness in many communities and provide many opportunities for exchange. The number of sports associations per thousand inhabitants is hence included as a fifth indicator (SPORT).

The conclusive finding within the milieu model is that start-ups are associated with qualities more related to individuals than to the collective. There are thus very strong correlations between firm formation and the share of the population employed in artistic activities (ART80) and the proportion of foreign citizens (FCIT) in the population. The latter two categories seem to represent dynamic contextual forces. Considering the findings of the resource model, it is not surprising that the existence of a university (UNI) in the region enhances firm formation. The weak and/or negative correlations between the more tacit cultural aspects of the context suggest that more accurate measuring devices must be developed.

$$N8589A = 2.863 + 0.263 \ ART80 + 0.171 \ FCIT$$
$$\text{Adjusted R Square: } 0.673 \qquad F = 24.7$$

The career model

In Sweden, as in most welfare countries, the diminishing role of the manufacturing industry in the economy reflects the move away from the industrial society. As an indicator of the lingering industrial society, the proportion of employees within the manufacturing industry of all privately employed (MIND) is calculated. This is supplemented with a 1987 indicator of unemployment (UNEMP87). As a potential for privatization, then, the ratio between the total municipal employment and the regional population is calculated (MEMP). Access to resident entrepreneurs, both symbolically as role models and with respect to concrete support and as resource providers and customers, may stimulate others to enter an entrepreneurial career. One indicator calculates the ratio between existing businessmen and households (BUHOU) and another the share of privately employed who work in small, over-managed firms with less than twenty employees (SMALL).

As expected, the career model suggests that in a region where, on the one hand, the Swedish business structure has developed beyond dependence on the manufacturing industry (*cf.* MIND), and on the other hand has a 'visible' small-business structure in terms of a high proportion of entrepreneurial households (BUHOU), the career of an owner-manager is recognized. In contrast to the assumptions of the model, the impact of owner-managers as role models on the small workplace seems to make employees refrain from starting their own firm. There are many possible explanations, e.g. appreciation of the small-scale advantages as an employee and insight into the demanding role of the owner-manager. According to the career model the privatization potential (MEMP) is still a rather negligible option for an own firm in the Swedish context.

$$N8589A = 3.096 - 0.027 \text{ MIND} + 0.456 \text{ BUHOU} - 0.025 \text{ SMALL}$$

Adjusted R Square = 0.659   F = 15.8

The findings are summarized in Table 5.2 below. The market model stands out as the most powerful. Each model must however be further elaborated, with respect to its conceptual base, adopted indicators and application to various subpopulations, e.g. industries. Such analyses are reported in Johannisson and Bång 1992. Considering these ambiguities all independent variables were

Table 5.2 Alternative models for interpreting regional variations in new-firm formation in Sweden, 1986–9

Model	Explained variation %	Included significant variables
Market model	83.0	Population density, household growth, income growth
Resource model	63.1	Level of education
Context model	67.3	Employed in artistic professions, foreign citizens
Career model	65.9	Employment in manufacturing industry (neg.), owner-managers in relation to households, employment in small firms (neg.)

included in a multiple-step regression analysis. In the regression model the following variables were included: the share of the population (aged 16–74) with a college education 1985 (CED85), the ratio between existing businessmen and households (BUHOU), total income per capita (20 years and older) 1985 (INC85) and the public expenses for the regional development funds 1985 (per capita) (FUND85) (Adjusted R Square: 0.930, F = 79.0). Thus, abandoning the conceptual design, i.e., four competing (sketched) frameworks, only increases the explained regional variation in firm formation in Sweden by 10 per cent (since the market model explains 83.0 per cent). It is obviously not worth reverting to empiricism in this kind of research.

ALTERNATIVE SUPPORT STRUCTURES FOR ENTREPRENEURS

When the contextual approach to small business support is contrasted with the relevant public policy in Sweden the outcome is ambiguous. On one hand the focus on spatial objects such as counties and local communities seems appropriate. The Swedish industrial and regional policies are intertwined. As a matter of fact, ten times more financial resources are allocated to regional measures than to special small-business programmes. However, since most firms in the peripheral areas focused on in the regional policy are small, they benefit from available tax allowances, investment subsidies and employment grants. Although administered by other bodies the regional development funds are often involved in dealing with the applications within the regional policy field.

The ambiguous directions given to regional and local public bodies with respect to industrial policy make a contextual approach to small-business support appropriate. As indicated above, a lot of initiatives are taken locally and regionally in order to promote business. Although Swedish municipalities are financially very strong in an international perspective, they are legally very restricted with regard to content and volume of support to individual firms. Basically, they are limited to the provision of liaison services and physical premises. Eight out of ten of the Swedish local municipalities claim, though, that they aggressively promote business issues; 75 per cent of Sweden's 284 municipalities in the mid-1980s employed one or more industrial liaison officer (Hull and Bergendahl 1986).

Since the beginning of the 1980s the target group of public policy measures has successively become enlarged to include not just manufacturing but all small and medium-sized firms. It is now up to each regional development fund to give priority to resources that are scarce due to the unique characteristics of the regional industry. Generally, however, only firms considered to have a potential for growth should be supported. A 1991 government bill on economic expansion stresses technology and business growth, e.g. in terms of high-tech university spin-offs and internationalization. Considerable investment in infrastructure, such as transportation and telecommunication is planned as well. This focus on infrastructure seems to be inspired by Porter (1990). However, his suggestion to induce national competition for international competitiveness by nurturing industrial districts, i.e., contexts, has been neglected by Swedish politicians. This again reflects the Swedish irresolution with respect to which strategy to apply to small-business development.

The various approaches to small-business support adopted in Sweden can be classified as focusing on three different levels. On the micro level the individual firm is the recipient and on the macro level investments in infrastructure and other collective assets are made in order to support business development. On an intermediary level the emerging network of firms is the target of different measures (see Table 5.3).

The specific support measure provided reflects, implicitly or explicitly, which context model is used. The public support that is already offered in Sweden can provisionally be associated with different contextual perspectives. A survey of fifty different Swedish public policy measures for which new and/or small firms were eligible in the mid-1980s produces an uneven distribution over the four

Table 5.3 Alternative support strategies for business venturing

Focus	Target	Measures (examples)
Micro level	The budding individual venture/firm	Stimulate local outsourcing Train management locally Support innovators
Intermediary level	The emerging network of firms	Create a local personnel pool Encourage joint tendering Supply joint information services
Macro level	Infrastructure and socio–cultural institutions	Encourage pluri-activity Make public procurement locally Identify community entrepreneurs

contextual models provided here: eight are associated with the market model, twenty with the resource model, three with the milieu model and only one with the career model (Stödhandboken 1986). The remaining eighteen all concern various measures to deal with unemployment which, basically, is negatively correlated with firm formation in Sweden (see p. 122 and Johannisson and Bång 1992). Out of the fifty surveyed measures only three directly refer to new venture support; the remaining either concern (small) business development generally or measures aimed at reducing unemployment.

A contextual approach has three major implications for the feasibility and design of public support for new firms. First, the approach suggests that efficient support may not always be focused on individual firms but collective, aimed at substructures of firms and other contextual actors, or at the regional society at large. A contextual support policy is then inter-firm and inter-sectoral. Second, since contexts are partially defined by history, their resistance to external influence may be considerable; this inertia means that support for the creation of sustainable business contexts will need long pay-off periods. Third, since private and public lives intermingle in the context, private and public measures must be matched in local and regional economic development strategies. Accordingly, not only measures within stated public policy programmes, or potentially so, are illustrated below.

Induced public measures have to be locally administered for several reasons. First, only then can they be synchronized with spontaneously evoked private ambitions to develop business. Second, only on the local level can a holistic approach to business and community development across sectors be adopted. Local insight both facilitates the selection of appropriate measures and demands responsibility from the recipients. Third, a local organization is needed to pay due attention to specific territorial characteristics and make it possible to establish a personal relationship between the entrepreneurs and the representative of the support organization. Support has to be channelled through people and institutions that the entrepreneur trusts, e.g. business friends, existing business ties and the auditor. Only then can the support pay due respect to the impressionistic management style of the entrepreneur as well as safeguard the economies of overview which are the trademark of the small entrepreneurial firm. In Sweden this would imply a further decentralization of industrial policy and strengthening of the municipal industrial liaison offices.

I want to devote the rest of this section to optional measures to encourage firm formation and emerging ventures. The proposed private or public support is linked to each of the four models of firm formation. In Table 5.4 some of the suggested measures are cross-classified with respect to the focused level: micro, intermediary or macro. In presenting the various measures, I try to illustrate implications with respect to distinct demands on the recipients. The argument is that only if support implies establishing a relationship with mutual responsibilities can a support prove itself to both society and the business community.

Within the market model individuals would be encouraged to run temporary ventures with low entry costs in order to tap opportunities and gain general business experience. The support would be through market surveys which are systematically followed up. Further measures include sponsoring cooperation between small firms or between large and small firms in terms of subcontracting and joint marketing. 'Extrapreneurship', means supplementary spin-offs, often implying that the new entrepreneur launches his or her venture with the former employer as a major customer (Johannisson and Johnsson 1988). This seems to be a very efficient way to introduce a new business on to the market. It is also appropriate to intervene in spontaneously initiated production networks which, among other things, guarantee that the parties can get along. Recently a public

Table 5.4 Firm formation models and contextual support strategies

Formation model	Optional support measures on different levels		
	Micro	Intermediate	Macro
Market	Encourage local market surveys	Sponsor subcontracting and extrapreneurship	Organize local trade shows and promote privatization
Resource	Subsidize rented premises	Organize private investors' networks	Establish collective R&D centre
Milieu	Encourage immigrant internships	Stimulate local organizational activities	Invest in leisure and cultural infrastructure
Career	Establish a 'marriage' agency for partnerships	Create a pool of role models and mentors	Promote an enterprising community in the schools

programme encouraging strategic partnerships between large and small firms, preferably in a customer/supplier relationship, was introduced in Sweden. A preliminary evaluation suggests, though, that the larger partner especially has difficulties in mobilizing true commitment and reciprocating public subsidies. Obviously such interventions must be made with great care.

Local outsourcing and public procurement are also important measures within the market model. Such efforts can be enhanced by organizing local exhibitions which also will expose opportunities for privatization of parts of the public sector as well as for joint tendering.

Public measures within the resource model, which are common in Sweden, include venture capital in regional organizations and an elaborate consultancy organization in the regional (county) development funds. Most municipal authorities also offer industrial premises for rent, usually subsidized at least during the first years of the start-up process, in peripheral regions for longer periods. The resource model, furthermore, suggests that information access is crucial and therefore information centres should be established, for example, in cooperation with the public library. The service in return from the new firm using the information would be to register in the databank that encompasses local firms. In addition to this the databank must scan information outside the context. Such support, to be meaningful, requires preconditions, such as the entrepreneur's general experience in the marketplace. Such experience will, among other things, probably provide the individual with an information network and thereby visibility in the marketplace.

Training programmes for new entrepreneurs are to a great extent organized by the regional development funds (in 1989, 9 per cent of business founders stated that they had joined such a programme). Spontaneous initiatives providing resources are organized for example by the private organization Jobs & Society through enterprise agencies. In Sweden these agencies are often the outcome of joining central and local, public and private interests. A general impression is that these programmes lack sufficient effort *vis-à-vis* following up and that they all demand too little involvement on the part of the entrepreneurs.

Socio–cultural resources are not easily activated by way of planned initiatives but municipal support of local industrial associations will both encourage networking among entrepreneurs and strengthen commitment to place, which in turn will encourage networking. Since a contextual approach underlines the social dimension of all business activity including technology transfer, local/regional collective R&D

centres are crucial to competence enhancement in small firms (Pyke *et al.* 1990).

The milieu model, in welfare-state Sweden, encompasses many ingredients originating in different sectoral policies and with major regional implications. My own research into the borderland between urban and rural Sweden shows that even quite small municipalities can offer a favourable milieu with respect to general public services. In Sweden, as well as in many other industrialized states, the recession in the early 1980s gave spontaneous impulses to local initiatives for economic development (Stöhr 1990). There have been various points of departure for such initiatives – the cultural, the educational or the business part of community life. These initiatives have benefited in some cases from an elaborate public-service sector while others have been played down as not very much needed because of the existence of this sector.

The milieu model suggests that, in general, concern for the cultural heritage will make potential entrepreneurs more able and committed to consider the context as an area for serendipitous initiation of new ventures. This can be achieved, for example, by encouraging local organizational life and employment of qualified immigrants in the businesses. Support of amateur theatres and choirs will add to both the creative potential and collective self-confidence. Sometimes leadership is needed to create a milieu which integrates commercial and socio–cultural concerns. Elsewhere we have labelled these leaders community entrepreneurs and positioned their characteristics against those of autonomous entrepreneurs (Johannisson and Nilsson 1989). One of the missions of the community entrepreneurs is to capitalize on the creativity that a broad mobilization of the region may release and, jointly with other parties, support innovators.

The career model takes the socio–economic background of the entrepreneur as a point of departure. In the Scandinavian context, research has identified three basic ways of life: the independent, which includes artisans, small proprietors and farmers; the wage-earner; and the professional. Hjalager and Lindgaard (1984) argue that public support must be adapted to each of these ways of life. New venturing originating in the independent way of life would thus call for general management training, industrial premises for rent and joint study trips to other contexts. Within contexts dominated by the wage-earner's way of life, business venturing must be supported by active recruitment of entrepreneurs from the public sector, encouraging the creation of cooperatives and municipal local acquisition, for example. In order to create contexts for the cosmopolitan members of the professional way of life, measures must include the recruitment of potential entrepreneurs among people who once left the community for educational qualifications and positions in the urban areas. A diversified local labour market is needed to tie the entrepreneur's spouse to the community and advanced communications will help entrepreneurs to retain their cosmopolitan outlook parallel with local commitment.

After decades of expansion, the public sector in Sweden in the early 1990s has begun to lay off personnel. Switching from a career as a public servant to that of an entrepreneur will call for training programmes, not least to unlearn the cost-oriented logic of the public sector and train for opportunity management. A possible measure would be to facilitate partnerships between people from the private and public sectors. Salaried senior entrepreneurs could contribute to career transition processes as mentors and by generally 'walking the community'. Further role models and experienced mentors could be paid by the authorities for providing guidance through the fragile transition process. Partial leave of absence, for example, would make it possible for the individual to search carefully in the community for a venture which trades on his/her profile and on what is needed locally. Pluri-activity may be generally promoted as a strategy for learning the versatility needed for running a firm. Even more important is to create a favourable entrepreneurial spirit in the local and regional context that will legitimate the owner-manager career. The spirit of enterprise must be founded among children, partly through the school system.

FURTHER RESEARCH CHALLENGES

The linkages between reasoning, empirical findings and appropriate public measures provided need further scrutinizing. Several firm formation determinants and public measures may be appropriate in more than one model context. I will indicate here some areas where additional research is needed.

Although I have argued theoretically for a territorial, contextual, approach to firm formation, the dependence upon public statistical data has only provided blunt empirical tools to prove the case. The public database used obviously means that hard facts dominate. This may have favoured a certain way of arguing for defining and understanding entrepreneurial activity. Considering my focus on the territorial dimension of the firm formation context it seems important to reflect on whether the approach has favoured a cosmopolitan or a local outlook. With respect to the definition of 'new venture', initiatives within the informal economy, presumably more elaborate in rural areas, obviously have been disregarded. The operationalization of the determinants of firm formation also seems to treat the local logic unfairly since socio–cultural factors reflecting territorial identity and personal networking are excluded in the model. Further research is thus needed to state the true entrepreneurial potential of different contexts.

The empirical findings concerning entrepreneurial networking reported in the second section of this chapter and firm formation, discussed in the fourth section, suggest that each of the proposed models in the third section are valid in different phases of the venturing process. This is important to consider since the definition of 'take-off' in the venturing process varies between national and international studies in firm formation: it may be the conceptualization of the venture, the formal registration of the firm, the first order received or the first employee hired. While the career and milieu models seem to be appropriate in the early stages (the milieu also in late ones), the resource and market models apply when the venture has become established on the market. Qualitative data may however be needed in order to create a better understanding of how the entrepreneur and her/his venture interplay with the spatial context throughout the venture cycle.

The explanatory power of the various models may vary with respect to the line of business of the new firm. It can, for example, be hypothesized that startups in the service industries are especially dependent on a large regional market and new establishments in the construction business on a growing market, while manufacturing firms can only be started with a minimum of physical and financial resources. Further research therefore must consider industry differences (*cf.* Johannisson and Bång 1992).

The enhanced recognition of human and socio–cultural resources calls for more respect for local capabilities in an increasingly international society. This paradox suggests both that spontaneous initiatives will be more common in all sectors and that much more effort has to be put into tailoring support structures and their implementation to each business context. These are, to a varying degree, already claimed by organically developed support networks (*cf.* Hull and Hjern 1987). Only further research into contextual organizing can provide the information needed for this endeavour.

The linear regression models used to interpret assumed causal relationships is limited in at least two respects. First, the assumption concerning linearity should be tested (*cf.* Johannisson and Bång 1992). Second, the interaction between the independent variables should not only be managed by controlling for multi–collinearity but more actively dealt with. Such interactions may *per se* have a decisive influence on firm formation.

The region as defined in the analyses reported here, i.e., the county, is in a Swedish setting not necessarily the most appropriate territory for understanding the context of firm formation. On one hand the counties are geographically quite large, at least in the northern part of the country; on the other, they represent administrative units with only limited influence on the making of a business environment. The notion of context calls for an operationalization such as the local labour market or a territory with a distinct identity.

APPENDIX

Table A5.1 Correlation coefficients in adopted firm formation models

Dependent variable in all models:
Average annual number of genuinely new firms 1985–9 per thousand households (N8589A).

Independent variables	Correlation coefficients
The market model	
Total income per capita (20 years and older) 1985 (INC85)	0.79**
Income growth over the period 1980–99 (INC8088)	0.32
Increase in number of households over the period 1985–9 (H8588)	0.65**
Population density 1987 (PD87)	0.80**
The share of population that is economically active, i.e. aged 15–64 1987 (P1564)	0.61**
The resource model	
The portion of the families/households which either own their own homes or run farms 1987 (HOUSE)	−0.61**
The portion of the working population employed in banking and professional services 1987 (FINPRO)	0.70**
The share of the population (aged 16–74) with a college education 1985 (CED85)	0.80**
Total public regional industry location support 1985–9 per thousand households 1987 (LOC87)	−0.19
Public expenses for regional development funds 1985 per thousand inhabitants (FUND85)	−0.19
The milieu model	
The share of the population being employed in artistic professions 1980 (per mille) (ART80)	0.80**
Location of a full university 1985 (dummy) (UNI)	0.54*
The share of foreign citizens (per cent) 1987 (FCIT)	0.77**

A5.1 continued

Independent variables	Correlation coefficients
The municipal budget for spending on culture 1988 (per capita) (MCB88)	0.11
The number of sports associations per thousand inhabitants 1987 (SPORT)	−0.35
The career model	
The portion of employees within the manufacturing industry of all privately employed 1986 (MIND)	−0.70**
Unemployment 1987 (UNEMP87)	−0.39
Ratio between the total municipal employment and the regional population 1987 (MEMP)	0.23
Ratio between existing businessmen and households 1987 (BUHOU)	0.55*
The share of privately employed who work in small firms with less than 20 employees 1987 (SMALL)	−0.37

*Significance on the 0.01-level
**Significance on the 0.001-level

REFERENCES

Aguilar, F.J. (1967) *Scanning the Business Environment*, New York: Inter Book.

Aldrich, H., Rosen, B. and Woodward, W. (1987) 'The Impact of Social Networks on Business Foundation and Profit: A Longitudinal Study', paper presented at the 1987 Babson Entrepreneurship Conference, Pepperdine University, Malibu, CA: 29 April–2 May.

Aldrich, H., Reese, P.R., Dubini, P., Rosen, B. and Woodward, B. (1989) 'Women on the Verge of a Breakthrough?: Networking among Entrepreneurs in the United States and Italy', paper presented at the 1989 Babson Entrepreneurship Conference, St Louis, Missouri.

Birley, S., Cromie, S. and Myers, A. (1989) 'Entrepreneurial Networks: Their Creation and Development in Different Countries', Unpublished paper, Cranfield: Cranfield School of Management.

Carland, J.W., Hoy, F. and Carland, J.A.C. (1988) '"Who is an Entrepreneur?"; Is a Question Worth Asking', *American Journal of Small Business* Spring: 33–9.

Coleman, J.S. (1989) 'Social Capital in the Creation of Human Capital', *American Journal of Sociology* 94: Supplement, S95–S120.

Driver, M.J. (1988) 'Careers: A Review of Personal and Organizational Research', in C.I. Cooper and I. Robertson (eds) *International Review of Industrial and Organizational Psychology 1988*, New York: Wiley.

Gartner, W.B. (1989) '"Who is an Entrepreneur?" Is the Wrong Question', *Entrepreneurship Theory and Practice* Summer: 47–68.

Hjalager, A-M. and Lindgaard, G. (1984) *Livsformer og lokale erhvervspolitiske initiativer* (Way of Life and Municipal Industrial Initiatives), Oslo: NordREFO.

Hjern, B. and Bergendahl, U. (1986) *Kommunal näringspolitik – ansvar och kompetens* (Municipal Industrial Policy – Responsibilities and Competences), Stockholm: Svenska kommunförbundet.

Hull, C. and Hjern, B. (1987) *Helping Small Firms Grow. An Implementation Approach*, London: Croom Helm.

Johannisson, B. (1983) 'Swedish Evidence of the Potential of Local Entrepreneurship in Regional Development', *European Small Business Journal* 1(2): 11–24.

—— (1988a) 'Regional Variations in Emerging Entrepreneurial Networks', paper presented at the 28th Congress of the Regional Science Association, Stockholm: 23–6 August.

—— (1988b) 'Business Formation – A Network Approach', *Scandinavian Journal of Management* 4(3/4): 83–99.

—— (1990a) 'Building an Entrepreneurial Career in a Mixed Economy: Need for Social and Business Ties in Personal Networks', paper presented at the Academy of Management Annual Meeting, San Francisco, CA: 12–15 August.

—— (1990b) 'Economies of Overview – Guiding the External Growth of Small Firms', *International Small Business Journal* 9(1): 32–44.

—— (1991) 'University Training for Entrepreneurship: Swedish Approaches', *Entrepreneurship and Regional Development* 3: 67–82.

—— (1992) 'Entrepreneurship – The Management of Ambiguity', in T. Polesie and J.-L. Johansson (eds) *Responsibility and Accounting*, Lund: Studentlitteratur: 155–79.

Johannisson, B. and Bång, H. (1992) *New-Firm Formation and the Regions*, (Nyföretagande och regioner – modeller, fakta, stimulantia), ERU, Stockholm: Ministry of Labour.

Johannisson, B. and Johnsson, T. (1988) *New Venture Network Strategies: The Case of Extrapreneurs*, reports from Växjö University, Ser. 1 Economy and Politics 18, Växjö: Växjö University.

Johannisson, B. and Nilsson, A. (1989) 'Community Entrepreneurship – Networking for Local Development', *Journal of Entrepreneurship and Regional Development* 1(1): 1–19.

Kanter, R.M. (1983) *The Change Masters*, New York: Simon & Schuster.

Light, I.H. (1972) *Ethnic Enterprise in America*, Berkeley, CA: University of California.

Lorenzoni, G. and Ornati, O.A. (1988) 'Constellations of Firms and New Ventures', *Journal of Business Venturing* 3(1): 41–57.

Marshall, A. (1920) (1979) *Principles of Economics*, Eighth edn, London: Macmillan.

Miller, D. (1983) 'The Correlates of Entrepreneurship in Three Types of Firms', *Management Science* 29: 770–91.

Monck, C.S.P., Quintas, P.R., Porter, R.B. and Storey, D.J. (1988) *Science Parks and the Growth of High Technology Firms*, London: Croom Helm.

Piore, M.J. and Sabel, C.F. (1984) *The Second Industrial Divide*, New York: Basic Books.

Porter. M. (1990) 'The Competitive Advantage of Nations', *Harvard Business Review* March–April: 73–93.

Pyke, F., Becattini, G. and Sengenberger, W. (eds) (1990) *Industrial Districts and Inter-Firm Co-operation in Italy*, Geneva: ILO.

Schumacher, E.F. (1975) *Small is Beautiful*, New York: Perennial, Harper & Row.

Shapero, A. and Sokol, L. (1982) 'The Social Dimension of Entrepreneurship', in C.A. Kent, D.L. Sexton and K.H. Vesper (eds) *Encyclopedia of Entrepreneurship*, Englewood Cliffs, N.J.: Prentice-Hall: 72–90.

Stödhandboken (*The Public Support Manual*) (1986), Stockholm: Liber.

Stöhr, W. (ed.) (1990) *Global Challenge and Local Response*, London: Mansell.

Storey, D.J. (1991) 'The Birth of New Firms – Does Unemployment Matter? A Review of the Evidence', *Small Business Economics* 3: 167–78.

Vesper, K.H. (1990) *New Venture Strategies*, Second edn, Englewood Cliffs, N.Y.: Prentice-Hall.

Ward, R. (1987) 'Ethnic Entrepreneurs in Britain and Europe', in R. Goffee and R. Scase (eds) *Entrepreneurship in Europe*, London: Croom Helm: 83–104.

Zeitlin, J. (ed.) (1989) *Local Industrial Strategies*. Special issue of *Economy and Society* 18(4).

p 117;

DISCUSSION

142 – 44
SWEDEN
L11 R12 M13

Paul D. Reynolds

The objective of this chapter, to understand the basis for region-to-region variation in firm formation across the twenty-four regions/counties of Sweden, is important and timely. Four alternative conceptions of fertile contexts for entrepreneurship are presented: the market model emphasizes the demands for products and services in the region; the resource model emphasizes the availability of inputs (e.g. capital) needed to start a new firm; the milieu model emphasizes a positive orientation towards entrepreneurial activity as an integral feature of the region's economic specialization; and the career model emphasizes the positive value placed on entrepreneurship as a suitable career option for the residents. The analysis, based on existing data from national sources, attempts to determine if there is a correspondence between the conceptual models of fertility and actual new-firm births.

The primary research issues are: is there empirical evidence to support the influence of any of these models on firm births? And, if more than one has an impact, what is their relative influence? In other words, how much of the variation in firm births across the twenty-four regions of Sweden can be accounted for by these four conceptions of regional fertility?

The empirical data starts with counts of new firm births for 1986–9 across the twenty-four Swedish regions. New-firm births are standardized with respect to the number per 1,000 households, reflecting an emphasis on the need for a household effort for successful firm births. (This unusual choice of a base may not affect the results, for the number of households probably correlates highly with the total population, number employed, number in the labour force, percentage over 25 years old, or any of the other various bases used for normalization in such research.) A variety of indicators considered relevant to the four different 'fertility models' are taken from standard national statistical sources and then used in linear models in attempts to predict variation in the firm birth rate. These indicators reflect a number of different time periods, some prior to and some concurrent with the period for which birth rates are measured.

Despite the limitations imposed by having only twenty-four regions in the analysis, there is systematic support for each of the four models. The supportive evidence is, first, in the form of a single linear model for each of the four conceptions of regional fertility. These linear equations contain from three to five indicators reflecting their respective conceptions and explain individually from 57 per cent to 81 per cent of the explained variance. When all eighteen indicators are included in one overall model, the multiple regression step-wise procedure retains one indicator representing each of the four models in the final equation, explaining 91 per cent of the variation in the firm birth rates.

There are a number of issues regarding the methodology that could be addressed. For example, the desire to have a causal explanation is not consistent with a large proportion of the indicators taken from the same time period as the measure of birth rates. Second, there is likely to be some ambivalence over a regression procedure that involves eighteen independent variables applied to twenty-four units of analysis. In such an effort, there are few degrees of freedom and the regression procedure is almost forced to create a single, optimum fit linear model. The absence of opportunity for the procedure to make mistakes reduces the information conveyed by a high explained variance.

While the number of Swedish regions cannot easily be increased, it might be possible to combine the individual measures to create a single index representing each of the four conceptual models. A regression analysis with four independent variables and twenty-four regions would provide more possibility for error and a more stringent test of the success of explaining variations in birth rates. It would also provide an opportunity to determine if there is variation among the regions with regard to the presence of different types of 'fertility'. For example, are those regions with a high 'market index' the same regions with a high 'resource index'?

There are several strategies that may be used to increase the number of units of analysis. One would be to use more time periods. Perhaps break the 1986–9 period into three one-year periods. If nothing else, this would allow for an estimation of the temporal stability of the birth rates. If there is high stability, it suggests that firm birth rates are a stable characteristic of the region, slow to change, and not easily affected by small changes in the start-up processes. A second strategy would be to differentiate both birth rates and independent variables by industries. If nothing else, it would allow for a separation of those firms in industries that rely on a local market (such as retail, consumer services, and construction) and are highly affected by the features of the region from those that emphasize an export market (manufacturing) and are likely to be more responsible to conditions outside the region or even outside Sweden. It would allow an estimate of the relative impact of the four conceptions on different productive activity. This may increase the accuracy of the predictions and the precision of the under-standing provided by this theoretical framework.

No analysis or research is perfect, and this chapter is not without unresolved issues. However, no research can advance without efforts to structure the problems and develop some form of analysis. This is a good beginning and the results are encouraging; it suggests that additional cross-regional comparisons may enhance understanding of the processes affecting entrepreneurial activity. One can ask no more of any scholarly effort.

6   Regional characteristics, business dynamics and economic development[1]

Per Davidsson, Leif Lindmark and Christer Olofsson[2]

INTRODUCTION

A sound market economy is characterized by dynamic change. According to the theory, competitive pressure should result in the birth and expansion of companies or entire industries that satisfy consumer demands better or at lower cost, whereas other companies or industries are punished for their relative inefficiency and therefore contract out or are wiped out entirely. The process thus yields efficient use of scarce resources over time. Hence, business dynamics – including business births *and* deaths, expansions *and* contractions – increases economic well-being. And indeed, the evidence for the importance of structural change for economic development is overwhelming (*cf.* Armstrong and Taylor 1978).

Accordingly, structural change, startups, and expansions are actively promoted in many countries. At the same time it is evident that dynamics is not always good, at least not for individual firms and individual people. Some resources, not only obsolete machinery and other material resources but also human skills and self-respect, may simply be destroyed in the process. Besides unmeasurable costs at the individual level this destruction of resources can be a cost to society as well. Furthermore, in less than perfect markets agglomeration of capital can result in monopoly power that makes dynamics *per se* no guarantee for increases in economic well-being even in the long run.

Not surprisingly, policy makers tend not to rely entirely on the self-regulating operations of the market and introduce measures designed to reduce dynamics as well. Companies on the verge of bankruptcy may be saved, and other companies that (temporarily) need to reduce the number of employees may receive support for keeping them, in order to avoid sky-rocketing unemployment figures. Along with the good intentions, of course, comes the risk of actually decreasing rather than increasing well-being in the long run by hindering efficient resource allocation.

It has been shown empirically that the pattern of dynamics differs considerably among countries and geographic regions (see Illeris 1986; Keeble and Wever 1986; Cramer 1987; Cramer and Koller 1988; Reynolds and Maki 1990). Sociologists and psychologists (Weber 1930; McClelland 1961; Etzioni 1987) have sought to explain the differential levels of entrepreneurial spirit among regions by differences in cultural values. McClelland (1961) and others (see Bellu 1987) have also provided systematic empirical evidence to support such ideas.

Other researchers have focused on more tangible characteristics of geographic regions as explanations for regional differences in general economic vitality as well as specific aspects such as start-up, survival and growth rates (see Bruno and Tyebjee 1982; and Keeble *et al.* 1990 for reviews). While the studies converge on some points, it is safe to say that our knowledge as to the causes and effects of regional economic dynamics is far from complete.

The above discussion is in line with the model shown in Figure 6.1.

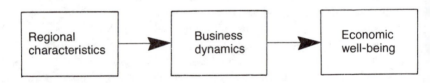

Figure 6.1 Regional characteristics, business dynamics and economic well-being

This model guided a large-scale study of business and job volatility in the US in the 1976–86 period (Reynolds 1988; Reynolds and Maki 1989; 1990). Using a 382-region framework based on US labour market areas (LMAs) and empirical data from the US Small Business Administration, they found strong empirical relations between regional characteristics and small-firm births, and a positive relation between business volatility and subsequent economic well-being. An intriguing result is that this includes a positive (although weak) effect of *death* rates on economic well-being, suggesting that deaths indeed led to resources being re-allocated to better use. They further conclude that 'it would be reasonable to assume that up to half of all economic growth is directly related to the volatility of business establishments (births and deaths) and job changes (gains and losses). Another substantial proportion is related to interaction between regional (LMA) characteristics and business volatility' (Reynolds and Maki 1990: 49).

Although this study is a comprehensive one it obviously cannot give definite answers to all the intricate questions of theoretical as well as practical interest that the model evokes. Do more dynamics lead to increased well-being? Is *any* type of dynamics advantageous? What are the causes of business dynamics? Is the pattern the same or strikingly different across industries, countries and regions? Can policy measures be designed to promote the positive effects of change and reduce the negative ones? Or is any intervention bound to be counter-productive, as radical liberals would have it?

The purpose of the study presented in this chapter is to address some of these questions by means of an investigation of (nearly) all Swedish business establishments in the 1985–9 period. While the study also covers the large corporations, special attention is devoted to the small-firm sector. More specifically, the purpose of the study is to:

1   provide a disaggregated *description* of business dynamics. This involves detailed analyses of gross changes among establishments of different types grouped in various ways.
2   attempt to *explain* differences in regional business dynamics by differences in regional demographic and economic-structural characteristics.
3   attempt to *explain* differential development of economic well-being by differences in business dynamics and background characteristics of the regions.

As analyses of the full data-base have as yet not been conducted, our purpose is to describe the research project and present some examples of analyses from one labour market area. The focus lies on the description of business dynamics.

A CLOSER LOOK AT ECONOMIC DYNAMICS

Dynamics over time

While academic as well as political interest in economic dynamics has been around for a long time, the focus of interest has changed over the years. This change has largely mirrored the actual economic situation. The first half of the twentieth century was dominated by the continuous transfer of resources from agriculture to the manufacturing sector. The result was considerable economic development interrupted by a few major downturns, and a great academic and policy-making interest in structural change, business cycles (Keynesianism) and production costs.

In summary, the 1960s was the era of the big corporations, general policy measures to support the creation of a rational industry structure, and economic growth to a great extent achieved by economies of scale. The 1970s (in Sweden) was the decade of crises, characterized by stagflation, structural rationalization and selective policy measures aimed at developing new firms and industries and slowing down the speed of the restructuring process in the economy.

The rapid expansion of the service sector began in the 1970s and continued during the 1980s. Forecasts predict that the importance of business services in creating new jobs will increase further in the 1990s (Statens industriverk 1990). The development of the service sector is both cause and effect of the increasing specialization and division of labour in highly developed economies. The more developed the economy, the more firms are involved in the value added chains transforming raw materials into final products (Christensen *et al.* 1990).

Another feature of the last decade is the growth of high-tech manufacturing, albeit perhaps less so in Sweden than in other countries, causing some authors to voice concern over de-industrialization or insufficient renewal (Erixon 1991; Lundberg 1991).

The last decade also brought a revival of smallness, entrepreneurship and individual initiative. Large corporations realized that big isn't always beautiful. Therefore, their growth-through-diversification efforts have come to a halt or reversal, and power and responsibility have been decentralized in order to make the organizations more adaptive and cost-effective. At the same time, studies in several countries have claimed that the number of new firm startups has risen and that the relative importance of the small-firm sector as creator of new employment has increased, which has resulted in a dramatically increased interest in the small-firm sector among academics and policy makers as well as in the media. This apparent turbulence among small as well as large companies will be discussed in greater detail in the next subsection.

Most empirical studies of changes in the economy focus on *net* changes, while very few actually examine the dynamics by studying

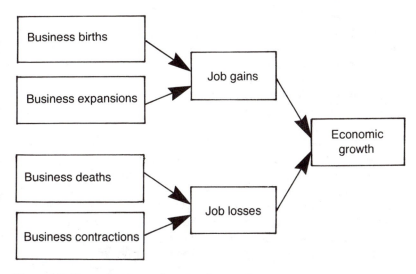

Figure 6.2 Gross changes and economic growth

gross changes at the company or establishment level. More detailed studies are badly needed since it certainly makes a differences if, for example, a zero net change in employment means that the same people are employed by the same firms, or if it is the net result of turbulent change. As mentioned earlier, the purpose of this paper is to describe the dynamics of the Swedish economy at a disaggregate level. This involves tracking business births, expansions, contractions and deaths, and the resulting job volatility. Figure 6.2 displays the model for this part of the study.

Tracking the components according to the model shown in the figure has considerable advantages over just studying net changes. Further breakdowns may be required in order to get a detailed understanding of business dynamics itself, as well as its causes and effects. Breakdowns by region, industry sector, size class, etc. are called for, judging from empirical research reviewed and discussed in the next sub-section.

Business dynamics and job creation

The presence of regional variations in economic development is well documented (see pp. 145–7). Sweden is no exception: empirical studies show, for example, regional variations in new-firm formation and economic growth (Statistics Sweden 1990).

An intensive debate about the importance of small firms in the job creation process was initiated by David Birch in 1979 and the question has now been on the agenda for more than a decade. One reason for the ongoing controversy is lack of accurate data, but the evidence seems to favour the importance of small firms in the job creation process. Reynolds and Maki (1990) report that on average 66 per cent of the total jobs gained in the US economy 1969–84 were provided by firms with less than 100 employees, while between 1976 and 1984, 54 per cent of total job gains were in autonomous, locally-headquartered firms. According to Reynolds and Maki it is clear that a major source of new business jobs are new-firm births and small-firm expansions. Another conclusion is that SME births and expansions play an independent and positive role in regional economic change in the US. In a Swedish study on the development of manufacturing industry in a county over a ten-year period (1974–83) it was shown that only new establishments provided new jobs, on average 1.7 per cent per year, while closed down establishments lost 1.1 per cent on average (Olofsson *et al.* 1986). The net figure for surviving establishments was a yearly loss of 2.4 per cent.

Empirical data from European countries support the idea of the importance of new-firm formation and small autonomous firms in the job creation process (Aronsson 1991; Ettinger and Weereld 1988; Keeble *et al.* 1990; Karlsson and Löwstedt 1990). However, lack of accurate data, problems with separating autonomous small firms from branch plants, and other methodological problems give reasons to be careful about making far-reaching conclusions concerning the role of small firms in the job creation process.

In a review of research on regional variations in SME births and development in European countries Keeble *et al.* (1990) point out that the studies thus far have been more restricted than in the US, with a marked bias towards the manufacturing sector. They also point out that many European researchers have adopted a qualitative rather than quantitative approach describing and discussing regional variations and possible influences. There is thus a need for quantitative approaches to testing many of the hypotheses generated.

More research is also needed into the development of large multinational companies and changes in their internal structure and localization pattern over time. Another important research question concerns their importance in the national economies as creators of new jobs.

Empirical studies also show important sectoral and subsectoral variations over time in development (Statens industriverk 1990). The relative importance of births, expansions, contractions and deaths can also be assumed to vary between sectors and subsectors in the economy depending, for example, on maturity and barriers to entry. This underlines the importance of paying attention to sectoral variations in empirical studies of business volatility and regional economic growth.

According to Reynolds and Maki (1990) the percentage of business jobs gained and lost has increased markedly over time. In the period 1976–8 the percentage of jobs gained and lost was 8.5 per cent and 5.2 per cent respectively. Less than a decade later (1984–6) the corresponding figures were doubled, 15.4 and 12.3 per cent, respectively. In the 1980s more than one in four jobs in the business sector was created or eliminated each two-year period, according to Reynolds and Maki. It is open to discussion whether the data reflect real changes in the US economy or if they are, at least to some extent, artefacts created by changes in data collection and up-dating. But there is no doubt that there are changes over time in job turnover, depending on the aggregate demand in the economy, structural crises, etc.

This short review has shown that we lack accurate information on several important issues and that there are many interesting research questions that can be addressed, analysing gross changes in the economy on firm or establishment level. One crucial point in a study designed to monitor changes over time on the level of individual establishments is access to accurate data. In the project discussed in this chapter, considerable time and effort has been spent on compiling a high quality data set that can be used for analysing the relationships between regional characteristics, business volatility and economic growth. In the next section the data set used for studying business volatility will be discussed in more detail.

THE DATA SET

For the purpose of describing and analysing business volatility in the Swedish economy a data set has been created to meet certain criteria. The most important of these are that the data set should make it possible to:

(a) monitor individual establishments over time in order to identify births, deaths, expansions and contractions with accuracy,
(b) identify different types of establishments, i.e., autonomous firms, corporate headquarters and branch plants,

(c) group the establishments according to sectorial affinity
(d) group the establishments according to size of employment
(e) relate the establishments to labour market regions
(f) locate geographically the ownership of branch plants, including foreign ownership.

The work compiling relevant data for the project has taken more than a year. That is in spite of only using data already collected by Statistics Sweden (SCB). In close cooperation with register experts and programmers at SCB, data from various data-bases and different (annual) versions thereof have been combined and checked in order to achieve the highest possible quality of the input data. In addition, samples of register data have been checked against reality by means of telephone interviews and other sources. All together, data from four data-bases have been matched. These are:

(a) the Central Establishment Register (CFAR)
(b) the Register on Regional Employment (ÅRSYS)
(c) the Register over Groups of Companies (KCR)
(d) the Register over Establishments and Firms with Foreign Ownership.

By the comparison of different annual versions of CFAR, births, deaths, expansions and contractions can be tracked. The period studied is 1985 to 1989, allowing five static descriptions and four year-by-year comparisons. In 1985 a major change in data collecting and recording procedures occurred, increasing the quality of the CFAR. This makes analyses of data prior to 1985 more uncertain, and the research group therefore settled on the 1985–9 period. Data for 1990 onwards were not ready for compilation but can be added later.

By choosing establishments rather than legal firms as the basic unit of analysis, *monitoring changes over time* is made possible. In CFAR, each establishment has a unique code that in principle is not altered by single changes such as transfer of ownership, change of legal form, or geographic move, whereas combinations of changes as a rule result in a new code. In some cases, though, the code is altered and an ongoing business is classified as a death and a birth in the data-bases used. The over-estimation of births and deaths can be checked by special analyses of the individuals working in these establishments. The over-estimation stays around 10 per cent in the data sets used. Also, unique codes exist for legal firms, but these are often changed even if no real birth or death has occurred. The legal firm as a unit of analysis is therefore more problematic than is the establishment.

Perhaps the trickiest part of data compiling has been the *identification of establishment types*. Following Reynolds and Maki (1990), three types of establishments are identified:

1 Simples, which are autonomous, one-establishment firms
2 Branches, which are either units other than headquarters in company groups, or units other than headquarters in independent multi-establishment firms
3 Tops, which are headquarters in either of the two internal structures described under Branches.

The identification involves extensive search and matching of data in CFAR, KCR, and the Register over Establishments and Firms with Foreign Ownership. Especially cumbersome is the identification of Tops in company groups, and the accuracy of these classifications was therefore checked separately.

As to *industries*, fairly broad categories have to be used in order to make the study manageable. Another reason for working with broad categories is that the quality of 4- and 5-digit classifications is highly questionable, whereas the degree of uncertainty in this regard is not as serious a problem at the 2-digit level. Based on SNI-codes (a Swedish version of the ISIC-system) the following industry sectors were created:

(a) High-tech manufacturing
(b) Knowledge-intensive services
(c) Forest-based industry (pulp, paper, lumber, wood products)
(d) Engineering (metal goods, machinery, vehicles, appliances, etc.)
(e) Mining and steelworks
(f) Other manufacturing (food, textile, chemical, etc.)
(g) Construction
(h) Trade (wholesale and retail)
(i) Transportation
(j) Finance (bank, insurance, etc.)
(k) Other services (repairs, cleaning, etc.)
(l) Unclassified

Primary industries like agriculture and forestry, and non-commercial public services, are not included in the study.

The logic behind the aggregation has been the degree of homogeneity, significance for the Swedish economy, a special interest in some relatively small but growing industries (a) and (b), and data limitations (1). For establishments that start out small, industry classification can lag behind. In order to reduce this problem, original blanks are exchanged for later classification through checks of subsequent versions of CFAR. This does not reduce category (1) to zero, but there are possibilities of estimating the proportion of blanks per sector. Preliminary checks indicate that small Simples, that should be classified in category (b), knowledge-intensive services, make up a large proportion of the establishments in category (1).

Our delineation of geographical units is based on the 111 Labour Market Areas in Sweden (see Figure 6A.1 in the appendix). Our concept of LMAs is similar to that used by Reynolds and Maki (1990) although there are some differences between Sweden and the United States when it comes to local and regional organization of administrative units that add up to LMAs.

The Swedish LMAs have recently been defined by Statistics Sweden's unit for labour market statistics on the basis of commuting statistics. The population of the areas differs considerably, from a couple of thousands to over a million (Greater Stockholm). For the purpose of this study, Greater Stockholm has been divided into three areas. Very small areas have been combined into another area with similar demographic and economic–structural characteristics if they are geographically adjacent. The combination of LMAs has been done according to a cluster analysis of LMAs that had already been prepared by Statistics Sweden for other purposes. The end result of these adjustments is a division of the country into eighty areas.

Data on the *location of ownership* (within the same LMA, within other Swedish LMAs, foreign) for Branches is not contained in CFAR. By linking Branches to their respective Top in KCR and also checking for foreign ownership, this classification is fairly straightforward and mis-specifications occur only in cases of recent changes of ownership location.

For all three establishment types (Tops, Simples, Branches) six *size classes* are specified based on number of employees: 0, 1–4, 5–19, 20–49, 50–199 and 200+. As data quality of the CFAR was judged unsatisfactory in regard to employment figures, the original size measure is exchanged for more accurate figures from the register ÅRSYS, that tracks specific individuals. The business establishments covered by the two registers do not match completely, so in some cases the original employment figure has to be retained. For industry sector (g), the original figure is retained throughout. For some legal entities, e.g. limited companies, partnerships etc., the owner(s) are not counted in the employment figures. Corrections have been made so that the owner-manager(s) is counted as an employee irrespective of legal entity.

Special problems occur when establishments change categorical affinity (LMA, type, size, etc.) from the first to the second year of an analysis period. As a general rule such problems have been solved so as to ascribe negative changes to the category of origin and positive changes to the new category.

The empirical analysis from the Linköping LMA presented in the following section is the result of the last major data check used in the study.

A DISAGGREGATED ANALYSIS OF THE BUSINESS DYNAMICS IN ONE REGION

In order to test the model, concepts and measurements discussed on pp. 149–54, one labour market area, Linköping, was chosen for a test run. In this section we present some data from that test and in the final section of this chapter we will make some comments on the measurements, quality of the data set and computer programs used.

The Linköping labour market area

The Linköping labour market area is one of the larger LMAs in the southern part of Sweden. It is composed of eight local municipalities of which Linköping is the largest one (see Table 6.1). The municipality of Linköping is the site of the county administration, a regional hospital and a university. The headquarters and production units of one of Sweden's largest companies, Saab, is also located in Linköping.

Table 6.1 The Linköping labour market area

	Population
Boxholm	5,600
Kinda	10,200
Linköping	120,500
Mjölby	26,000
Motala	41,700
Vadstena	7,400
Åtvidaberg	12,700
Ödeshög	5,900

Table 6.2 Establishments by industry, 1985

Industry	%
High-tech	1.8
Knowledge-intensive services	7.6
Forest-based industry	3.0
Engineering	6.5
Mining and steel works	1.1
Other manufacturing	5.8
Construction	15.1
Trade	45.1
Transportation	8.8
Finance	6.4
Other services	8.7

The total number of business establishments in the industries included in this study is about 8,000, employing approximately 55,000 people. In the public service sector (not included), there are another 2,000 establishments, employing 37,000 people, and in the agricultural sector (not included) there are about 4,000 establishments with 5,000 people employed.

The relative shares of business establishments for different industries in terms of the industry classification described in the previous section are shown in Table 6.2 above. Most establishments are found in the trading sector, relatively few in manufacturing. Only about 10 per cent of the total number of establishments are in the forest based industry, engineering or mining and steel industries.

Simples, Tops, and Branches in the Linköping LMA

In the Linköping region, as well as in other labour market regions in Sweden, small establishments make up the dominant share of all establishments. Around 80 per cent of all establishments have up to four employees, 14 per cent have between five and nineteen employees and the remaining 5 per cent employ twenty or more persons. The relative shares of the size groups in terms of numbers of establishments have remained fairly stable over the time period studied (see Figure 6.3).

The industry structure of the Linköping labour market area can also be described by using the three types of business establishments discussed in the previous section: SIMPLES, TOPS, and BRANCHES. In Figures 6.4 and 6.5 the relative shares of types of

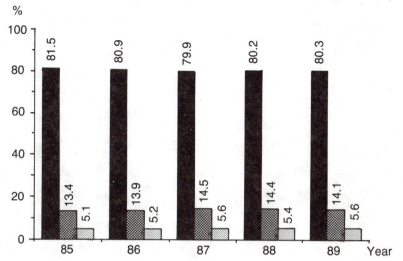

Figure 6.3 Establishments by size groups (%)

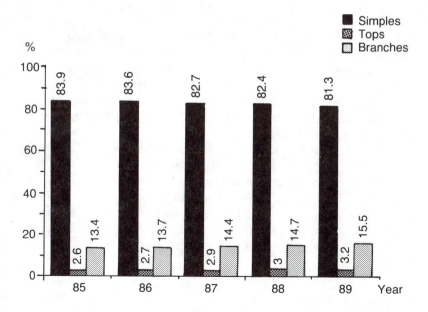

Figure 6.4 Establishments by types (%)

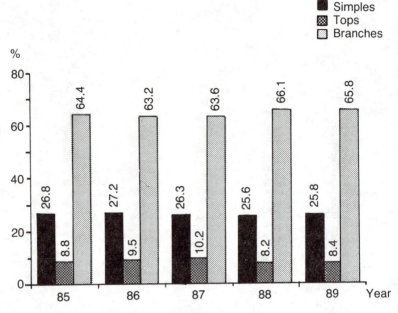

Figure 6.5 Employment by type of establishments (%)

establishments and their shares of employment in the industries covered in the study are presented.

Simples represent more than 80 per cent of the establishments in the region but only a little more than a quarter of the employment. The number of Tops is relatively small and less than 10 per cent of employees work in Tops. More important from the viewpoint of employment are Branches. Around one out of seven establishments can be classified as a Branch representing two-thirds of the employment in the industries studied.

Over the five-year period studied, the relative share of Branches has slightly increased and the share of Simples decreased. These changes are also reflected in the employment figures for Simples and Branches. This should not be interpreted as showing that the small firm sector is diminishing. Other results suggest the converse. Instead, the main reason for this pattern is that an increasing number of small firms are run as multi-establishment entities, e.g. as a Top with a Branch.

Births and deaths

Net figures about changes in the number of establishments and

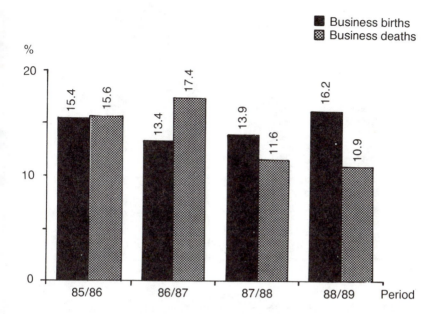

Figure 6.6 Births and deaths of establishments (%)

employment by type of firm give rather limited information about the underlying dynamics in the economy. More information can be obtained by studying gross changes. Such a model was introduced in Figure 6.2 (see p. 149) using births, deaths, expansions and contractions as analytic tools.

A large proportion of the business establishments are subject to change every year. In the Linköping LMA changes in employment figures occurred for two out of three establishments. In this section births and deaths of establishments are discussed in more detail, in the next section the focus is on expansions and contractions.

Figure 6.6, displaying births and deaths in the Linköping LMA, indicates a rather high degree of economic dynamics in the region. On average one out of seven establishments are new firms and about the same proportion go out of business each year. For the first two years studied the proportion of deaths was higher than births, for the last two years it was the other way round.

Nine out of ten new establishments each year are Simples. Very few are Tops, only 1–2 per cent. This is quite understandable since few firms start out as multi-establishment entities. Worth noting is that the share of new Simples has decreased slightly over time; a

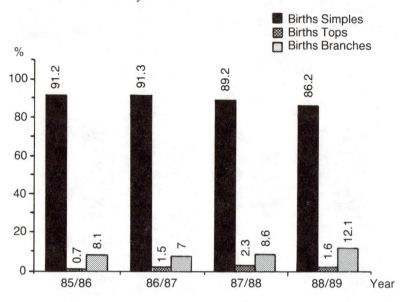

Figure 6.7 Business births by type of establishment (%)

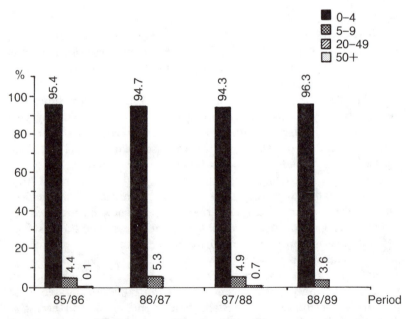

Figure 6.8 Size structure of new Simples (%)

larger proportion of the new establishments are either Tops or Branches (see Figure 6.7).

Not unexpectedly the vast majority of the new establishments are very small. Out of the Simples, about 95 per cent have less than five employees at the end of the first calendar year (see Figure 6.8). Other data (see Figure 6.3) suggest that most firms which start as Simples also remain very small. As indicated above, some may, however, become multi-establishment firms and thus cease to be Simples.

A large number of new firms are established in the trade sector – retailing, restaurants, etc. Other sectors with a high business volatility in terms of new establishments are the finance and knowledge-intensive service sectors. On the other hand, the proportion of new establishments is relatively small in the manufacturing sectors.

The death rate of Simples varies over the four-year period studied, from 12 to 19 per cent of the total number at the beginning of each period. Compared with Branches and Tops the approximate death rate is twice and three times higher, respectively, for Simples. Over time, though, there is a marked decline in the death rate for Simples, less so for Tops and Branches (see Figure 6.9).

A closer look at the Simples shows that with few exceptions the deaths occur among establishments in the smallest size bracket, up to four employees (see Figure 6.10). A comparison between Figure 6.8

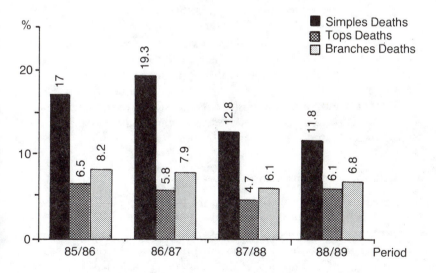

Figure 6.9 Death rate by type of establishment (%)

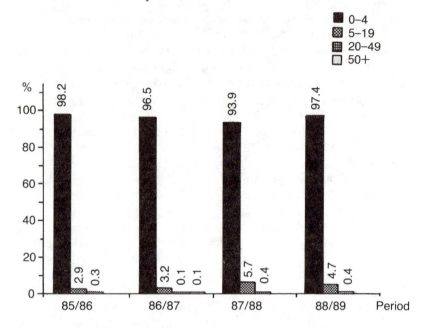

Figure 6.10 Deaths of Simples by size (%)

displaying the size structure of births and Figure 6.10 with corresponding figures for deaths, shows that the share of deaths among the smallest Simples is slightly higher than the share of births.

The trade sector is not only one with many new establishments during the period studied; it is also a sector with many business deaths. The number of deaths is slightly higher than births. The same goes for the finance sector. Among knowledge-intensive services, on the other hand, new establishments definitely outnumber deaths. Transportation and other services are other industry sectors with more births than deaths during the period studied.

Expansions and contractions

Expansions and contractions add to the business dynamics of a region as well as business births and deaths. Figure 6.11 shows that 35 per cent of the existing stock of establishments either expand or contract each year, not counting births and deaths. For all the periods studied the number of expansions in the Linköping LMA has been larger than the number of contractions (see Figure 6.11). This can probably

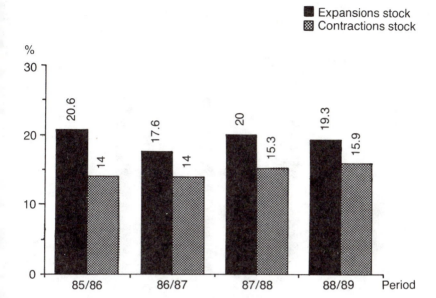

Figure 6.11 Expansions and contractions (%)

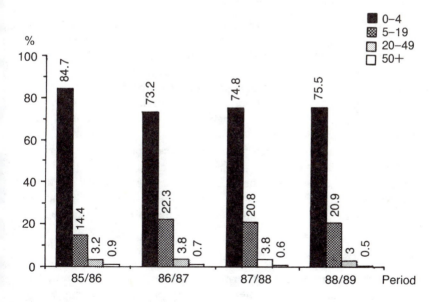

Figure 6.12 Expanding Simples by size (%)

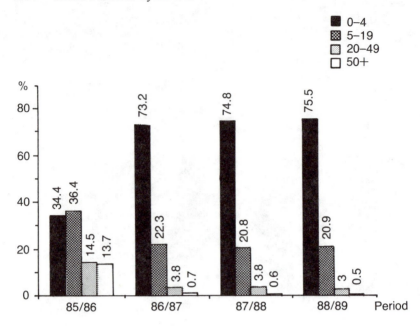

Figure 6.13 Expanding Branches by size (%)

be explained by the economic cycle, with a marked, continuous upswing during the second part of the 1980s. It should be noted that roughly 70 per cent of the expansions are Simples and about 25 per cent are Branches. For contractions the corresponding figures are 65 per cent for Simples and close to 30 per cent for Branches.

In Figure 6.12 the distribution of expanding Simples over size groups is shown. About 95 per cent of the expanding Simples have less than twenty employees.

In contrast to the pattern for Simples, the Branch expansions are more evenly distributed over the size brackets, which is a reflection of differences in size structure between Simples and Branches. As much as 30 per cent of the the expansions in Branches takes place in establishments with more than twenty employees (see Figure 6.13).

Business dynamics and employment

A high business volatility in terms of births, deaths, expansions and contractions of establishments characterizes the Linköping LMA. Two-thirds of the establishments each year report changes in

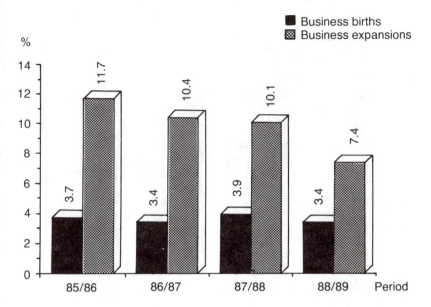

Figure 6.14 Job gains each year as percentage of total number of jobs.

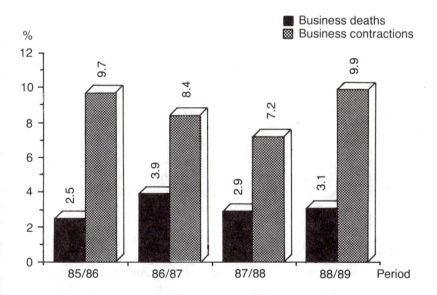

Figure 6.15 Job losses each year as percentage of total number of jobs.

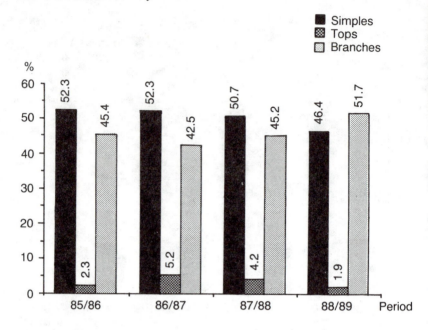

Figure 6.16 Job gains from births by type of establishment

employment figures. The net effect of these changes is a small increase over time of the total employment in the industries studied.

If we look at gross instead of net figures the changes in employment are quite substantive. The number of new jobs created each year by new and expanding establishments varies between 11 and 15 per cent of the total number of jobs at the beginning of the year. About one-third of the new jobs are created by births, the rest by expanding establishments (see Figure 6.14).

The job losses from deaths and contractions of establishments vary between 10 and 13 per cent for the time period studied. The absolute majority of job losses is related to contractions (see Figure 6.15). It may be worth noting that at the end of the period studied there is a decline in new employment and a rise in lost jobs, producing a net loss of jobs (1989).

More than half of the new jobs from establishment births come from Simples, somewhat less from Branches as shown in Figure 6.16. A slight decline in the share of new jobs created by Simples can be noticed over the period studied. A more detailed analysis shows that of the contribution from births of Simples, more than 50 per cent of

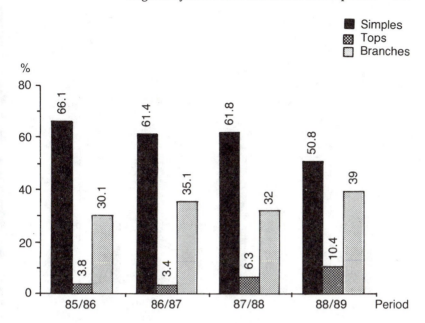

Figure 6.17 Job losses from deaths by type of establishment

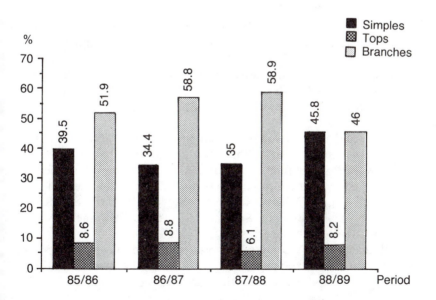

Figure 6.18 Job gains from expansions by type of establishment (%)

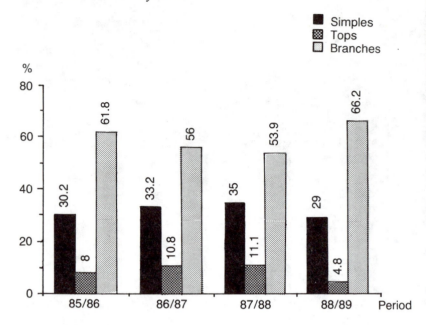

Figure 6.19 Job losses from contractions by type of establishment (%)

new jobs are created by establishments in the smallest size group and about 40–45 per cent of the jobs are gained by establishments with between five and nineteen employees. For the Branches there is quite another situation. Of the new employment contributed by Branches only between 30 and 45 per cent comes from establishments with less than twenty employees, the rest being created by more sizeable establishments.

Job losses from establishment deaths are displayed in Figure 6.17. It shows a declining trend in the share of job losses from deaths of Simples, from two-thirds in the beginning of the period studied to about 50 per cent at the end of the period. This parallels the declining trend for Simples' share of the number of establishment deaths (Figure 6.9). Accordingly, the trend for Tops and Branches is the opposite: their share is increasing.

Job gains from business expansions broken down by type of establishment is presented in Figure 6.18. In the beginning of the period less than 40 per cent of the gains were contributed by Simples and about 50 per cent by Branches. The relations change slightly towards the end of the period, when Simples and Branches both contribute about 45 per cent of the gains.

As shown in Figure 6.19 the main source of job losses are Branches, which, in two of the periods, account for more than 60 per cent of the losses, while 30–35 per cent of the losses come from Simples whose share of job losses is slightly larger than their share of employment. Data not displayed here indicate that two-thirds of the losses from contractions in Branches are produced by the two largest size groups.

SUMMING UP

The data produced in the test run for the Linköping LMA are preliminary. However, the data do support the point of the departure for the study, namely the important study of gross changes in the economy at the establishment level. These kind of data make it possible to understand the dynamics of the regional economy and the role of dynamics for regional economic growth and well-being.

In the Linköping LMA two-thirds of the establishments reported changes in employment figures each year during the period studied. This means that business volatility in terms of births, deaths, expansions and contractions seems to be the rule rather than the exception in the Linköping LMA. The new jobs created and lost each year by the studied establishments account for 10–15 per cent of the stock of jobs in the region. About one-third of the new jobs are created by births, the rest by expanding establishments. The empirical results are consistent with Reynold and Maki's (1990) observations of the joint presence of births and deaths, expansions and contractions for economic growth.

The test run also supports the models, concepts and measurements developed for the study. The preliminary data from the Linköping region show that the data set can be used for descriptive purposes and for analyses of business volatility at the regional level.

However, using empirical data from just one labour market area makes it difficult to identify and analyse patterns in the material. The possibilities to study and interpret the patterns in regional business volatility will increase dramatically with the full scale study using data from eighty labour market areas. In the full scale study the data set will be explored more systematically than in this preliminary report, also using information about industry classification, localization of ownership, etc. The analyses will also be more sophisticated and will include data about regional characteristics and economic well-being at the regional level.

To sum up, the test run has shown that models, concepts and measurements used are relevant for studying business volatility at the regional level. The test run has also shown that interesting empirical results are obtained which can be used for further analyses of the relationships between regional characteristics, business dynamics and economic development.

NOTES

1   Project sponsored by National Board for Industrial and Technical Development.
2   Gunnar Petersson has acted as research consultant and had the main responsibility for technical communication with Statistics Sweden as concerns extracting and combining information from various data registers.

APPENDIX

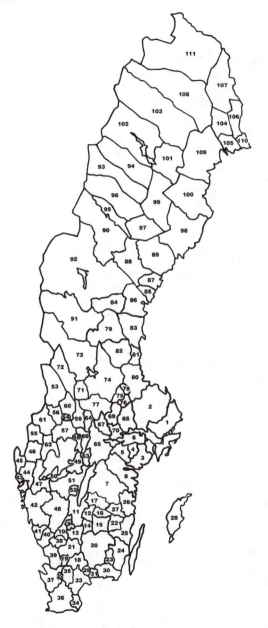

Figure A6.1 Swedish labour market areas according to commuting statistics, 1988

172   Small business dynamics

REFERENCES

Armstrong, H. and Taylor, J. (1978) *Regional Economic Policy and Its Analysis*, Southampton: Philip Alan.

Aronsson, M. (1991) *Nyföretagande i Sverige* (Business startups in Sweden), Stockholm: The National Industry Board.

Bellu, R.R. (1987) 'A Behavioral Explanation of the Differential Economic Development of the Center-North and Mezzogiorno of Italy', Working Paper, New York: Kingsborough College of the City University of New York.

Birch, D.L. (1979) 'The Job Generation Process', Working Paper, Cambridge, Mass: MIT.

Bruno, A.V. and Tyebjee, T.T. (1982) 'The Environment for Entrepreneurship', in C.A. Kent, D.L. Sexton and K.H. Vesper (eds) *Encyclopedia of Entrepreneurship*, Englewood Cliffs, NJ: Prentice-Hall: 288–316.

Christensen, P.R., Eskelinen, H., Forsström, B., Lindmark, L. and Vatne, E. (1990) 'Firms in Network: Concepts, Spatial Impacts and Policy Implications', NordREFO:1.

Cramer, U. and Koller, M. (1988) Gewinne und Verluste von Arbetisplatzen in Betrieben – der 'Job Turnover' – Ansatz. Mitteilungen aus der Arbeitsmarkt- und Berufsforschung, 3/88, 361–77.

Erixon, L. (1991) 'Den tredje vägen – inläsning eller förnyelse?' (The third path – lock-in or renewal?), in R. Norén (ed.) *Struktur och tillväxt* (Structure and Growth), Stockholm: SNS Publishing Company.

Ettinger, J.C. and van Weereld M. (1988) 'The Training of Entrepreneurs: A Key to the Success of the Creation of Business Ventures', paper submitted to the Second Workshop on Recent Research on Entrepreneurship, EIASM, Vienna: 5–6 December.

Etzioni, A. (1987) 'Entrepreneurship, Adaptation and Legitimation. A Macro-behavioral Perspective', *Journal of Economic Behavior and Organization* 8: 175–89.

Illeris, S. (1986) 'New Firm Creation in Denmark: The Importance of the Cultural Background', in D. Keeble and E. Wever (eds) *New firms and regional development in Europe*, Beckenham: Croom Helm: 141–50.

Karlsson, A-K. and Löwstedt, E-L. (1990) *Nyföretagande i Frankrike* (Business startups in France), Stockholm: The National Industry Board.

Keeble, D. and Wever, E. (eds) (1986) *New Firms and Regional Development in Europe*, Beckenham: Croom Helm.

Keeble, D., Potter, J. and Storey, D.J. (1990) 'Cross National Comparisons of the Role of SMEs in Regional Economic Growth in the European Community', Working Paper, University of Cambridge and University of Warwick.

Lundberg, L. (1991) Svensk industristruktur – basindustri eller högteknologi? (Sweden's industrial structure – basic industries or high technology?) in R. Norén (ed.) *Struktur och tillväxt* (Structure and Growth), Stockholm: SNS Publishing Company.

McClelland, D.C. (1961) *The Achieving Society*, Princeton, NJ: Van Nostrand.

Olofsson, C., Petersson, G. and Wahlbin, C. (1986) 'Opportunities and Obstacles – A Study of Start-Ups and their Development', in *Frontiers of*

Entrepreneurship Research, Wellesley, MA: Babson College: 482–501.

Reynolds, P.D. (1988) 'Organizational Births: Perspectives on the Emergence of New Firms', Academy of Management Best Papers Proceedings.

Reynolds, P.D. and Maki, W.R. (1989) 'Regional Characteristics Affecting Business Growth', proposal to the Ford Foundation, University of Minnesota, Departments of Sociology and Agricultural and Applied Economics.

——— (1990) 'Business Volatility and Economic Growth', final project report submitted to the US Small Business Administration.

Statens industriverk (1990) *Privat tjänstesektor* (The Private Service Sector) Stockholm: The National Industry Board.

Statistics Sweden (1990) *Nyföretagandet i Sverige 1988 och 1989* (New firms in Sweden 1988 and 1989), Statistical Reports F15 SM 9001.

Weber, M. (1930) *The Protestant Ethic and the Spirit of Capitalism*, London: Allen & Unwin.

DISCUSSION

Will Bartlett

This chapter has presented an analysis of part of a new establishment level data-set on company births, deaths, expansions and contractions in Sweden. The authors have been able to merge information from disparate sources to create a valuable source of information for the analysis of business dynamics over time (1985 to 1989), across sectors and regions, and by type of firm (autonomous firms or 'simples', branch plants and headquarters). As yet the analysis is preliminary, focusing on only one of the 111 labour market areas included in the data-set (Linköping), but even so it provides convincing evidence that the most important determinants of employment change over the period studied were expansions and contractions of establishments, rather than births and deaths (entry and exit). Specifically, only one-third of job gains came from firm births, compared to two-thirds from firm expansions; only a quarter of job losses come from firm deaths, compared to three-quarters from firm contractions. This is a useful finding, as it suggests that, to the extent that job creation is associated with small firms, a major impact in the Swedish case may be coming through growth of existing firms rather than just through new-firm entries. Unfortunately it is not really possible to link these findings to the debate on the importance of small firms in the job creation process, since the major analytical dimension in the analysis is the type, rather than the size, of the enterprise. A breakdown of the sources of job growth and job loss (in terms of births, deaths, expansions and contractions) by size group would be needed to really address this key issue.

A further issue addressed in this chapter is the linkage between business dynamics and welfare. According to the authors, 'a sound market economy is characterized by dynamic change'. Whilst this is no doubt correct in so far as the operation of the price mechanism will bring about welfare-enhancing reallocations of resources through the mechanisms of entry and exit and firm expansions and contractions, there are varieties of modes of such dynamic change which may have very different effects on welfare. For example, in terms of the distinction between Simples and Branches which is the central dichotomy of the study, it may matter very much to the welfare of a local community whether the decisions to expand or contract, to enter or leave the market, are made within Simples, by local entrepreneurs informed by a sensitive understanding of the local environment, or by remote headquarters of local Branches. The former may be much more likely to make decisions which are welfare-enhancing for the local community, whereas the latter may be making decisions which are welfare-enhancing for groups and individuals (shareholders, employees, managers) located in other regions or in other countries. Thus, the distributional consequences of a given level of business dynamics are quite variable. In addition, even within a region or locality, the way in which welfare effects change with the intensity of business dynamics is of interest. Whilst low levels of business dynamics may be undesirable, there may be levels of business dynamics which are too intensive, in terms of the costs imposed by rapid rates of turnover and adjustment. This suggests that there may be an optimum level of intensity of business dynamics, in a given environment. Whilst this chapter is clearly only preliminary and descriptive, it does raise the issue of the link between differences in business dynamics and the differential development of economic well-being. This is an interesting area for future research which deserves to be carried forward, and this carefully compiled data-set provides a useful basis from which such research questions can begin to be addressed in a systematic fashion.

7   A macroview of the Gnosjö entrepreneurial spirit[1]

Charlie Karlsson and Jan Larsson

GNOSJÖ AND THE GNOSJÖ SPIRIT

Gnosjö is a municipality with 9,659 inhabitants (1 January 1991) located in the south-western part of the county of Jönköping, Sweden. Gnosjö is well-known all over Sweden and also internationally for its extraordinarily strong entrepreneurial spirit, known in Sweden as the Gnosjö spirit. To give one indication of the strength of the Gnosjö spirit, we can compare the development of employment in the manufacturing industry in the municipality during the period 1980–8 with the national average. During the period in question employment in manufacturing (plants with more than four employees) in Gnosjö rose by 28.5 per cent while in the country as a whole employment in manufacturing declined by 12.8 per cent.

Manufacturing employment in Gnosjö is concentrated in small and medium-sized plants. On average, in 1988, they employed thirty-five people according to official statistics for manufacturing industry in Sweden (covering only plants with more than four employees). This can be compared with a national average of eighty-two. The average size of plants in Gnosjö is, however, increasing: in 1980 the average plant had twenty-eight employees.

Compared with the total national figure for employment in manufacturing of 752,247 in 1988, the 2,973 employed in manufacturing industry in Gnosjö is, of course, insignificant. On the other hand, we must admit that the growth record is quite significant, particularly, as it is based on growth in small and medium-sized independent enterprises and not the result of larger companies moving in from outside and creating employment in branch plants.

We can also give some information about the structure of the manufacturing industry in Gnosjö. First, we may conclude that, using the definitions developed by Ohlsson and Vinell (1987), the manufacturing

175

industry in Gnosjö is highly labour-intensive. If we define regional concentration as the share of the industry in the region/share of the industry in the country as a whole × 100, the regional concentration of labour-intensive industries in Gnosjö was 266 in 1985. Second, we may conclude that the manufacturing industry in Gnosjö is strongly dominated by price competing industries. Using the definitions we developed earlier (Karlsson and Larsson 1989; 1990) the regional concentration in Gnosjö of price competing industries with declining employment was 193 in 1985.

Given the unusual growth record and the strong orientation towards entrepreneurship in small and medium-sized enterprises, it should be no surprise that Gnosjö has caught the eyes of scientists with an interest in entrepreneurship and small business development (Johannisson and Gustavsson 1984; Gidlund *et al.* 1988; Sollbe 1988). Most explanations of the Gnosjö phenomenon point to the existing tightly knit local networks which are said to have the many free churches in the municipality as their main nodes. Within these local networks established business concepts are preserved and new ones are developed in a trial and error process where the individual entrepreneurs cooperate with each other while at the same time continuously learning from each other. Within the tight local network a kind of mutual dependence is developed that makes the border between competition and cooperation fluid. The tight local networks in Gnosjö mean, in effect, that the knowledge and business contacts of every individual entrepreneur become the knowledge and business contacts of all entrepreneurs in Gnosjö.

Almost all research done on the Gnosjö phenomenon thus far has studied it from below, in the form of case studies of different kinds, often with a considerable number of in-depth interviews with entrepreneurs. Overall assessments of the Gnosjö phenomenon in terms of productivity, profitability, etc. are, however, generally lacking. This means that irrespective of the major research efforts we have surprisingly little information that can be used to evaluate the long-term sustainability of the phenomenon. This does not mean that entrepreneurship does not matter. It matters a lot. However, we believe that the entrepreneurial spirit as such, even though it is a necessary condition, is not a sufficient condition for long-run sustainability. External conditions may very well change in a way which makes the entrepreneurial spirit as such insufficient, given the overall location conditions in Gnosjö, to guarantee long-run employment growth or even to preserve the current employment level.

The aim of this chapter is to make an overall assessment of the

Gnosjö phenomenon in terms of employment, productivity, wages and profitability in the manufacturing industry. We will compare the situation in Gnosjö with that at the national level and we will also look at how the situation has changed in Gnosjö during the period 1980–8. As the composition of manufacturing industry in Gnosjö differs a lot from the national average we will also study the relevant subset of manufacturing industry. Given the results of the overall assessments, we will try to evaluate the long-run sustainability of the Gnosjö phenomenon and to indicate what policy measures might be necessary to increase sustainability, as well as make some suggestions for future research.

In the following section we discuss the long-term sustainability of regional economic systems and in the third section we introduce the methods used in the empirical analysis. The data for the empirical analysis are presented in the fourth section, while the fifth is devoted to a presentation of the empirical results. The results are discussed in the subsequent section and the final one we summarize our main results and make some suggestions for future research.

THE LONG-TERM SUSTAINABILITY OF REGIONAL ECONOMIC SYSTEMS

We may characterize Gnosjö as a regional economic system because of its well developed local networks which contain flows of information as well as flows of goods and services between the numerous small and medium-sized enterprises. The long-term sustainability of a regional economic system is determined by a dynamic interplay between external forces, internal change and accommodation processes and the sluggish transformation of localized resources. It is these factors which create the locational advantages of regions, which make it desirable to locate different types of production in different regions and thus generate a regional specialization. When these locational advantages are reduced the probability of a reduction in the volume of production increases. The opposite is true when the locational advantages increase.

A forward-looking analysis of a regional economic system and its long-term sustainability should therefore be based on an evaluation of the region's locational advantages. Such an approach is motivated, in particular, by the fact that many of the factors or system qualities that create the locational advantages are, or can be, influenced by political measures.

Locational advantage is a relative quality. The size of the

advantage must be estimated by comparing different locations. Every region's profile of advantages (and disadvantages) has its background in the region's set of resources in relation to other regions. Lasting advantages and the specialization that builds on them are based on resources that are sluggish and change at a slow pace both within and outside the region. Table 7.1 contains a schematic description of such resources.

Some of the factors that are significant for specialization and the change in specialization have a local or regional origin. Other factors are to a greater extent determined by the qualities of the external environment; to an increasing degree these have come to be associated with formal and informal networks of enterprises, organizations and/or individuals. Furthermore, we must understand that many locational advantages and disadvantages are created by stern forces in the international competitive environment.

The costs of a certain type of production can at any given moment be derived from prices of inputs and of local resources in the actual region. The income from production is determined by the price level and the sales costs in the markets within reach. In this connection we may note that there are also links between different markets and location qualities, which are important for locational decisions. For example, improvements in transportation and communication technologies are making it easier to produce customized products far away from the market.

Two processes – the spatial product cycle and the process of structural change (Karlsson 1988) – are stern in the sense that they often cannot be neutralized by actions and measures taken at the local level. It is possible, however, to take advantage of and avoid being influenced by the actual processes if the actors in the local economy can successively adapt their own technology and renew the composition of their own production. If, however, the need for adaptation and renewal is caused by a fundamental change in locational advantages, such adaptation and renewal processes may be dependent upon a parallel adaptation of localized resources in the region. We intend to concentrate on the process of structural change and see what information an analysis of this process might produce concerning the long-term sustainability of the Gnosjo phenomenon.

METHOD

Conventional analyses and predictions of the development of productivity, costs and profitability of manufacturing industry are as a rule based on average values. The problem with this type of evaluation is that much useful information is averaged out. Phenomena like the renewal or closing down of plants are not average phenomena. They are processes that must be connected with special conditions. The closing down of plants is primarily determined by the existence of low productive – marginal – plants with obsolete products and processes and inferior knowledge and competence. The rate of renewal, on the other hand, is mainly determined by the conditions for highly productive activities, new products and processes, technical and market competence and modern education.

The value added per employee is the most commonly used productivity measure. The value added not only reflects the physical productivity of a firm but also its pricing policies and its costs for the running inputs used in the production process. Technical development based on internal, original or imitation R&D, product cycles and other market changes result in a skewed productivity distribution in manufacturing industry as a whole as well as within different subsets of manufacturing industry. This is normal for all subsets (industries, regions, etc.) where industry has passed through a longer development period.

Plants or firms with products adjusted to market needs, advanced marketing, technological leads, modern production equipment, and well-educated labour will, as a rule, exhibit high productivity. At the same time, in the same industry or region there are usually units with obsolete products and old-fashioned, technically worn-down production equipment which, as a result, have low productivity. The best units, therefore, often have productivity that is several times higher than that of the worst units. Thus, the main reasons behind the skew productivity distributions are technical changes, investments and market changes.

The productivity distribution and its connection with the process of structural change is analysed by means of the diagram in Figure 7.1. This diagram gives a picture of the productivity (= value added per employee) distribution within an industry (Salter 1966). The production units (plants) in the actual industry are ranked on a falling scale of productivity from left to right. Along the horizontal axis the share of employees in every production unit or every productivity group of production units is given as a percentage of total employment in the industry in question. In Figure 7.1 a plant's relative competitive power is indicated by its position on the vertical axis (productivity) in relation to that of other plants. Such productivity or technique distributions are characterized by a high degree of structural

Table 7.1 Location qualities that influence a region's specialization

Type of specialization factor	Location quality	Change process
Product markets	Accessibility to customer groups in different regions of varying size and purchasing power. Transportation and accessibility qualities	Changes in the geographical distribution of price levels and demand. Changed relations between costs for transportation and communication
Input markets	Accessibility to suppliers and inputs and production services	Changes in techniques and relocation for suppliers of inputs and services
Localized resources	Natural resources. The supply of different kinds of land. Infrastructure including networks for transportation, communication and distribution. Enterprise structure and entrepreneurial capability and flexibility. Existing production capacity and technology. Labour and varying competence and experiences. Supply of higher education and R&D	Land use and location policy. Investments in infrastructure. New enterprise forms and new business concepts. Investments in new capacity and new techniques. Education, training and migration
Global resources	Accessibility to international R&D and innovations. Experience of participating in international competition	Niches and networks for knowledge building and distribution. Import of ideas and technology. Swiftness in accommodation of local resources to new conditions

Sources: Adapted from Snickars *et al.* (1989)

invariance, which means that the process of structural change is a slow one. It is very probable that the individual production units will keep their relative position over time on a Salter curve of the type illustrated in Figure 7.1 (Johansson and Marksjö 1984).

The curve in the figure describes how the wage paying capability falls when we move down the curve, since the productivity indicates the maximum wage paying capability of a production unit. The

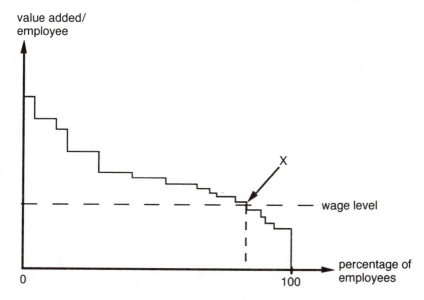

Figure 7.1 Productivity distribution

diagram also illustrates the average personnel cost level (= direct and indirect wage costs) in the industry. The productivity curve cuts the wage level at point X. To the left of this point productivity is higher than personnel costs, which means that the gross profits are positive. To the right of this point gross profits are negative. The gross profit is equal to the difference between the plant's position on the Salter curve and the wage level. We must, however, add that the position on the Salter curve is also influenced by capital intensity. A high value added per employee in relation to the wage cost per employee may be due to a high capital intensity, which means that the net profit can diverge substantially from the gross profit measure we use (Braunerhjelm 1990).

When analysing this type of diagram we study the different parts of the curves and their shape and how they change over time. Two important moments of the process of structural change within the total manufacturing industry or a subset of it can be illustrated by means of a productivity diagram. In the left part of the diagram we find those production units that have the highest productivity in the industry in question. Productivity is high because new technology has been introduced by means of investments, which means that these

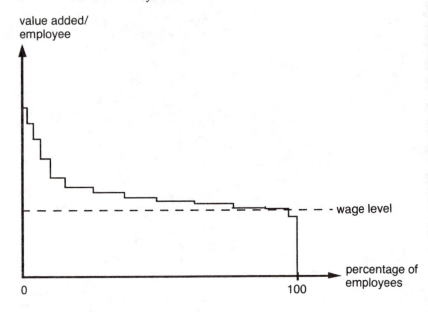

Figure 7.2 The concave case – a vulnerable structure in an industry

production units have been partly or totally renewed recently either in terms of products or processes or both. This means that here we find, on the one hand, large production units whose high productivity is a reflection of successful price competition and, on the other, plants with a high rate of product renewal engaged in product (dynamic) competition. Given that modern production technology and investments imply higher productivity than the average for the industry, the best part of the curve should be connected with technical change and investment opportunities. This means that the introduction of new production capacity resulting in productivity that is higher than the average for existing capacity, takes place to the left in the diagram. In practice, of course, the new capacity is to a varying degree distributed over all the productivity steps in the diagram.

To the right of the diagram we find the production units with a low or negative gross profit, i.e. plants with a comparatively short remaining life if they continue to use their current techniques. If the productivity is lower than the wage level, the production unit is not able to cover its variable costs, which means that a share of its personnel costs must be covered by using its own capital or by some type of external financing, e.g. subsidies from the government. If such a structural situation prevails over a longer period, most production units will have to consider either a reduction of their operations or even a total withdrawal from the market. Thus, the worst part of the curve should be connected with threats of reduced operations and the need for renewal by means of investments. This means that a major part of the production capacity that disappears during any given period can be found to the right of the diagram, in units with low productivity and without the ability to cover their costs. The survival of these plants normally presumes technique and product renewals on such a scale that the renewal investments can be compared with the costs of creating totally new plants.

In a productivity diagram for a particular subset of the manufacturing industry the structural change of this subset can be described as the addition over time of new production capacity with high productivity to the left of the diagram and the disappearance of low productive capacity to the right. As the composition of the labour force in the units that are added and the units that disappear normally diverge in a marked way, the transformation of the production structure also means that the labour market is gradually restructured. Hence, it is justifiable to place heavy emphasis on the way the transformation of the labour market (and other localized resources) limits the transformation of industry as a whole. Structural shifts between different subsets of industry are also influenced by a similar mutual interaction with the conditions on the labour market.

As regards the shape of the curve, we distinguish two typical cases: the concave case and the convex case. The concave case is illustrated in Figure 7.2. This form of productivity curve indicates a slow expansion or renewal process; and that the industry in question is sensitive to wage increases, which means that a large share of all production units after a wage increase (*ceteris paribus*) will have a negative gross profit and thus face the threat of reduced operations.

The convex case is illustrated in Figure 7.3. This form of curve indicates a rapid expansion and renewal process; major differences between modern and old production units, i.e. an uneven capital structure, which indicates a relatively rapid growth in the industry and/or a rapid renewal of the production technology; and that the industry is relatively insensitive to increases in personnel costs, which means that if the wage level increases, a relatively small share of the production units will face a negative gross profit.

Similar considerations are relevant for diagrams illustrating the distribution of gross profit shares. Given that the network story told above is a good description of the Gnosjö phenomenon, it points in

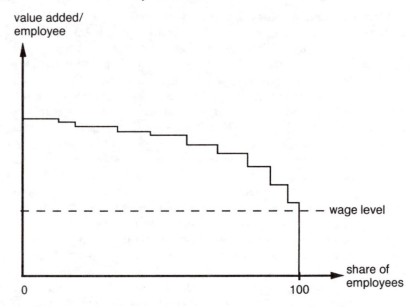

Figure 7.3 The convex case – a robust structure in an industry

the direction of a very homogeneous entrepreneurial society. Hence, we should expect that the variability in measures like productivity and profitability should be much less in Gnosjö than is the case for total manufacturing industry in Sweden as a whole. And this hypothesis should hold even when we study the relevant subsets of the manufacturing industry.

It is also possible to use the technique introduced here to make comparisons between different industrial subsets (sectors, regions, etc.) or between the situation within the same subset (or the total manufacturing industry) at two different points in time. We illustrate this possibility in Figure 7.4. Here we see, for example, that the difference between the best and the worst part is much greater for sector 1 than for sector 2. Such differences are not only the result of the faster introduction of new techniques in the most productive part of sector 1; equally important are differences in the shut-down and renewal policies in older production units in the two sectors.

It is also possible to use the productivity distribution to study the investment process and its focus in different subsets of the manufacturing industry. By comparing the shape of the Salter curve at different points in time it is possible to describe the focus of the

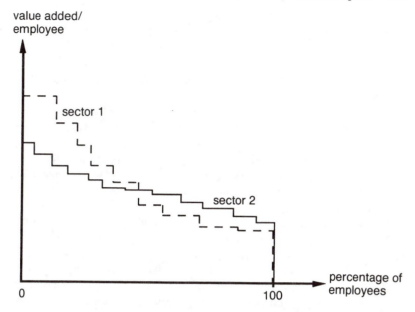

Figure 7.4 Productivity distributions for two different industrial subsets (sectors)

technique introduction and the product renewal processes by studying how rapidly productivity grows at different points on the productivity curve. A large share of product competition probably means that the productivity of the first (best) quartile, in particular, grows quickly and, hence, the productivity curve becomes steeper. When price competition, market stagnation and rationalization dominate, we could instead expect that a large part of the worst techniques would disappear at the same time as productivity is increased in the middle section of the curve. Such a process leads to a less steep curve. Figure 7.5 illustrates two extreme cases of the type described above. In case (a) capacity expansion has been rapid whilst production techniques have only improved slowly; case (b), on the other hand, describes a change with slow capacity expansion but rapid technique improvement.

New capacity in the best quartile of the productivity distribution normmally has a labour force that is more knowledge-oriented than capacity in the worst profile. The disappearance of activities with low productivity and the introduction of production based upon product renewal and product competition will thus not only lead to quantitative but also qualitative changes on the labour market. The accommodation ability of a region in this respect is therefore an important location quality. In regions where the accommodation of the labour market is rigid, the supply of labour with the required qualities becomes a factor that limits the renewal of manufacturing industry as well as other parts of the private sector towards product competition. Hence, unemployment can be high among certain employment categories at the same time as addition is slow when it comes to labour with education and labour market experience that correspond to the demands in those areas where capacity expansion is possible. The specific needs of different categories of labour are thus an important aspect when specifying the techniques that are available for enterprises in different regions when they are to renew their production system

It is well known that the Gnosjö phenomenon does not rest upon a rich supply of highly educated entrepreneurs and white- and blue-collar workers. On the contrary, the formal educational level is surprisingly low in Gnosjö (and in the surrounding municipalities as well). The low formal educational level in Gnosjö may be assumed to create problems when it comes to adopt new technology, since, as has been shown elsewhere (Karlsson 1988), the early adoption of new technology by enterprises is heavily dependent upon the formal educational level of their employees. Given that the early adoption of new technologies is important for the rate of productivity growth, we should expect a slower growth in productivity in Gnosjö than in the country as a whole. And, as before, this hypothesis should hold even when we study the relevant subsets of the manufacturing industry.

THE DATA

The data used in this study are drawn from the information collected annually by the Swedish Central Bureau of Statistics from all plants in the manufacturing industry employing more than four employees. The data used provide us with information about total sales value, total value added, total wage costs for both blue- and white-collar workers and the total number of employees for each plant. Using this information we are able to calculate (labour) productivity and gross profit shares. The productivity is calculated as value added per employee and the gross profit shares as the difference between total value added and total wage costs divided by the total value added.

In the first step we use data for all manufacturing industry in the municipality of Gnosjö and compared them with the same data for all

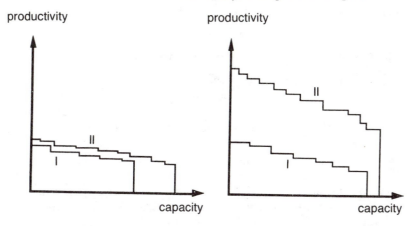

Figure 7.5 Technique improvement and capacity expansion between two points in time

manufacturing industry in Sweden. As the manufacturing industry in Gnosjö has a heavy bias towards labour-intensive industries, in a second step we try to neutralize the effects of the composition of manufacturing industry in Gnosjö. To do this we use the grouping of industries developed by Ohlsson and Vinell (1987), namely sheltered industries, (unskilled) labour-intensive industries, capital-intensive industries, knowledge-intensive industries, and R&D-intensive industries. As plants in the capital-intensive and the R&D-intensive industries are very rare in Gnosjö (as well as in the surrounding municipalities) we only analyse the three remaining subsets of the manufacturing industry. To preserve the confidentiality of the data we merge the data for the Gnosjö plants with the same data for all plants from the three municipalities that surround Gnosjö (Gislaved, Värnamo and Vaggeryd). When we use the merged data, we talk about the Gnosjö region. The loss of information due to this procedure should not be overestimated since much of the same entrepreneurial spirit can be found in the surrounding municipalities. Given the financial limits for our study we only use information for two years, namely 1980 and 1988.

THE RESULTS

The Gnosjö phenomenon – a preliminary assessment

We start the presentation of our results in the traditional way by giving some information about the average development of the manufacturing industry in Gnosjö compared with the national situation. This information is presented in Table 7.2. In 1980 the manufacturing industry in Gnosjö on the average paid lower wages and had a lower productivity than the total manufacturing industry in Sweden but had, on the other hand, higher gross profit shares. If we compare the situation in 1988 with that in 1980, we can see that the difference between Gnosjö and the national average has increased both in the case of the wage level and in the case of the productivity level. The gross profit share in Gnosjö is now, as an average, lower than in the country as a whole.

Table 7.2 shows that the expansion of employment in manufacturing industry that has taken place in Gnosjö between 1980 and 1988 has been an expansion of work places with relatively low productivity compared with the national average. It also tells us that, even if the wage costs in Gnosjö have not increased as rapidly as the national average, the manufacturing plants in Gnosjö have not been able to preserve their relative position in terms of gross profit shares.

But, as has already been pointed out, average figures tend to hide a lot of information. So now we turn to the productivity distributions and see what their shape is and how it has changed over time. In Figure 7.6 we compare the productivity distribution for the total manufacturing industry in Gnosjö with the corresponding distribution for the country as a whole. We can immediately see that our hypothesis about a lower variability in productivity distribution due to

Table 7.2 The manufacturing industry in Gnosjö compared with the national average (index, national average = 100)

	1980	*1988*
Average wage level	90	87
Average productivity (value added per employee)	93	86
Average gross profit shares	105	97

Source: Calculations based upon the official statistics for manufacturing industry in Sweden

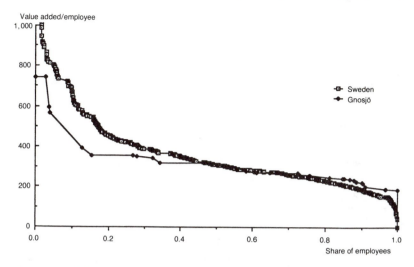

Figure 7.6 Labour productivity in total manufacturing industry in Gnosjö and in Sweden, 1988 (SEK 000s)

the dense local networks is certainly not rejected. If we then compare the two curves, we see that for the greater part, productivity for the best 45 per cent of the plants is distinctly higher for the country as a whole than in Gnosjö. For about 30 per cent of the plants in the middle of the productivity distribution there is no difference and for the worst 25 per cent the plants in Gnosjö exhibit the highest productivity. Thus, we can say that while Gnosjö certainly lacks really bad plants, it also lacks really good ones in terms of productivity.

If we look at investment behaviour within the manufacturing industry in Gnosjö and in the whole of Sweden, respectively, we find distinct differences. The relevant information can be found in the two Figures 7.7 and 7.8. In Figure 7.7 we see that the dominant investment pattern in Gnosjö has been capacity expansion with modest technique improvement. In the country as a whole we have had capacity reduction (in terms of the number of employees) with a distinct technique improvement (Figure 7.8).

We end the presentation of results in this section by comparing the distribution of gross profit shares in the manufacturing industry in Gnosjö with the same distribution for manufacturing industry in the country as a whole. This is done in Figure 7.9. First we see that the variability of gross profit shares is significantly lower in Gnosjö than in the country as a whole. We also see that the best plants in Gnosjö

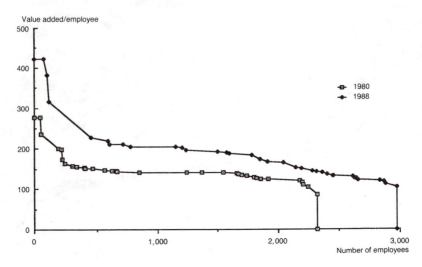

Figure 7.7 Investment behaviour in total manufacturing industry in Gnosjö during 1980–8 (SEK 000s) (price level 1980 = 100)

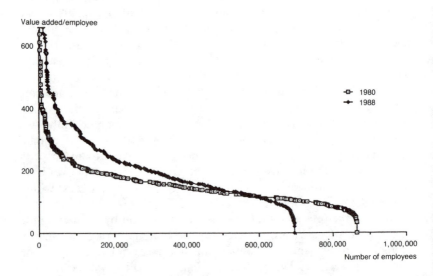

Figure 7.8 Investment behaviour in total manufacturing industry in Sweden during 1980–8 (SEK 000s) (price level 1980 = 100)

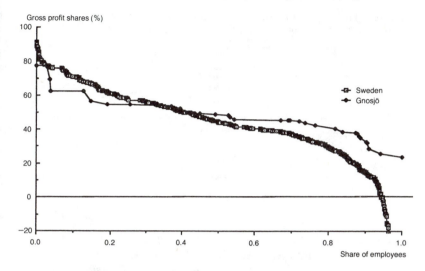

Figure 7.9 Gross profit shares in manufacturing industry in Gnosjö and in Sweden, 1988 (%)

have lower gross profit shares than the best plants in the country as a whole while the opposite is true for the worst plants.

The results presented thus far do not really fit with the traditional success story told about Gnosjö. The Gnosjö phenomenon clearly looks less impressive than we had expected. What is the clue? One important factor to draw attention to is the fact that the industrial composition of the manufacturing industry in Gnosjö is very different from the industrial composition of the manufacturing industry in Sweden as a whole. In the next section we neutralize the influence of this background factor and tell the Gnosjö story once again.

The Gnosjö phenomenon – an alternative assessment

In this section we shall try to make a new assessment of the Gnosjö phenomenon. We use data from the Gnosjö region and study the three dominant subsets of the manufacturing industry in the Gnosjö region, namely labour-intensive industries (10,445 employees in 1988), knowledge-intensive industries (3,506 employees in 1988) and sheltered industries (1,910 employees in 1988). Table 7.3 gives some information about the development of these three subsets of the manufacturing industry in the Gnosjö region compared with the national situation.

Table 7.3 Three subsets of the manufacturing industry in the Gnosjö region compared with the national average (index, national average = 100)

	Labour-intensive		Industries Knowledge-intensive		Sheltered	
	1980	1988	1980	1988	1980	1988
Average wage level	98	103	93	96	97	94
Average productivity	103	103	94	88	93	91
Average gross profit shares	108	100	102	91	92	97

Source: See Table 7.2

Here a somewhat different picture emerges. If we first consider the labour-intensive industries that in 1988 had 63.3 per cent of all employment in the manufacturing industry in the Gnosjö region, we can see that in terms of average productivity they are doing fine in comparison with labour-intensive industries in the rest of Sweden. What has happened during the period 1980–8 is that the wage level has increased faster in the Gnosjö region than in the rest of Sweden with the obvious result that the average gross profit shares in 1988 were at the same level in the Gnosjö region as in the rest of Sweden, while eight years earlier they had been significantly higher in the Gnosjö region than in the country as a whole.

In the subset of knowledge-intensive industries the Gnosjö region is, however, facing problems. Here productivity growth has not matched productivity growth in the country as a whole and as the wage level has increased faster in the Gnosjö region than in the country as a whole the average gross profit share in the Gnosjö region in 1988 was significantly below the national average. Obviously, the knowledge-intensive industries in the Gnosjö region have not been able to match the performance of knowledge-intensive industries in the country as a whole. Sheltered industries in the Gnosjö region are facing similar problems even though they have been able to improve their gross profit shares due to a slower increase in the wage level.

We now leave the world of averages and start to look at productivity distributions and how they have changed over time. In Figure 7.10 we compare the productivity distribution for labour-intensive industries in the Gnosjö region for the year 1988 with that for the country as a whole. We can clearly see that for the best 20 per cent – in terms of productivity – of the employment in labour-

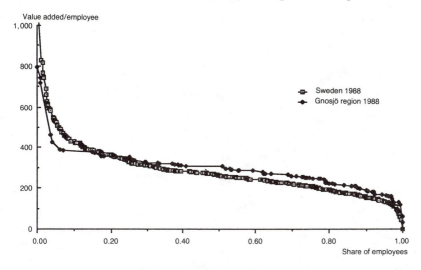

Figure 7.10 Distribution of productivity in labour-intensive industries in the Gnosjö region and in the country as a whole (price level, 1988)

intensive industries, productivity is lower in the Gnosjö region than in the country as a whole. For the remaining 80 per cent of employment, however, productivity is higher in the Gnosjö region than in the country as a whole. As before there is lower variability in productivity distribution in the Gnosjö region than in the country as a whole, which seems to confirm our hypothesis about the role of entrepreneurial networks in that region.

We now consider the productivity distribution for knowledge-intensive industries in the Gnosjö region and compare it with the corresponding distribution for the country as a whole. This is done in Figure 7.11. Here we can see that for the best plants employing some 20 per cent of employees, productivity in the country as a whole is between 50 amd 100 per cent higher than in the Gnosjö region. For the plants employing about 30 per cent, in the middle of the productivity distribution, productivity is somewhat lower in the Gnosjö region than in the country as a whole. For the worst plants, employing about 30 per cent of employees, there is no significant difference between the Gnosjö region than in the country as a whole. Once again we see that the variability in productivity distribution is lower in the Gnosjö region than in the country as a whole. However, in this case the entrepreneurial spirit is not strong enough to bring productivity up to national standards. One reason might be that

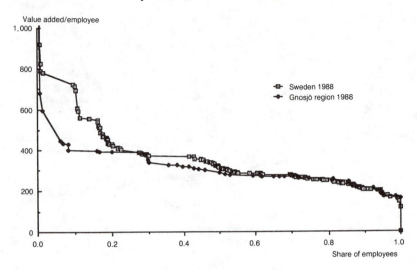

Figure 7.11 Distribution of productivity in knowledge-intensive industries in the Gnosjö region and in the country as a whole (price level, 1988)

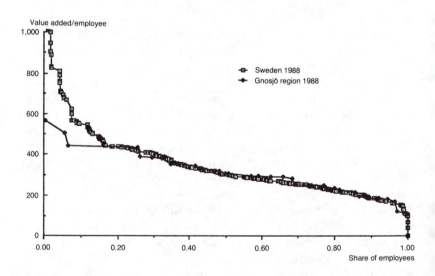

Figure 7.12 Distribution of productivity in sheltered industries in the Gnosjö region and in the country as a whole (price level, 1988)

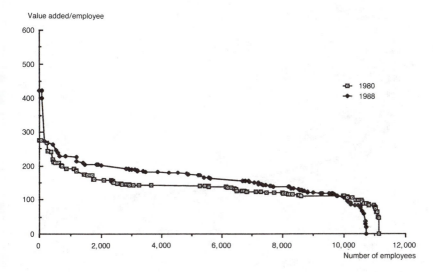

Figure 7.13 Investment behaviour in labour-intensive industries in Gnosjö during 1980–8 (SEK 000s) (price level 1980 = 100)

knowledge intensity is too low in the Gnosjö region. The share of white-collar workers, for example, was only 26 per cent, compared with 30 per cent in the country as a whole.

The productivity distributions for the sheltered industries can be found in Figure 7.12. For 85 per cent of employment there is no difference between the Gnosjö region and the country as a whole. However, for the best 15 per cent, productivity is much higher in the country as a whole than in the Gnosjö region.

We now turn to the investment patterns in the three groups of industries. If we start with the labour-intensive industries, we notice that the investment pattern in the Gnosjö region (Figure 7.13) has resulted in a modest employment contraction as well as a modest technique improvement. In the country as a whole (Figure 7.14) the investment pattern has been characterized by substantial employment contraction and only modest technique improvement. The shape of the productivity distribution in the Gnosjö region has not changed very much during the period while at the national level it has become somewhat steeper, indicating that part of the actual industries work under conditions of product competition.

As regards investment patterns in the knowledge-intensive industries we see that the Gnosjö region exhibits a pattern of capacity

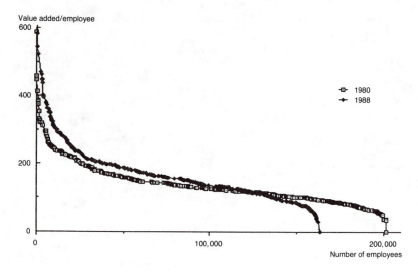

Figure 7.14 Investment behaviour in labour-intensive industries in Sweden, 1980–8 (SEK 000s) (price level 1980 = 100)

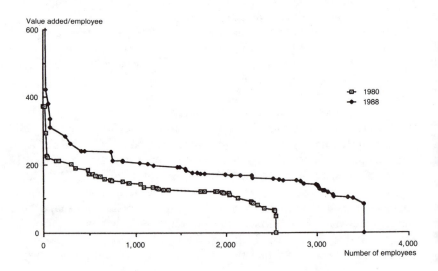

Figure 7.15 Investment behaviour in knowledge-intensive industries in the Gnosjö region, 1980–8 (SEK 000s) (price level 1980 = 100)

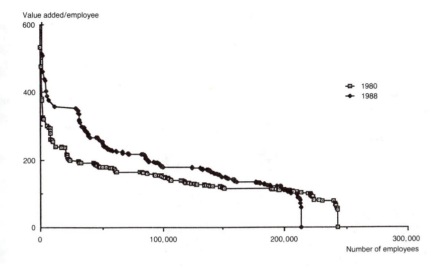

Figure 7.16 Investment behaviour in knowledge-intensive industries in Sweden, 1980–8 (SEK 000s) (price level 1980 = 100)

expansion (in terms of employment) and distinct technique improvement (Figure 7.15). For the country as a whole we have technique improvement combined with capacity reduction (Figure 7.16). Once again we observe that the shape of the productivity distribution in the Gnosjö region has not changed very much during the period, indicating that these plants are working under conditions of price competition. At the national level the productivity distribution has become distinctly steeper, indicating the existence of substantial product competition.

The investment patterns for sheltered industries can be found in Figures 7.17 and 7.18.

DISCUSSION

Our analysis of the Gnosjö phenomenon has shown that the entrepreneurs in the Gnosjö region are doing an excellent job in the labour-intensive sector while they are less successful in the sheltered and the knowledge-intensive sectors. In the capital- and R&D-intensive sectors they are only engaged to a very minor degree. Earlier in this chapter we raised the long-run sustainability of the Gnosjö phenomenon as an interesting and important question. This

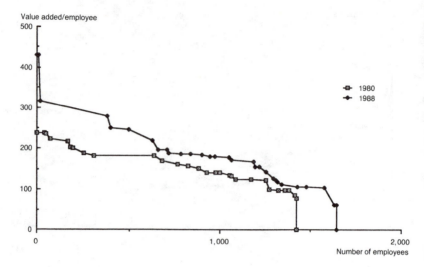

Figure 7.17 Investment behaviour in sheltered industries in the Gnosjö region, 1980–8 (SEK 000s) (price level 1980 = 100)

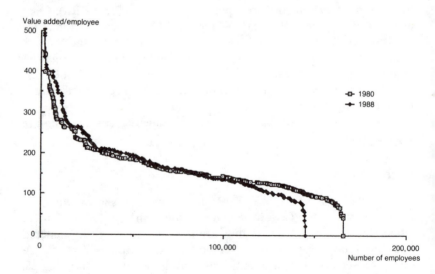

Figure 7.18 Investment behaviour in sheltered industries in Sweden, 1980–8 (SEK 000s) (price level 1980 = 100)

phenomenon can lose its sustainability as a result of either internal or external factors, and this discussion will concentrate on some possible external threats.

We will first consider the labour-intensive sector which is the dominant employer within the manufacturing industry in the Gnosjö region. In all, forty-three sub-industries are classified as unskilled labour-intensive industries (Ohlsson and Vinell 1987). It is self-evident that these industries do not have the same competitive power although they have the mutual characteristic of using labour-intensive technology. The differences within the sector in competitive power can be seized by using the following two criteria:

1   the dependence upon natural resources; and
2   the geographical reach of the products in international trade (for industries not based on natural resources).

The part of the labour-intensive sector that is not based on natural resources contains a number of industries whose products are to a large extent global. The wage-cost sensitivity due to the technology used has made the developing countries price leaders for a number of such products. The relevant industries are classified as industries competing with developing countries.

Other industries in the labour-intensive sector have a more limited reach – the competition is European rather than global. As a result, major competitors are normally enterprises in other industrialized countries. The relevant industries here are classified as industries competing with industrialized countries.

The labour-intensive sector in Gnosjö is heavily dominated by industries competing with industrialized countries. In 1988, 85 per cent of employees in the labour-intensive sector were employed in this sub-sector. The corresponding figure for the country as a whole is 56 per cent. This sub-sector will meet strongly intensified competition when Sweden joins the EC and also when the countries in Eastern Europe start to build up a competitive manufacturing industry. The range and depth of this intensification of competition will depend on the degree to which the labour-intensive enterprises in the high-wage countries within the EC relocate production to low-wage countries within the EC and in Eastern Europe to minimize their production costs and the degree to which those areas succeed in building up competitive industries of their own (Braunerhjelm 1991).

This development will certainly hit the Gnosjö region sooner or later. In the longer run, entrepreneurs in Gnosjö will tend to find it impossible to compete with their new competitors. If employment in the manufacturing industry is to be preserved in the region, entre-preneurs will have to find new products. In a more open Swedish economy specialization in quality products is a basic prerequisite for strong competitive power in labour-intensive industries. Hence, the labour-intensive industries should be restructured in a knowledge-intensive direction. This also holds for the Gnosjö region but here a paradox emerges. As we have seen, attempts to develop the knowledge-intensive sector in the Gnosjö region have up till now not been very successful. One possible reason for this is that due to its historical specialization the region has not had a high enough knowledge intensity in its labour force to meet the needs of the knowledge-intensive industries. If this hypothesis is true the Gnosjö phenomenon faces a serious threat, because the necessary restruc-turing of the manufacturing industry will be seriously hampered by a lack of the relevant labour supply. Of course, such a situation could be avoided by a massive educational campaign with the object of raising the knowledge intensity of the labour force in the region and by recruiting key personnel from other regions. If such a policy were pursued it would mean that a new arena would be opened up for the entrepreneurs in the Gnosjö region, giving them a new chance to demonstrate the superior flexibility of their networks.

SUMMARY AND SUGGESTIONS FOR FUTURE RESEARCH

We set out to investigate the long-run sustainability of the Gnosjö phenomenon. We were able to demonstrate that the manufacturing industry in the region is dominated by labour-intensive industries and that the plants in these industries have been quite successful when compared with plants in the same industries in the country as a whole. However, during the period 1980–8 a restructuring took place in the region with employment growth in the sheltered and the knowledge-intensive industries while employment declined in the labour-intensive industries. This restructuring was not very successful and the plants in the Gnosjö region in the two growth sectors were not able to compete in terms of productivity and profitability with their counterparts in the rest of Sweden. We launched the hypothesis that the main reason for this was the lower knowledge intensity of the labour force in the region. We also maintained the view that the labour-intensive industries in the future will face much harder foreign competition which will force them to find new knowledge-intensive products, but that a restructuring in that direction in the Gnosjö region will be seriously hampered by the low knowledge intensity of the labour force. If this conjecture holds, the relevant policy response is a massive educational campaign that will create a new arena for the entrepreneurs in the region.

Of course, what we have presented here is just a hypothesis. It would be a relevant object for future research to study whether the unsatisfactory performance of the knowledge-intensive and sheltered industries in the Gnosjö region is actually a result of the low knowledge intensity of the labour force in the region or if there are other reasons. It would also be a relevant object for future research to study whether the entrepreneurial spirit in the region could be preserved if a massive educational campaign were carried through and a significant number of highly educated people were recruited to the Gnosjö region from other regions. A third relevant object for future research would be the educational needs of the entrepreneurs during the transformation process from labour-intensive to know-ledge-intensive industries.

NOTE

1   The research in this chapter was funded by the ERU (The Expert Group on Regional Development Studies within the Swedish Ministry of Industry). We wish to express our thanks for this financial support. We also want to thank Johan Karlsson who typed the chapter and prepared Figures 7.1–7.5. The authors divided the work between them in such a manner than Jan Larsson was responsible for data management, computations and the preparation of statistical diagrams while Charlie Karlsson made the analysis and wrote the report.

REFERENCES

Braunerhjelm, P. (1990) *Svenska industriföretag inför EG 1992. Fövänt-ningar och planer* (Swedish Manufacturing Enterprises on the Eve of EC 1992. Expectations and Plans), Stockholm: Industrins Utredningsinstitut och Överstyrelsen for Civil Beredskap.

—— (1991) *Svenska underleverantörer och småföretag i det nya Europa. Struktur, kompetens och internationalisering* (Swedish Suppliers and Small and Medium Sized Enterprises in the New Europe: Structure, Competence and Internationalization), Stockholm: Industrins Utredningsinstitut.

Gidlund, J., Ekman, A.-K., Lagergren, M., Lindström, B., Rudebeck, K. and Wigren, R. (1988) *Periferins renässans* (The Revival of the Periphery), Stockholm: Allmänna förlaget.

Johannisson, B. and Gustavsson, B.Å. (1984) *Småföretagande på småort: nätverksstrategier i informationssamhället* (Small-Scale Entrepreneurship in the Small Place: Network Strategies in the Information Society), Högskolan i Växjö: Centrum för småföretagsutveckling.

Johansson, B. and Marksjö, B. (1984) 'Interactive Systems for Integrated Regional Planning', in Nijkamp and Rietveld (eds) 231–50.

Karlsson, C. (1988) *Innovation Adoption and the Product Life Cycle*, Umeå Economic Studies 185, Umeå: Umeå University.

Karlsson, C. and Larsson, J. (1989) 'Product and Price Competition: A Characterization', Working Paper from Cerum 1989:3 CERUM, Umeå University.

—— (1990) 'Product and Price Competition in a Regional Context', Papers of the Regional Science Association, Vol. 90: 83–99.

Nijkamp, P. and Rietveld, P. (eds) (1984) *Information Systems for Integrated Regional Planning*, Amsterdam: North Holland.

Ohlsson, L. and Vinell, L. (1987) *Tillväxtens drivkrafter* (The Forces of Growth), Stockholm: Industriförbundets förlag.

Salter, W. (1966) *Productivity and Technical Change*, Cambridge, Mass. and London.

Snickars, F., Hjern, B., Johansson, B. Lindmark, L. and Åberg, R. (1989) *Chans för Norrbotten* (Opportunity for Norrbotten), Luleå: Norrbottens Museum.

Sollbe, B. (ed.) (1988) *Tjugohundra: sju svenska kommuner bygger sin framtid* (The Year 2000: Seven Swedish Municipalities Building Their Future), Stockholm: Statens råd för byggnadsforskning.

DISCUSSION

Bengt Johannisson

This chapter has attempted to evaluate the long-term sustainability of the Gnosjö phenomenon, by comparing productivity and investment behaviour in the manufacturing industry of the Gnosjö region to the national figures. The three dominant subsets of manufacturing industry in the region are evaluated, namely labour-intensive, knowledge-intensive and sheltered industry. Two sets of data are used, from 1980 and 1988. The study contains average values of productivity and investment behaviour, as well as the productivity and investment distribution within the industries.

The main results of the study are:

1   The variability in the productivity and investment distribution is considerably lower within the Gnosjö region compared to the corresponding distribution for the country as a whole.

2   The difference in productivity and investments between the different subsets of industry (labour-intensive, knowledge-intensive and sheltered industry) is considerably smaller within the Gnosjö region compared to the country as a whole.

3   The average values of productivity and investments are higher within the Gnosjö region for the labour-intensive industry but lower for the knowledge-intensive and sheltered industries compared to the country as a whole.

4   The number of employees within manufacturing industry in the Gnosjö region has increased. Labour-intensive industry has lost jobs whereas knowledge-intensive and sheltered industries have gained jobs. All three subsets of industries have lost jobs at the national level.

The chapter concludes that there are two major threats to the long-term sustainability of the Gnosjö phenomenon. First, the labour-intensive sector is too large within the region. Second, productivity and the variability in productivity of the knowledge-intensive industry is too low within the region.

The theoretical framework of the study suggests that companies with high productivity will grow whereas companies with low productivity eventually will disappear. From this point of view it is a paradox that the knowledge-intensive industry of the region has expanded. The average productivity level is low, as is the variability in the productivity distribution.

However, it is possible to draw other conclusions from the data presented in the paper. The small differences concerning productivity and investments support the results of other studies of the Gnosjö region (see Sabel 1989 and Johannisson 1984). These small differences are due to an extensive exchange of information and knowledge within the region. Sabel calls this 'flexible specialization' and Johannisson 'entrepreneurial networks'. From their point of view, the flexibility, adaptivity and innovation of the regional industry determines the long-term sustainability. From this point of view the growing knowledge-intensive industry, in spite of low productivity, could be explained by the strong entrepreneurial spirit, the competence of the entrepreneurs and the co-operation and flexibility of the region. The skills of the entrepreneurs and the dynamics of the regional networks rather than the productivity determine which companies expand and which do not.

This is merely one alternative hypothesis that can be drawn from this study. The chapter is interesting because it contains new facts about the Gnosjö region that can be used in forthcoming studies. Thus it contributes to the knowledge of the Gnosjö phenomenon.

The paradox (according to the model used) of the growing knowledge-intensive industry indicates that the use of a few macro variables is insufficient when explaining such a complex phenomenon as the long-term sustainability of a region. The explanatory power would drastically increase if other variables were added. It would be interesting, for instance, to add variables concerning the entrepreneurial behaviour of the companies in the Gnosjö region.

8   Regional network processes: networks for the service sector or development of entrepreneurs?

Mette Mønsted

INTRODUCTION

The concept of network has been used for a whole variety of applications in analysis. The application of such a 'fashion concept' implies a lot of confusion about the exact content, and some themes and findings from earlier research are suddenly renamed. The problem with using this concept for so many different phenomena, earlier called by different names, is not only that communication on the content of the concept is confused, but that some apparently contradictory findings arise.

In regional development studies linkages have been an important issue much before network was a fashion concept. The coupling of industries and mutual interchange between local industries in regional development has been perceived as a must since the 1950s. The emphasis on linkages, and the kind of linkages necessary is varying according to period, region and discipline, though the perspective being the start off of a regional growth or blocking mechanisms (Perroux 1950; Amin 1973; Judet 1988).

Many earlier studies of regional linkages are tied to dependency patterns and growth centres, defining local linkages as the strong ties supporting a self-sustained regional development and avoid some of the problems of a regional dependency of other areas (Mønsted 1974; Sundin 1983b; Lindmark and Lundmark 1982). Even if most of these studies only deal with industrial structure, the whole complex of services and subsuppliers, i.e. the formal ties and trade structures, and some of the relations between suppliers, subsuppliers and customers, are very complicated and methodologically complex.

In a regional context the many different personal ties may often be one of the important factors for understanding the diffusion of ideas and changes in the areas. Outside large urban areas, the overlap of professional ties with personal and social ties makes the interaction pattern much more complex. It is necessary to understand these ties in order to appreciate why things happen, or why they do not happen.

The methodological reflections are closely tied to the type of network and to the perspectives of the network. The patterns may be interpreted very differently depending on the methods and the perspectives. Some of the contradictions may reflect some of these differences.

REGIONAL DEVELOPMENT PERSPECTIVES OF NETWORKS

The importance of linkages between firms to push for economic development is an old discussion.

The perspectives of the strong development firm 'the growth pole', which would trigger spin-off development in a region, was the point of departure for the study of the linkages. Perroux's original studies of the deconcentration of the industry, and the expectation of economic development around the chemical plants emphasized the need for local economic transactions to produce spin-off development in the region. Most of the large firms that where constructed in development areas had few local ties. They had many contacts in the metropolitan areas, and brought technical staff with them. Little employment was developed locally, as the linkages did not tie up with the local industry (Perroux 1950; Mønsted 1974).

Different studies have stressed a pattern where high-tech firms especially had few local ties (Sundin 1983a). Thus such a firm placed in an area with no other high-tech firms is not likely to generate spin-off growth or to be able to link up with any local industry, and will thus remain a 'cathedral in the desert' (Judet 1988).

The pattern should be different in areas with many firms in similar or related industries even if these are small and medium-sized industries. In Denmark, some of the areas earlier perceived as deprived and poor in terms of development surprised everybody by rapid growth, both in terms of economic growth and employment. The development was not in the large urban centres and not in the few large enterprises either, but apparently tied up with many small enterprises. A few such areas or communities have developed an 'entrepreneurial culture'.

The studies of the content of linkages and even the structure of subsuppliers, however, have proven quite complicated. Even if the study is only looking at the formal ties between firms, the general impression is a very diversified and complex pattern. Grøn's study of subsuppliers in Southern Jutland collected empirical evidence on the trade patterns between firms, but the pattern was so complex and difficult to structure that he ended up structuring the role of firms as subsuppliers by use of qualifications. The other complexity of trade linkages was not used (Grøn 1984), and the complexity of the dynamics of the networks were not even touched upon.

Regional studies covering only vertical trade relations are very complex. The complexity multiplies when other aspects of the network perspective are included, especially such things as personal, informal networks and through these also potential networks. Johannisson and Spilling (1986) expanded this and developed the use of networks, as they combined many different ties in the region, as an important characteristic of economic potential. Later the character-istic of networks of a prosperous small business area was compared to the types of networks developed in the IDEON science park and showed the poverty of the urban science park networks (Johannisson 1987a). The problem with this analysis is the lack of comparison with prosperous technological development areas such as the Silicon Valley or some other science parks. The close personal network tied to the same region may not be that important in a development perspective in a high-tech community. This raises the issue of the different kinds of network for service and maintenance or for pushing new initiatives.

Working empirically with regional networks, the barriers set up between different networks seems just as important as the access through networks.[1] Local power structures form the basis for access through networks, implying that totally different pictures of the opportunities in a community are formulated by competing networks.

NETWORK PROCESSES

The purpose of measuring and documenting network ties has changed over time. In earlier studies in the mid-1980s the interest centred on using them as a field or sphere outside the strict economic relations, a set of relations which could not be described and measured in the same way as the economic transactions (Johansson and Mattson 1982). In these studies networks are seen more as a perspective analysing the inertia in trade relations, i.e., the lack of change expected on the basis of the analysis of pure economic rationality. The emphasis therefore is on the strength of the ties, but not a measurement of characteristics, or the factors favouring or hindering expansion of networks.

In studies of resource networks for information, the access channels of information and the size of the network become more important. The 'old-boys' and stars of information become important as resource persons, being those who know who to contact to find information. For new entrants to the network the important thing is to get access to these stars to be passed on in the network (Mueller 1986).

Szarka (1990) provides a good overview of different network analysis. In a regional context, however, the focus of network analysis is fruitfully tied up with at least three different perspectives:

1 service and assistance;
2 seeking specific information, and structuring of information;
3 entrepreneurship and product development.

The purposes, the channels of communication, and the methodology to study the network are dependent on the type of network, on the power structure in the region, and the dynamic processes in the network.

The channels of information may reflect professional or personal ties or the type of information which is possible to standardize. Other factors could be related to the type of communication – a one-way communication, data-bases, libraries, or dependence on dialogue.

The focus may be on documenting the existence and shape of linkages, such as in the IDEON science park in Lund (Johannisson 1987a). In other studies the number of contacts and size of the total network is more important (Aldrich 1989), or the size combined with the homogeneity of the network (Andersen and Arnestad 1990).

The heterogeneity of networks does not allow for a general and standardized methodology covering the range of sociology, trade, industrial relations and regional development. The field builds only to a relatively limited extent on reference studies, both in sociology (Granovetter 1973) on social contacts/friendship-interaction patterns, and in industrial geography on the industrial linkages (Sundin 1983b; Lindmark and Lundmark 1983).

Some of the most difficult aspects of the concept are not the actual use of contacts reflecting the sociometric pattern, but the potential network relations. The documentation and evaluation of the potential, which is not used and may never be used, is hard to measure. It may be earlier contacts, which suddenly open access to relevant information, which are hardly predictable. But the problems should not deter us from trying to evaluate the potential network through different indirect measures, as it is one of the clues to prediction, and an important element for understanding the dynamics of network, not only describing a static picture.

In an entrepreneurial context, the change potential of dynamic networks is much more interesting than the general subsupplier relations or general service and support network functions. Most of the methods used to characterize networks, such as network density, reachability, centrality, strength of ties (Aldrich and Zimmer 1986) are static measures, where the dynamics and the potential resources are not only not registered, but also outside the focus.

Whereas some of the measures provide some hints as to whether a person has access to a large and strong network for general information, this does not characterize the change or the content of the network contacts. Pubs may provide the basis for a wide and strong network, but do not necessarily provide information on access to resources for development. Some local religious communities and local ministers may have high scores in network contacts, and on the openness of the network, but may not use them for any other purposes.

The use of network contacts for other purposes, such as using friends and family for business contacts, varies in different cultures. The possibility of generalizing from the United States to Scandinavia may be limited, because mixing friendship and social contacts with business is far less acceptable in Scandinavia.

An attempt to change a social acquaintanceship to a business relationship may be interpreted as bad taste, or associated with the *nouveau riche* in some Danish communities, making it difficult to use these contacts in the same, positive, way as in US network theory. This does not mean that business and personal ties are not closely interlinked, but that there are much larger barriers to be overcome in order to change or 'exploit' social ties than is generally perceived in the network literature.

Looking at network studies, there are many paradoxes or contradictions in the findings, which may well reflect not only the different types of networks and different perspectives of the analysis, but also cultural differences.

During interviews both in relation to the use of consultants and in relation to the introduction of IT, the network perspective has been touched upon. The findings referred to draw on two of these case studies.[2]

DIFFERENT PURPOSES AND TYPES OF NETWORKS

The different types and functions of networks may be one way of organizing the perception and use of the concept. The purposes here are not the analysis and picture of the overall structure, but delimited to the use by persons and firms to apply the network resources in an area.

Networks for service and assistance

Methodologically, the service and assistance type of network is easy to identify in discussions with firms, as it is often close to a more sociometric description. Who is servicing the firm, where does the firm buy different kinds of business service? and how formal are the relations with these people and firms? The questions are obvious, but it may be very difficult to find a pattern. Which relations are the decisive contacts, and which are easy to replace by any type of service or supplier firm?

Looking at the purpose and content of the network, it may be a service system as part of the formal service, and several studies have analysed only these aspects as a network (Frederiksson and Lindmark 1978). Often, however, we have to add the informal networks, especially where relations to the formal system are frustrated (Mønsted 1989). Also, the choice of the formal service may often be linked to the personal network, recommending firms for this function.

The geographical proximity in the industrial areas of the provincial townships could form a basis for industrial networks as part of the infrastructure. This may provide certain technical services and give access to equipment which may be borrowed. This has happened in firms interviewed in such areas, but to a very limited extent, and only if other ties between firms support the contact, such as certain informal relations already established between owners and/or staff of the firms.

The introduction of administrative information technology to small firms is hard to analyse without the informal networks of assistance. There are many firms where trouble-shooting in the early introduction phase is not only the hot line to the supplier, but also friends, colleagues, grown up children, etc. The personal and informal network is supplementing the formal structures of assistance (Friedman and Mønsted 1989).

This does not necessarily provide a better support structure or a more safe service. The quality is not necessarily better in the informal structures. But this system may assist in acute situations, and may be more important, help to structure the situation in order to use the formal service, i.e. getting access to mediators or assistance to continue, when bogged down with problems. Many of the functions could also be related to the roles of consultants as experts or sparring partners. The small firms mainly seem to find the sparring partners within informal networks (Mønsted 1989).

In a dynamic perspective, the analysis of when formal or informal networks are used is important. It could be a hypothesis that the more complex the problem is, the more likely is the use of informal contacts to help structure the situation and define specific problems to be settled by the formal service structure. When the formal system does not work well, trouble shooting is yet another field, where informal network structures provide assistance.

This last perspective, however, is close to the use of networks for structuring information.

Networks for information and structuring

The use of networks to find specific solutions to a problem is relatively close to the service network. The structure is more related to informal structures, but it is still an effort to use network contacts to find information and decide on a solution to a specific problem. The search is therefore related to specific types of information. Sometimes the person who has the problem (a) knows which person to contact (b), and uses the network contacts only to get access to that person.

In order to find the relevant information, different channels can be used. Some are personal and some may be formal and even standardized, such as brochures and data-bases. The most important thing is to get a feeling of finding the exact information to obtain an overview and be able to act.

The use of networks for this kind of search is hard to predict, especially if the information explored is new. Then the SME-owners will start off by contacting people and institutions they know. Some of these people may have access to contacts able to find a solution. The problems of prediction, however, are related to the fact that the network contacts used are not only contact people they see regularly, but may be people they have met at some earlier time. Which earlier contact can be used as a 'potential', and which cannot be 'reactivated' is not understandable from outside.

In a regional context the search for information in networks is

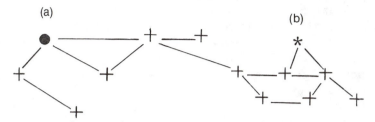

Figure 8.1 Access networks from a to b

related to the access to broader networks, with open access to broader groups. In a regional area where the person seeking informa- tion only knows people who all know each other in a close and strong relationship, the network does not lead to new information, and there is a barrier against gaining access to new information and solving other than earlier, known problems, tied to a common frame of reference.

These features have implications for an outside researcher to enter the community and get access to information and acceptance to work on projects. An open-ended organization may be seen as the access to many sources via acceptance by only a few core people. Methodologically, however, the structure of networks is surprising even in small regional areas, as there may be different core-networks, and communication between them may be very poor or even blocked. In a regional perspective there seem to be factors other than the open-ended organization, leading more to a study of subgroups. Understanding networks has to be supplemented with understanding groups and power bases of different groups in an empirical study of the networks.

The case of information technology in small firms illustrates the problems of being tied to a uniform, closed network. If the people who are being asked for information have the same level of knowledge, or lack of knowledge, then there is no sense of being passed on to new people. The access to other groups with other information is crucial, and the whole meaning of using networks to gain access to new information.

The structure of the network may be relatively flat, with uniform entities, or it may consist of different layers and roles. Some people function as opinion leaders, both to disseminate information and to change attitudes, as illustrated in much earlier studies of diffusion of technology (Rogers 1962). The methodological identification of the network structure is difficult as the network patterns revealed, e.g. in relation to solving certain problems such as the introduction of new technology, are quite different, both in terms of people, and of structure of networks in the same area revolving around the same person dealing with other issues, such as, for example, exports or cultural activities.

The application of the concept of networks for specific, closed problem areas also implies the structuring of information. This is related to the search for information, where the search involves a lot of information which is difficult to evaluate and structure. For example, in the late 1980s the gap was great between what information suppliers offered and what the customers understood and could relate to their problems. The communication process was quite poor. The implication of this was that many people searched for and found lots of information, but many of the sources of information turned out to be dead-ends, not leading to a structured overview providing a basis for decision. The period between taking a decision to acquire information technology and actually buying it, could easily be a year. This long period was not one of thorough examination of information and possibilities; the collection of information in the first round often resulted in confusion and long passive waiting periods without any result (Mønsted and Neergaard 1986; Mønsted 1989). The main problem was to evaluate the information and decide what to choose. 'Information pollution' distresses the overview and the capacity to decide.

The role of mediator in the decision process, the person whom the small business owner trusts and leans on when the information picture is too overwhelming, is clearly a network contact. In some cases the person may be a professional, formal consultant, who has proved reliable and good in other contexts, and the trust is transferred to a new field. In other cases the role is taken up by a colleague, who has been through some of the same problems. The most important thing is that decision-making does not follow a 'rational' decision model. The information is to some extent sorted out by a solid evaluation of the facts, but most of the structuring of information is given priority based on personal trust (Mønsted 1989).

In the study of information technology to small firms, those most capable of dealing with the problems were groups of small firms with many other professional and social contacts, i.e., a large network proved to be a good potential network for new types of problems. They had much more information from other firms, and a better contact network with people whose decisions they trusted. They found people whom they trusted to help play the role of opinion leader and help them structure the information for a decision.

The informal network replaces professional evaluation with personal trust. The information and evaluation base for the decision on who to trust could be based on many sources. If there is a clear pattern in communications the decision is easier for the manager to take. If not, then new contacts have to be made, as the contradictory information blocks the decision and needs the network to structure it.

In network terms this is somewhat of a contradiction. The network is applied to seek and structure the information in order to get an overview which makes it possible to act. But if the network is large, and information gathered through it is contradictory, then a new process has to go on, either seeking more information, or evaluating the quality or trustworthiness of informants and information.

This process may not look much different from other decision processes, reevaluating contradictory data, and using information from other sources, such as data-bases, courses, and consultants. What makes the network approach fundamentally different is the emphasis on personal trust rather than on professional evaluation. This also implies that contradictions less often happen, as the personal, trusted contacts are rarely equal. There is a clear priority in the trust, making structuring easier, though not necessarily better.

Some of this culture of personal trust is related to the community, and the sense of mutual ties between the customer and the supplier of information technology. Many small firms prefer local supplier and service firms to metropolitan firms, because they want to build mutual relations, and make sure that the service firm is also dependent on them as customers. This reflects both mutual culture and an effort to be equal, i.e., small firms trading with small firms. However, one aspect of this was that all firms who had had some bad experience decided to change, in order to avoid a repetition of the problems. Small firms which had been dealing with metropolitan firms changed to local ones, for the reasons just stated, and those which had been dealing with local firms changed to large metropolitan ones, arguing that local ones were not professional enough, and you had to go to the 'real professionals of the large firms'.

The main characteristics of the type of network whose purpose is to find and structure information of a relatively standardized character, are the feeling of security and the personal trust. The network is established and used to help with specific problems, and the contacts are based on people well known to the person seeking information. The role of weak ties in gaining new information is important in the search procedure, but in the structuring and evaluation some strong ties may become important. The network contacts provide assistance in seeking information and getting an overview, but these do not have to be the same networks. The professional value of the information and service may be good or bad, but, most important, the system provides the overview on which to act, and if problems arise the network opens up access to support and help.

Networks for entrepreneurship and product development

In the early start-up phase of a business the need for information is immense, and many different kinds of information are needed, though not always defined very precisely. Success in the early stage of the business startup seems in recent literature to be related to the use of networks. But the findings do not totally agree on this issue. There seems to be a relationship in the studies by Aldrich (1989) and Johannisson (1988), but none in Birley's study (1985). The relationship is not very clear in the Norwegian study of high-tech entrepreneurs by Andersen and Arnestad (1990).

In several of the studies related to entrepreneurship and the use of networks to support business startups, the network is measured by the number of contacts with whom the entrepreneur talks for at least five minutes a week about the business (Johannisson 1987). This way of measuring contacts may reveal the dimensions of the maintenance net, but does not provide much qualitative information on the content and ability of the network to solve new problems. It is obvious that some quantitative measures have to be developed to measure differences in access to networks, but most often we have to have some qualitative data as well. Not all relevant contacts have to be used frequently, and not all the contacts used regularly are important network contacts in a development perspective.

In Andersen and Arnestad's (1990) study of high-tech entrepreneurs, the network support as an explanatory factor is included to find out the heterogeneity of the network in relation to the complexity of the work of the enterprise. The firms with complex products did not have more extensive and heterogeneous networks than did others. The explanatory value of the heterogeneous versus homogeneous networks was low.

In a Danish survey of the local electronic industry in Northern Jutland, the networks for innovations were studied, showing clusters of firms to be important, as the technicians have a set of informal contacts, which proved efficient for getting on with the work of product development (Gelsing 1989). The so-called knowledge networks were part of the local clusters and culture, and highly beneficial for the flexibility of the firms. Many of the data here are related to clusters of firms, where most were related to each other by spin-off. The clustering of innovations in a region, however, seems to be closely related to the exchange of information between the technicians involved in the development. This information infrastructure around innovations, indicates the dependency on both formal and sporadic contacts in pursuing a persistent process of innovation. This is also a basic characteristic of innovation processes in sectors dominated by large firms, such as the dairy sector (Lundvall 1985).

The clustering of innovations promotes the further innovation of ideas, and apparently keeps innovation processes more open. This may also be one of the reasons for a lack of development if only one 'growth pole' firm is placed in a basically different structure. All the firm's ties will then be outside the region, which makes the structure more formal, and instead of a process of innovation, the firm may more easily become a 'cathedral in the desert' (Judet 1988).

In product development and innovation cases, the search for information may also be vague and seeking different opportunities. These opportunities are usually phases which *ex-post-facto* are interpreted by the innovators as 'incidental' or 'luck'. Methodological they may indicate what small-enterprise owners do to give a higher likelihood of coincidence and luck. Old contacts, not used regularly, may be seen as some kind of potential network. In a series of case studies this seems to be one of the ways used, partly because it is easier to explain to well-known people, when vague perspectives and opportunities are discussed.

A few of these contacts could be formal, i.e., contacts developed at an exhibition, or earlier customers, but most are characterized by being not only formal, but also personally related. The kind of problems to be solved need personal interaction, as there are various opportunities, and the information cannot be sought in one-way communication or standardized information.

If the focus of entrepreneurship as well as innovation is on the 'process' and on the constantly amounting opportunities, then the network is an important concept for the understanding of the processes. As the target is not a clear one, the strategic management on the issue may give a blurred or wrong picture of the use of the network. Late in the process, when decisions are made, then ex-post-facto the pathfinder (referring to Leavitt 1986) will tend to rationalize

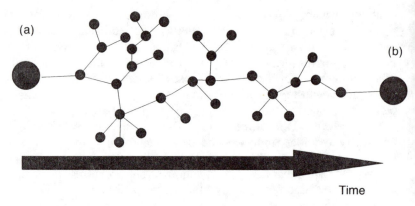

(a)

(b)

Time

Figure 8.2 Networks construction as a decision process

or legitimize the path which was actually created. After the total network used in the process is difficult to remember and restore. Some of the many 'dead-end' traces, apparently outside the focused planned direction, may be this search for opportunities. On this background some of these will not be irrational behaviour, but part of an innovative behaviour of pathfinding.

The evaluation of *ex-post-facto* will make a picture which is often more simple than the process itself. The successful contacts are always remembered, and many of the contacts proven to be dead ends will not be presented or are totally forgotten. The lack of information about the paths really followed makes the actual path look more like an 'incident', as the many other efforts to define the problem and approach the problems are not really defined.

The interpretation *ex-post-facto* would have a tendency to be illustrated in the perspective of the closed information searching system, as the result (b) is now known, and thus interpreted as some kind of strategic management. The perception of the process as a backward view of the steps may give the impression of irrational sidesteps and dead-ends, where resources have been obsolete, because afterwards the result is given.

In a forward perspective the end result or target is not given, but could be different. This implies that the so-called dead-ends are not only a waste of time, but a part of the process of sorting out information and possibilities, which may prove to be very important for the actual result. The follow up on case studies reveals some of the problems, if viewed as a process, where the perspective and possibilities are many. Options are searched and evaluated rather broadly, and then after the decision on the product or process is made, the precise search for further information is initiated.[3]

ACTIVE NETWORKS FOR DEVELOPING ENTREPRENEURS

It is possible to identify regional networks for the regular service of an enterprise even if the pattern may be complex. The other types of network, especially for entrepreneurial processes and innovation, are harder to identify. The weak ties and potential networks cannot be measured in the same way.

The models of networks tend to simplify and identify parts of the formal network, as well as the very close and regularly used personal contacts. This part of the network provides some essential information about the patterns of the network, but in relation to the innovative processes it does not appear to reflect the crucial patterns. The potential network and the contacts generating new information and new ideas and activating the processes are hardly reflected in any sociometric pattern of frequent contacts.

Many of the frequent contacts may be part of a passive network for service or maintenance or for information and support, but where no really new issues or aspects are discussed or initiated. Many networks have as their social context the culture, norms and rules, which are stabilized and hard to break. This implies that in research terms it is hard to predict whether and when new initiatives suddenly crop up and disturb the social balance of the network.

With the case-studies from local communities, it could be raised as a hypothesis that in a regional context the many social ties seem to be much stronger in making up networks for services and assistance and for the structuring of information than for the innovative processes. The personal ties are symmetrical, and the service and assistance will be tied to this kind of mutual assistance.

Restrictions and barriers to innovative networks may be part of the structure. Some perspectives of initiating innovation processes or activating networks still have many social barriers. In a local community the influence of the political structures may have an impact on how new ideas are transferred, accepted and implemented. The central people in different networks are important to the support of new ideas. But the experience from a local development project in Western Zealand show the necessity of using the political, centrally placed groups for the access and acceptance of new ideas, but these same people were in a passive network. They legitimized ideas, but did not act. While the top of a network hierarchy has to give access to further initiative, it can kill ideas by passivity, even if it formally take responsibility and promises that its own bureaucracy will carry through the ideas for implementation.

A study of innovations and entrepreneurship reflects the problems of diffusing the culture of entrepreneurship and change.[4] Whereas personal ties and engagement seem to be necessary for the processes of innovation, access to weak ties and relations outside the community are an important part of the innovative culture in the studied SME metal workshops. The community's social pressure towards uniformity and symmetrical balance may be difficult to maintain in innovative processes with innovators and entrepreneurs, who as change masters will destroy some of the balance, and may be perceived as deviants in the community context.

It is always necessary to delimit the contacts in the network for measurement. Methodologically it becomes a serious problem, if the total pattern of contacts (i.e. the sociometric pattern) provides the main basis for the understanding of the network and the potential network of the person to innovate and search new information. In some of the local development projects, many newcomers to the local community are active entrepreneurs (ex. in a small region in Sweden, Järvsöö, and interviews in Slagelse in Denmark). The newcomers both have a much wider network and more varied experience than most people from the local community, and they are also less restricted by the social norms.

It is hard to measure and stimulate entrepreneurial cultures. We may study the rise and fall of entrepreneurial networks, but what are the implications of this for the stimulation of new entrepreneurial cultures in an industrial policy? In this perspective it is more important to establish conditions for these networks and to train people to establish network contacts and make projects.

The conditions may be related to the infrastructure and personal resources in the area, i.e., whether or not there are relevant firms and research/training institutions. But just as important is the stimulation of personal resources, to avoid supporting only the areas already favoured. Most important is to train the methods in the process as 'projectmaker', the capacity to establish projects and use existing networks both inside and outside the region. If infrastructural conditions and trained teams of entrepreneurs are available, the entrepreneurial potential of the region is increased (Herlau and Tetzschner 1990).

The training is carried out as a combination of projects generated in brainstorming sessions, and projects brought from the trainers. The training of the methods is perceived as much more important than the outcome of the first project. The first projects suggested are usually petty types. The process, however, shows that the use of network contacts for development is not a natural process, either for MA students or for different groups of employed or unemployed people in a local community. The training in perceiving, opening and exploiting networks may provide a basic methodology for later projects.

CONCLUSION

The use of networks in a regional context is tied very closely to the kind of tasks to be solved. The patterns of regular communications and the type of information to be found in the local networks are important for the understanding of service and structuring of information. The network contacts outside the region may be crucial for access to new information, but the close contact and personal trust secures the structuring of an 'information-pollution', which may hinder the overview and action. Generalizations between different types of network may not be very relevant.

The entrepreneurial processes related to entrepreneurship are, however, more complicated. They seem to demand both the close two-way communication processes and access to people with other experience and information. This may reflect something of a contradiction in a local community, especially as the entrepreneurial activities and innovation processes create a process of change, which may disturb a balance. Thus the study of the community networks may be perceived as open-ended organizations, or loose-coupled organizations, but the conditions may be power struggles and contradictions within the communities or sub-groups, in which certain networks try to keep their power base and stability. The creation of entrepreneurial cultures and potentials is an unstable balance, pushing new network contacts, and training people how to overcome the barriers created by networks.

Networks are hard to identify, apart from regular sociometric patterns, which may not be very important in innovative contexts. Active networks may be established to make a fertile ground for breeding and training of entrepreneurs and creating an entrepreneurial culture.

APPENDIX: DATA COLLECTION

The empirical evidence is based on three different studies, where the support structure of services has been an important issue, though not analysed mainly in the network perspective in all of them.

1984–5 Seventy small firms with less than fifty employees were interviewed in non-standardized one–two hour interviews' on the issues of management, organization, qualifications and use of external resources, such as financial support and use of different types of consultants.

The use of consultants and support structure was not at that time put in a network perspective, but related to the process of solving the technical and/or economic problems.

1988–9 As part of a larger project on the computing field, twenty-five small firms with less than fifty employees in North and Western Zealand were interviewed on the introduction of administrative information technology. Interviews with the implementing firms were supplemented with interviews with different groups of mediators of the new technology: computing firms and auditors. The interviews covered the whole process of diffusion of innovation with special emphasis on networks to seek information, to decide on the configuration and to assist in the implementation process.

1990–1 As part of a larger project on regional development in a Western Zealand township, local manufacturing firms and metalwork-shops were interviewed on product development, the service structure, and collaboration between firms. This is an ongoing project and interviewing is still in process. In the first phase fifteen firms have been interviewed. At the same time, different public institutions have been participating, and many other sources of information from local networks.

NOTES

1 See appendix for data collection.
2 See appendix. Seventy firms in construction and metal workshops were interviewed on the use of different consultants and advisers in 1984–5. Twenty-five within the same groups in Western Zealand were interviewed on introduction of IT in 1988–9.
3 This perspective is developed by Henrik Herlau in teaching materials at the Copenhagen Business School 1991.
4 The project (LOKE) is a local development project initiating new projects in the community and teaching and training local people to work with the processes of entrepreneurship and innovation.

REFERENCES

Aldrich, H. (1989) 'Women on the verge of breakthrough?: Networking among entrepreneurs in the United States and Italy', *Journal of Entre-*

preneurship and Regional Development I(3).

Aldrich, H. and Zimmer, C. (1986) 'Entrepreneurship through Social Networks', in Sexton, D.L. and Smilor, R.W. (eds) *The Art and Science of Entrepreneurship*, New York.

Amin, S. (1973) *Le Développement Inégal. Essai sur les formations sociales du capitalisme Périphérique*, Paris: Les Editions de Minuit.

Andersen, S.S. and Arnestad, M. (1990) 'Betingelser for entreprenørsuksess: Nettverk some strategisk ressurs', Research report 90/1, Oslo: Norwegian School of Management.

Birley, S. (1985) 'The Role of Networks in the Entrepreneurial Process', *Journal of Business Venturing* 1.

Christensen, P.Rind. (1991) 'The Small and Medium-Sized Exporters' Squeeze. Empirical Evidence and Model Reflections', *Entrepreneurship and Regional Development* 1.

Drucker, P.F. (1986) *Innovation and Entrepreneurship. Practice and Principle*, New York.

Frederiksson, C. and Lindmark, L. (1978) *From Firms to Systems of Firms*, Umeå: University of Umeå.

Friedman, A. and Mønsted, M. (1989) 'Purposive and Potential Networks in the Diffusion of Computer Systems to Small Firms', CHIPS Working paper 11, Copenhagen: Copenhagen Business School.

Gelsing, L. (1989) 'Knowledge Networks, Industrial Flexibility, and Innovation', in F. Borum, and P. Hull Kristensen (eds) *Technology Innovation and Organizational Change – Danish Patterns of Knowledge, Networks and Culture*, Copenhagen.

Granovetter, M. (1973) 'The Strength of Weak Ties', *American Journal of Sociology* 78(6).

Grøn, J. (1984) *Arbejde, virksomheder, regioner – en analyse af arbejdsdelingen i industrien*, Esbjerg: Sydjysk Universitetscenter.

Hägg, I. and Johansson, J. (eds) (1982) *Företag i Nättverk – ny syn på konkurenskraft*, Stockholm.

Herlau, H. and Tetzschner, H. (1990) *Danske iværksættere – model 2: Innovation, netværksopbygning og projektledelse*, Copenhagen.

Johannisson, B. (1987) 'Entrepreneurship and Creativity – On Dynamic Environments for Small Business', Växjö: Reports from Växjö University, Economy and Politics 7.

—— (1988) 'Emerging Female Entrepreneurship: Network Building Characteristics', Paper prepared for 18th European Small Business Seminar, Gent.

Johannisson, B. and Senneseth, K. (1990) 'Paradoxes of Entrepreneurship', Paper presented at the 4th workshop of Recent Research in Entrepreneurship, Köln, 29–30 November.

Johannisson, B. and Spilling, O. (1986) *Lokal Næringsutvikling – entreprenørskap og nettverksstrategier i noen norske og svenske kommuner*, Oslo.

Johansson, J. and Mattson, L.G. (1987) 'Interorganizational Relations in Industrial Systems: A Network Approach Compared with the Transaction-Cost Approach', *Organizing: the network metaphor. International Studies of Management & Organization* 17(1).

Judet, P. (1988) 'Small and Medium-Sized Enterprises, Networks and the

Industrialization Process', *Industrial Flexibility and Work – French and Danish Perspectives,* Grenoble: Cahiers d'IREP/Developpement.

Kanter, R.M. (1983) *The Change Masters. Corporate Entrepreneurship at Work,* New York.

Leavitt, H.J. (1986) *Corporate Pathfinders. Building Vision and Values into Organisations,* Homewood: Dow-Jones Irwin.

Lindmark, L. and Lundmark, K. (1982) 'Small Firms in a Mixed Economy', *Umeå University Research Papers FE-publ.* 43.

Lundvall, B.Å. (1985) 'Product Innovation and User-Producer Interaction', Industrial Development Research Series 31, Aalborg: Research Report AUC.

Mønsted, M. (1974) 'Francois Perroux's Theory of "Growth Pole" and "Development Pole" – A Critique', *Antipode: A Radical Journal of Geography,* 6(2).

—— (1989) 'Small Enterprises Coping with the Challenges of Information Technology', in F. Borum and P. Hull Kristensen (eds) *Technology Innovation and Organizational Change – Danish Patterns of Knowledge, Networks and Culture,* Copenhagen.

—— and Neergaard, P. (1986) EDB i mindre virksomheder (Microcomputers to SMEs) in Neergaard, P. (ed.) *Økonomisk styring i mindre virksomheder,* Copenhagen.

Mueller, R. (1986) *Corporate Networking: Building Channels for Information and Influence,* London.

Perroux, F. (1950) 'Economic Space, Theory and Applications', *Quarterly Journal of Economics* LXIV.

Rogers, E.M. (1962) *Diffusion of Innovation,* New York.

Sundin, E. (1983a) 'Olika sätt at förklara företagsamhet', in Lundin, R., Glader, M. and Sundin, E. (eds) *Små Företag i brännpunkten,* Umeå.

—— (1983b) 'Små lokala företagare – förlorarna i organisationsekonomin', *Regionalvetenskap i Norr,* Stockholm: ERU rapport 27.

Szarka, J. (1990) 'Networking and Small Firms', *Small Business Journal,* 8(2).

DISCUSSION

Ray Oakey

This is an interesting paper in which the author raises a number of issues concerning the impact of networking on the process of regional development in Denmark. The concept of networking is well established in Scandinavian literature and has many features similar to the agglomeration economies noted in much Anglo-American literature on the successful growth of industrial complexes, ranging in temporal terms from Victorian industries to the new concentrations of high technology production.

While the initial assumption of the paper that networking is an important contributor to growth within regional economies is valid, further work on this subject by the author might tackle the fundamental problem of how conducive networks are first established. A 'chicken and egg' problem appears to exist in which regions with poor networking conditions for entrepreneurs do not develop and therefore do not nurture the 'critical mass' of material and information economies which make industrial agglomerations 'the right place to be'. There is a serious problem here in that it is very difficult for depressed regions to develop the virtuous network characteristics which would ensure self sustained growth.

Another reservation that must be made when considering networks is the reality that much technical information of use to industrial enterprises is confidential in nature, and is not available for transfer within networks. Indeed, the most valuable technical data on product and process design are the source of 'competitive edge' between enterprises and remain closely guarded secrets. This assertion does not invalidate the truth that much useful secondary information may be transferred through networks to support R&D, and subsequently allow successful confidential innovations of major importance to occur within firms. However, it is probably safe to affirm that successful networking is a necessary, but not sufficient, requirement to assure the achievement of successful invention and innovation.

Finally, the concept of networking is essentially an informal process in which contacts are developed on a casual and informal basis. This point relates to the comment made above on the problem of stimulating networks in depressed regions. In particular, it is very difficult to 'artificially' stimulate from a regional development viewpoint a process that is inherently informal. There is a sense in which any attempt to establish networks through the establishment of formal structures is doomed to fail because such a process is forced and not the result of a 'natural' growth of local information supply and demand. Yet if networking is to seriously contribute to the regeneration of depressed industrial regions, this 'riddle' of network creation must be solved by the above author, and other advocates of the importance of networking to regional development.

9 High technology small firms: a more realistic evaluation of their growth potential

Ray Oakey

INTRODUCTION

The decade of the 1970s can now be seen as a watershed in the post-World War II industrial development of many Western economies. It was during this period that industries, including electronics, motor vehicles and mechanical engineering, which had led the post-war recovery in Europe, came under increasing pressure from industrializing countries in general, and Japan in particular (Rothwell and Zegveld 1981; 1985). This industrial decline, due to uncompetitive product quality and prices, grew throughout the 1980s, and was particularly pronounced in the United States and the United Kingdom. Ironically, in both countries, the 1970s ended with a change of political emphasis, in which Thatcherism and Reaganomics were seen as free market solutions to the previous decade of economic failure. Such an approach blamed much of the poor performance during the 1970s on excessive government interference in the economy in terms of the burden imposed on commerce and industry by punitive taxation, which, monetarist economists argued, was mainly needed to fund unnecessarily large government spending.

There was a particular irony in this doctrine, since the major example of success during this period was that of Japan, where the clear involvement of the government in directing and financially supporting technological and industrial growth through the Ministry for International Trade and Industry (MITI), pointed to more interventionist solutions to problems of poor industrial performance (Fransman 1991). None the less, by taking an extremely free market approach to industrial planning, governments in the United Kingdom and the United States achieved the twin objectives of reducing public expenditure (a major aim of the monetarist policies) and divorcing government from responsibility for the problems of poor industrial performance by arguing that investment decisions were best made by individual firm managements at the enterprise level.

However, the poverty of this approach to industrial planning was partly disguised by two major industrial trends that appeared to be emerging in 1980. First, the 1970s had ended in the United States and Europe with a growing interest in the contribution of small firms to industrial growth. Such interest had stemmed, both from Anglo–American studies that indicated the substantial short and medium term contribution of small firms to national and regional employment growth (Birch 1979; Fothergill and Gudgin 1979), and work that pointed to the neglect from which small firms had previously suffered (Storey 1982). Second, this concern for small firms coincided with, and was partly caused by, a sudden enthusiasm for the growth potential of new high technology industries. Indeed, much of the high technology industrial growth noted in the United States was provided by small firms in California that had experienced extremely rapid growth rates in the 1970s (Morse 1976). Thus, there was at least some evidence, as the 1980s began, to suggest that market forces, principally in the form of small firms in high technology industries, would provide the growth to soak up unemployment caused by the decline of the boom industries of the 1960s. The implicit assumption of this approach appeared to be that a combination of entrepreneurial spirit and leading edge technological power (embodied in small firms) would negate the need for government planning and support, since a natural form of free market growth would take place in an economic environment devoid of the macro-economic drawbacks of restrictive legislation and taxation. The enterprise zone concept, popular in both the United Kingdom and the United States in the early 1980s, was a physical manifestation of this approach.

One reason for the ease with which the United Kingdom and United States governments could accept the demise of industries that had been major driving forces in their economies since the turn of the century (e.g. motor vehicles, textiles), was the assumption that such sectors could be surrendered to emerging industrial nations as developed countries moved up the industrial product life cycle curve to concentrate on the lucrative 'start of cycle' industries, where value added was high and profit margin large. While Japan had been pursuing this path since the early 1960s (Rothwell and Zegveld 1985), the belief was that Europe and the United States would be able to keep ahead of Japan due to their greater expertise in producing basic scientific discoveries. Evidence from high technology agglomerations in the United States, of which Silicon Valley is perhaps the most famous, tended to support the view that a new high technology revolution, based on private venture capital and high technology production would be the blueprint for replication in Western Europe (Cooper 1970). The growth of the science park movement in the United Kingdom and Europe was based on the unsubstantiated premise that such actual American growth could be imitated in Europe. However, in terms of the United Kingdom, the establishment of science parks was a largely piecemeal exercise initiated by local authorities and universities, with no government coordination. None the less, this activity did create the illusion of a high technology policy, and filled the vacuum that would otherwise have been created by an obvious lack of any nationally coordinated technology policy for the United Kingdom (Oakey 1985).

The purpose of this chapter is the exploration of the explicit and implicit assumption of United Kingdom politicians and government agencies (e.g. the Department for Trade and Industry, the Scottish Development Agency) that new high technology industries would provide substantial economic and employment growth up to and beyond the year 2000. With the benefit of hindsight provided by the 1980s, and empirical evidence produced during this period, it will be argued that much of the enthusiasm for the growth potential of high technology industries, common in the early 1980s, was misplaced, and that any industrial policy dependent on high technology small-firm growth to suffice the nation's economic needs is an extremely risk laden strategy.

The survey results summarized below have been extracted from three substantial surveys of British high technology small firms (drawn from the planning regions of south-east England and Scotland), and the San Francisco Bay area of the United States (including Silicon Valley). First, data are included from a time series study of 174 British and American instruments and electronics firms initially surveyed in 1981 in Britain, and 1982 in the United States, when the total survey population equalled 174 independent enterprises of less than 200 workers. Of these original businesses, 131 surviving enterprises were re-interviewed in 1985 in Britain and 1986 in the United States to obtain accurate information on job change in these survey firms (for further details see Oakey *et al.* 1988). The second data set discussed below was produced by a postal questionnaire survey of 140 British biotechnology firms in 1988 (for further details see Oakey *et al.* 1990).

PROBLEMS ASSOCIATED WITH HIGH TECHNOLOGY INDUSTRIAL GROWTH

From a policy perspective, it is in many ways difficult to comprehend that the 1980s have passed. In the United Kingdom, much of this decade was spent waiting for the expected new high technology industrial growth to take place. In particular, the emergence of the new 'flagship firms' of the computer, electronics, and latterly, biotechnology sectors, were keenly awaited. In this context, the computer industry is a perfect example of lost opportunities. First Sinclair, then Acorn Computers, suggested that they might lead United Kingdom manufacture and become a major force in the world computer industry. Both these firms subsequently collapsed due to respective failures with new product selection and excessive marketing costs, and were acquired (Garnsey and Fleck 1987). Moreover Inmos, created by the outgoing Labour government in the late 1970s, was privatized in the 1980s, sold on to GEC, which then sold the firm to Thomson CSF, a French competitor. The decade ended on a similarly pessimistic note when ICL, the United Kingdom's only large mainframe computer maker, was sold to the Japanese firm Fugitsu. It is hard to escape the conclusion that, thus far, the manufacturing industries of the United Kingdom have largely failed to benefit from the massive international industrial growth provided by basic scientific discoveries based around miniaturized semiconductor technology in the electronics and other downstream industries (Freeman 1986). Not only has there been scant evidence of any individual large scale successes in the United Kingdom in terms of the emergence of a dominant domestic manufacturing firm from small-firm beginnings, but the aggregate performance of small firms in both the electronics and biotechnology sectors has been unimpressive (Oakey 1991a).

A major reason for the poor performance of the United Kingdom high technology computer-based industries is the previously mentioned government belief that the attractive profits possible in such industries would ensure that growth could be achieved through the provision of investment capital by the private sector alone. This argument was continued to the level of a self-fulfilling prophecy in which the eventual demise of a promising firm became simplistic proof that this firm, unable to survive in the open market, was not viable, and therefore not worthy of government support. However, had such a myopic policy been applied by the conservative government of the early 1970s, Rolls-Royce would not currently exist to employ thousands of workers throughout Britain. The lesson to be learnt from the Rolls-Royce example is that high technology industry is no soft option in terms of government industrial policy. Because the United Kingdom government throughout the 1980s was reluctant to support traditional indigenous industries in decline (e.g. motor vehicles), it should not have assumed that the new high technology industries did not need support and could be self sustaining. United Kingdom government assistance available during the 1980s was largely superficial in nature, offering assistance of marginal value which was biased towards new-firm formation at the expense of viable existing small firms, and, in keeping with much private sector finance available, tended to be small amounts lent over very short time periods. In particular, there was no long term commitment to the support of successful firms in key, strategically important sectors of the economy (ACOST 1990).

Survey evidence of the failure of external investment to penetrate high technology small firms, both in Britain and the United States, is provided by Table 9.1 in which 69 per cent of British firms in 1985 and 81 per cent of American firms in 1986 relied on internal profits as a main source of investment capital. A pervasive reason for the reluctance to become involved with external funding of individual businesses focused on risks associated with the onerous terms demanded by external lenders of money. Firm owners were generally not adverse to external assistance *per se*, since it was clearly a means of expanding their businesses at a faster rate. However, in practice it was generally believed, both in Britain and the United States, that the burden of risk was heavily biased in favour of the firm owner, while returns to the lender (partly due to this unbalanced risk), were excessive. Thus, individual small-firm owners generally preferred to move forward at a slower pace which was determined by the flow of profits into the business.

At a more general level in the United States, the experience of high technology growth throughout the 1980s was necessarily different from that in the United Kingdom for two major reasons. First, since there had not been a history of widespread government assistance, it was here a case of a general continuation of a previous non-interventionist policy rather than a dramatic retreat from government involvement, as in the United Kingdom (although the formation of the Small Business Administration (SBA) to support small business was a response to the transatlantic popularity of small firms in the late 1970s). Second, the United States had already experienced rapid high technology small-firm growth in the 1970s, which meant it was a case of consolidation or continued growth

Table 9.1 Main source of investment finance in instruments and electronics firms

| | Britain | | | | United States | | | | Total | | | |
| | 1981–2 | | 1985–6 | | 1981–2 | | 1985–6 | | 1981–2 | | 1985–6 | |
	No.	%	No.	%	No.	%	No.	%	No.	%	No.	%
Profits	84	74	60	69	45	75	35	81	129	74	95	73
Local bank	18	16	10	12	6	10	2	5	24	14	12	9
Venture capital	3	2	2	2	9	15	0	0	12	7	2	2
Other	9	8	15	17	0	0	6	14	9	5	21	16
Total	114	100	87	100	60	100	43	100	174	100	130	100

Source: Oakey *et al.* 1988

rather than the 'getting started' approach required in Europe (Freeman 1982). However, by 1985, the great promise of continued growth, evident in the early 1980s, began to be replaced by a familiar process. The decline in motor vehicle and electronics production as a result of a Japanese cornering of large parts of the market had provoked claims of Japanese 'dumping', and 'industrial espionage' by American manufacturers. This loss of market share often prompted a perceived need to specialize in up market products, as if the mass market had suddenly become unattractive. By 1985, the success of Japanese firms in the early 1980s in capturing increasing shares of the most lucrative 'volume' silicon chip market elicited similar responses from United States producers in Silicon Valley. American dominance of the high technology industry which they had invented and developed, had ceased (Langlois *et al.* 1988).

These developments have importance, not only for the future location of the world high technology semiconductor industry, but also for the above mentioned strategy of seeking protection from intense world industrial competition by taking refuge in 'start of cycle' manufacturing industries. In particular, the speed with which the Japanese were able to absorb the semiconductor technology originally developed by the Americans severely curtailed the breathing space that concentration on high technology industry theoretically offered. Put simply, the Japanese achieved in approximately ten years with a high technology sector, the same results that had taken thirty years to attain in motor vehicles, which was world domination of the most lucrative mass production parts of both industries. Indeed, it is perhaps not surprising that the success achieved in motor vehicles and semiconductors stemmed from an initial concentration on production efficiency and quality control, which produced the potent combination of low prices and reliability. However, from an industrial strategy viewpoint, the message implicit in the speed with which Japan absorbed and adapted this new high technology was that the retreat of western nations towards the upper reaches of technological development into 'start of cycle' industries would be unlikely to provide a substantial protection of their long term industrial bases.

This argument on the lack of protection provided by the movement of Western nations into the more basic 'start of cycle' areas of industrial production is further exacerbated by the issue of increased risk. A central problem confronting firms operating in high technology industries is that associated with the protection of technological assets produced by expensive long term R&D programmes. Clearly, for any R&D programme to be worthwhile, the cost of development and production must be exceeded by sales to allow an adequate profit. While in pharmaceuticals the ability of firms to protect new drugs is reasonably good, the potential for circumventing patents in semiconductor engineering often causes firms to negate the patent process due to its ineffectiveness. In other areas of high technology (e.g. software) there are also problems associated with the protection of intellectual output that does not take a physical form. In the case of the development of the semiconductor, the United States government might be seen as a major subsidiser of early development in the Japanese semiconductor industry through its initial funding of industrial R&D in American firms, which was then copied by Japanese competitors. However, as a general principle, there is no point in a firm spending massive amounts of capital on R&D to develop new products if this investment cannot be redeemed through the economic growth provided by the subsequent sale of high technology products. With the growth in importance of other South-east Asian countries to compete with Japan and the West in high technology markets (e.g. South Korea, Taiwan, Singapore), there is a danger that the economic bases of Western countries may become undermined in conditions where they bear most of the expense of inventing new high technologies through basic scientific discoveries, but do not enjoy the economic benefits of their commercial exploitation.

However, a more fundamental reason for increased risks associated with a concentration on high technology production is concerned with the unproved nature of a potential new sector in general, and individual products in particular. It is perhaps a sign of the desperation of western politicians and planners that they seek increasingly embryonic and unproven industries as candidates for economic salvation. For example, throughout the 1980s various sectors have been tipped as likely successors to the semiconductor industry as motors for growth in Western developed economies. Candidates have ranged from biotechnology through software, to materials technology, super conductivity and space technology. While it is clear that a number of these technologies have considerable potential (Freeman 1986), the desire of many planners to obtain new industrial growth has resulted in an over-estimation of both the actual and potential growth performance of these sectors. In particular, both at the individual firm level, and at that of its parent industry, there has been a tendency to optimistically foreshorten the lead time associated with the progression of a technology from its form as a basic scientific discovery to full commercial exploitation.

Problems with the rapid development of these new potential technologies have left a vacuum at the beginning of the 1990s in most Western developed economies, caused by the growing domination of the commercial exploitation of proven semiconductor-based electronic products by South-east Asian countries (e.g. fax machines, video recorders, micro computers), while none of the above mentioned potentially important technologies have yet emerged to offer the prospect of a new pulse of high technology-based production growth in the West. Indeed, the dominance of Japan has advanced to the stage where the invention of new basic scientific discoveries in Western research establishments, applicable in the semiconductor-based family of industries, might not find any Western owned firms left to exploit such discoveries. Indeed, the American government has been recently reminded of this depletion by the case of High Definition Television (HDTV). Although the applications for HDTV are estimated to be wide-ranging, the realization by the United States government that it had only one small domestic producer of conventional televisions rendered problematic the encouragement of the private sector exploitation of this new technology. Moreover, at the time of the recent Gulf War, most defence analysts largely ignored the strategic implication of the threat to world oil supplies, but were more concerned with the reality that much of the 'American' high technology hardware used in the conflict was critically dependent on Japanese semiconductor products.

While such strategic concerns have led to American government support, through the Pentagon, of the SEMATEC programme to foster leading-edge technical collaboration between American semi-conductor producers, a more enlightened approach might realize that military power and economic power are indivisible, and that there is no point in having strong defences if there is no manufacturing base to protect, or in the medium term, to pay for such military hardware. While this argument has recently been used in the Soviet Union, it equally applies to the United States, and other Western countries with large defence budgets (e.g. the United Kingdom). In summary, it is fair to conclude that the existing high technology industrial base of Western economies is in a weaker condition than was the case at the beginning of the 1980s. Moreover, if the strong defence orientation of much of the United States and United Kingdom electronics industries is considered, the reduction in defence spending as a result of the peace dividend is likely to cause severe problems of re-adjustment as both large and small firms seek to replace defence industry customers with civil patrons (Oakey 1991b).

EVIDENCE OF HIGH TECHNOLOGY SMALL-FIRM EMPLOYMENT GROWTH

The above general reservations about the employment potential of high technology small firms is supported by a consistent trend present in a number of studies performed by this author throughout the 1980s. In Table 9.2 evidence is provided on jobs created in new British and American instruments and electronics firms during the study described on pp. 226–8 (Oakey 1984). In this initial instance, only firms less than five years old, emerging from random samples of firms in the two countries, were analysed for job gains in 1981 in Britain, and 1982 in the United States. Although there is a clear difference in job generation between the two countries, with approximately equal numbers of firms recording an average job growth of seventeen workers in Britain and fifty-seven in the United States, this aggregate difference was mainly caused in the United States by only three firms, which grew to 125, 150 and 200 employees within five years, when the fastest grower in Britain was a firm of fifty-three employees. Thus, the main difference between the two countries appears to be the inability of British firms to show the rapid growth occasionally achieved in the United States. However, subsequent evidence indicates that rapid job growth in the United States can also be a precursor to rapid job losses.

Indeed, Table 9.3 clearly indicates that the American firms showed

Table 9.2 Jobs created in instruments and electronics firms of less than five years of age

	Britain (1976–81)	United States (1982–6)
Number of firms	19	14
Total jobs	329	796
Average jobs per firm	17	57

Source: Oakey 1984

both the largest job gains and job losses throughout the survey of all ages of instruments and electronics firms. From the 144 British firms that were trading in 1981, an additional 354 net jobs had been created by 1985, while the sixty American survey firms created 338 net new jobs between 1982 and 1986. The forty-three remaining American firms in 1986 produced 1,193 new jobs at an average of twenty-eight new jobs per firm, compared with an average of eleven new jobs per firm in the eighty-eight enterprises comprising the remaining 1985 British survey population. However, this initially superior American performance was dissipated by the severe recession that hit the American semiconductor industry between 1983 and 1985. The 619 jobs lost through the closure of American survey plants rendered the final figures for job gains far lower than they would otherwise have been. Two important general trends may be identified from these data. First, neither small size nor high technology status protects firms from employment decline during a

Table 9.3 Job gains, losses and net changes in survey firms

	Britain (1981–5)	United States (1982–6)
Job gains	+990	+1,193
Job losses	−384	−236
Job change	+606	+957
Closure job losses	−252	−619
Net job change	+354	+338

Source: Oakey *et al.* 1988

recession. Second, although the figures for employment growth from survey firms were drawn from small random samples of the total populations of firms in the survey regions, the average job growth in the total population is unlikely to be much different from the figures in Tables 9.2 and 9.3. Such patterns of job change in high technology small firms suggest that their medium term performance is unlikely, either in aggregate or individual terms, to compensate for the losses of jobs in more traditional industrial sectors. Moreover, these results on unimpressive job gains conform to results obtained for the British computer industry (Keeble and Kelly 1988).

This consideration of the rate of high technology employment growth is concluded by the presentation of evidence from the British biotechnology industry on employment growth. The data were collected in 1988 and represent a total population of the identified population of biotechnology firms in the United Kingdom at this time. The key information contained in Table 9.4 relates to the seventy-one firms founded since 1975. Although a number of enterprises included in this grouping were formed as subsidiaries of large chemical and pharmaceutical firms, only 10 per cent of these firms had exceeded 100 employees by 1988, while 73 per cent of them employed fewer than fifty workers. Indeed, the sub-sample of forty-three firms, founded as totally independent firms between 1976 and 1988, produced only one firm that exceeded 100 employees over the twelve-year study period (i.e. Celltech). Thus, in general terms, it may be concluded that the employment growth of new biotechnology firms is unimpressive, both in terms of the aggregate employment gains, and in terms of the individual performance of the fastest growing enterprises.

EVIDENCE ON THE RATE AT WHICH SELF-SUSTAINED GROWTH IS ACHIEVED

A number of the preceding points made on the limited growth potential of high technology industry can be supported by further evidence gained by the United Kingdom biotechnology industry survey (Oakey *et al.* 1990). In particular the above mentioned growing level of risk associated with an increased concentration on 'start of cycle' industries is readily apparent in this emerging sector. In the United Kingdom case, and probably in many other countries, the publicity concerning the new biotechnology industry has created an image of vitality and growth that is not substantiated by hard evidence. For example, in a detailed study of new biotechnology firm

Table 9.4 United Kingdom biotechnology survey firms: employment size by age

	Pre-1945		1945–74		Post-1974	
	No.	*%*	*No.*	*%*	*No.*	*%*
1–19	1	4	7	15	36	51
20–49	1	4	7	15	16	22
50–99	2	9	8	17	12	17
100–199	3	13	10	22	5	7
200+ >	16	70	14	31	2	3
Total	23	100	46	100	71	100

Source: Oakey *et al.* 1990

formations between 1978 and 1988 in the United Kingdom, only forty-eight new independent firms producing a legitimate biotechnology product or service (e.g. R&D), drawn from the postal survey referred to on p. 227 and discussed above, could be identified. Of these original target firms, forty-three enterprises agreed to take part in a detailed interview survey. This heterogeneous industry, which has no formal SIC listing in the United Kingdom, clearly is currently very small. However, it is ironic that this low level of formation probably overstates the value of the industry to national industrial output since much of the new-firm productive activity is directed at providing R&D oriented products and services for the support of R&D in larger firms and their subsidiaries, in the chemical and pharmaceutical industries.

Very little value added in this new sector is accounted for by the sale of products and services to other sectors, or to the final consumer. Both this incestuous form of productive activity, and later evidence on a slow transition to profitability in new small firms, is fundamentally caused by an over-optimistic assessment of the lead times on product development from basic scientific ideas, to a return on investment in the marketplace. Where large pharmaceutical firms are involved, the problems experienced by small, new biotechnology subsidiaries in not keeping to the new product lead times, agreed when their satellite enterprises were established, is a phenomenon with which they are very familiar, since such slippage occurs within their own internal R&D departments. Large firms such as Glaxo or ICI have the resources to accommodate such a miscalculation. However, in terms of the establishment of new, small independent

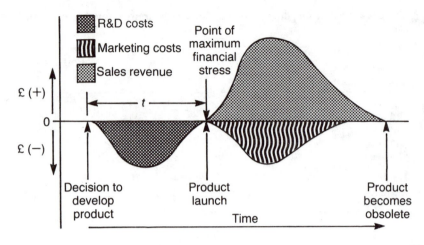

Figure 9.1 A complete product life cycle model

firms, an inability to break even and move into profitability at a time agreed in their business plans is likely to cause extreme nervousness on the part of external investors who are frequently short termist in mood.

The dilemma facing technical entrepreneurs establishing new firms is diagrammatically represented in Figure 9.1, which indicates the major outgoings and incomings associated with the formation of high technology small firms and the launch of an initial product. Unless most, or all, of the development work can be performed before formation, a critical amount of product development work must precede any income from product sales in a new firm. Figure 9.1 also notes that the product launch occurs at a time of maximum financial stress when R&D costs have been incurred, marketing needs to be funded, but no sales have been achieved. However, the key relevance of this diagram to the present discussion is the accuracy with which t is calibrated, which is the lead time between a decision to develop a product and the first receipt of sales from the marketplace. The estimation of this period of time is clearly a critical ingredient of the business plan, since it determines the point at which external investment can begin to be reduced and, hopefully, profits rapidly produce a return on investment.

It is not surprising to discover that firm founders in the bio-technology sector are frequently far too optimistic regarding the length of t. Clearly, an external investor will be easier to attract if t is three years than would be the case if this figure were eight years. However, the problem for the funding of new biotechnology firms is that eight years has become a more accurate estimate of a required lead time than three, resulting in a steady decline in the popularity of small biotechnology firms as targets for investment throughout the 1980s (Clark 1987; Martin 1989). Perhaps more importantly, at the government policy level, these over-optimistic individual estimates of biotechnology firm growth potentials might be aggregated to create an unrealistic view of the medium term employment potential of the whole sector. For example, the rapidity with which the Scottish Development Agency formed a distinct biotechnology division in the early 1980s is an example of this ill-informed enthusiasm. It is likely that, had the agency known the strong research orientation of this sector, its very limited medium term growth potential, and the cost-benefit involved, a special section to encourage small biotechnology firm establishment would not have been established. Indeed, evidence from the United States in the mid-1980s from the Office of Technology Assessment (OTA 1984), suggested that the emerging biotechnology industry would not replicate the small-firm growth experienced in the semiconductor sector, mainly because this new area of production was not supported by defence spending through the Pentagon to the same degree that R&D and production had been nurtured in the electronics industry between 1960 and 1980. While Western governments should be applauded for their support of basic science as a precursor to future industrial growth, the elevation of an emerging industry of uncertain potential to the status of leader of a

Table 9.5 Percentage of firms with internal profits as a main investment source: a comparison of instruments and electronics with biotechnology firms

Age of firm	Instruments and electronics (1970–80)		Biotechnology (1976–86)	
	No.	%	No.	%
1–5 years	17	55	7	26
6–10 years	42	75	4	25
Total respondents British and American instruments and electronics firms = 87				
United Kingdom biotechnology firms = 43				

Source: Instruments and electronic data: Oakey 1984
Biotechnology data: Oakey *et al.* 1990

current high technology-based industrial revolution, is an attitude stimulated more by desperation than hard evidence.

Detailed evidence on the poor growth performance of small firms in the British biotechnology industry is provided elsewhere (Oakey *et al.* 1990). However, limited specific evidence which highlights the point made above on unrealistic lead times in new biotechnology firms is provided in Table 9.5. This table compares the move towards self-generated profits as a main investment source in the new firms of two recent surveys into high technology small firms. Although the survey periods and national compositions differ slightly, with the instruments and electronic firms in Table 9.5 formed between 1970 and 1980, and the British biotechnology firms established in the 1976 to 1989 period, the questions asked these two groups on self-generated profits were identical. Since the question on self-generated profits is strategic in tone and categorical in form, macro-economic changes between the two periods are unlikely to be the cause of the sharp differences noted in Table 9.5. It is suggested that the comparatively slow transition from a reliance on external investment to self-generated profits in the biotechnology case is a result of the constraining influence of the activities available in this sector in terms of providing a basis for a rapid move to sales in newly formed firms, and consequent self-generated profits.

The two most striking features of Table 9.5 are, first, that a significantly lower 26 per cent of biotechnology firms had moved to self-sustained profits in the one to five year-period, compared with the larger 55 per cent of instruments and electronics firms. Second, while, as might be expected, this percentage increases in instruments and electronics firms in the five to ten year-period after formation to 75 per cent, the percentage for biotechnology firms was a marginal decline to 25 per cent. Expressed conversely, this evidence reveals that, after a minimum of five years in business, 75 per cent of the biotechnology firms relied on external capital for a majority of their funding. Such an inability to become self-sustaining resulted in a complex set of relationships with funders in which involvement ranged from total acquisition, to various forms of multiple external equity funding arrangements with external backers (Oakey *et al.* 1990). All these negative features stemmed from the inability of new biotechnology firm founders to produce marketable products of services on a substantial scale.

Conversations with individual entrepreneurs, and the widespread evidence of the restructuring of financial support, suggested that an under-estimation of the product lead time necessary to launch a firm into profitability was a major cause of such difficulties. A common problem appeared to be the transfer of many product ideas from the laboratory, well before a time when they were ready for commercial exploitation. As mentioned in general terms regarding high technology industry, a reliance on inventions from basic science carries with it increased risks, ranging from the total failure of a proposed new product, to a much longer period of development than was originally conceived.

CONCLUSIONS

This chapter has explored a number of issues concerning industrial policy throughout the 1980s in Western economies in general, and the United Kingdom in particular. Certainly in the United Kingdom's case, the 1980s must be judged a wasted decade of lost opportunities in terms of industrial development. The current deep recession in the manufacturing industry of the United Kingdom partly masks a worrying decline in productive capacity that is the result of a more long term demise of the manufacturing base. The extreme Thatcherite non-interventionist policies of the 1980s have meant that staple industries of the economy have been largely abandoned to their fate (e.g. motor vehicles, machine tools), while newly emerging sectors of high technology industry have been starved of much-needed long term support. Thus, by the start of the 1990s, large sectors of traditional manufacturing industry had become dominated by foreign ownership, either through full control, joint ventures, or the establishment of green field branch factories (e.g. in the motor vehicle industry). While the current government applauds such foreign direct investment, it fails to apply the valid test of additionality which it is keen to use in refuting the use of incentives in other contexts. Many of the new branch plant jobs created must have been at the expense of employment in indigenous United Kingdom firms, where local input material sourcing was higher, and in-house R&D and design ensured a continuing United Kingdom expertise, beyond the crude assembly of products designed elsewhere. Again, motor vehicle production is a strong example of this trend.

Neither new technology industries, nor small firms, have brought relief to this depressing picture of industrial decline in the 1980s. As already discussed, during the 1980s many large and medium sized high technology firms were allowed to become the acquisitions of foreign firms (e.g. ICL, Acorn Computers, INMOS). While, in principle, there is no automatic reason for the blocking of foreign ownership of industrial firms, there is an argument for the government to use the national interest defence of the monopolies and merger legislation on technological grounds, if the loss of a few key firms means the virtual demise of an emerging indigenous sector of industry. The failure of the current United Kingdom government to protect the small number of high technology firms that were established in the 1980s clearly stems from a lack of any strong technology policy which might indicate what might be the key productive sectors of the British economy beyond the year 2000. In this context, a reliance on market forces is a negation of a much needed governmental role of planning and nurturing the national economy to ensure continued industrial prosperity.

The hope of the early 1980s that entrepreneurship in small, high technology firms would be a free market solution of the United Kingdom's economic problems, has been dashed, both by the problems of longer lead times in these emerging industries as they developed, and the unwillingness of the government to understand that the short termism of private sector investment in the United Kingdom was creating a severe barrier to growth. Certainly, there has been no attempt to provide the necessary long term investment from public sources. Currently, there appears to be a policy vacuum in which, although it must be generally accepted that free market Thatcherism has served the industrial development of the country badly, the present United Kingdom government has no alternative approach on which to rely. This dilemma is exacerbated by problems associated with the peace dividend, because while the funding of high technology industry through defence expenditure was acceptable to both Reagan and Thatcher, finding an acceptable alternative means of spending peace dividend savings by the continuing right-wing governments of both the United Kingdom and the United States remains an embarrassing problem (Oakey 1991b).

It is certainly the case that in the United Kingdom and the United States over the past decade there has been a strong tendency to react to problems in a given sector of industry by adopting a fatalistic attitude, and arguing that the sector can be abandoned since new compensating employment will occur in some other new manufacturing or service sector activity, yet to emerge. This is an unrealistic attitude, and a reliance on new small firms or emerging technologies will not compensate for the loss of, for example, an indigenous motor vehicle industry. However, since no nation can be a world leader in all sectors of industry, it is clear that it is not possible to protect and nurture all sectors of industry. Thus, governments should concentrate their efforts on chosen sectors for development, which would be the basis of a nationally agreed technology policy. Such target sectors would not be either exclusively high technology, nor exclusively populated by small firms. Attempts to improve the industrial performance of sectors in the United Kingdom economy in the remaining years of this century should focus on a balance of high and low technology industries and the support of large and small firms within such technologically diverse sectors. In this context, the enthusiasm of United Kingdom government for small high technology firms displayed in the 1980s may be seen as a cynical attempt to divert attention from the otherwise obvious absence of a coherent industrial strategy towards all technological sophistications and sizes of industrial enterprise.

REFERENCES

ACOST (1990) 'The Enterprise Challenge: Overcoming Barriers to Growth in Small Firms', London: HMSO.

Birch, D.L. (1979) 'The Job Generation Process', Working Paper, MIT Program on Neighbourhood and Regional Change, Cambridge, Mass.

Clark, R. (1987) *Venture Capital in Britain, America and Japan*, London: Croom Helm.

Cooper, A.C. (1970) 'The Palo Alto Experience', *Industrial Research*, May: 58–84.

Fothergill, S. and Gudgin, G. (1979) *The Job Generation Process in Britain*, Centre for Environmental Studies Research Series 32, London: CES

Fransman, M. (1991) *The Market and Beyond*, Cambridge: Cambridge University Press.

Freeman, C. (1982) *The Economics of Industrial Innovation*, London: Frances Pinter.

—— (1986) 'The Role of Technological Change in National Economic Development', in A. Amin and J. Goddard (eds) *Technological Change and Industrial Restructuring*, London: Allen & Unwin.

Garnsey, E. and Fleck, V. (1987) '*Strategy and Internal Constraints in a High-Technology Firm: The Management of Growth at Acorn Computers*', Research Paper 2/87, Cambridge: University of Cambridge.

Keeble, D.E. and Kelly, T. (1988) 'Regional Distribution of NTBFs in Britain', in *New Technology Based Firms in Britain and Germany*, London: Anglo-German Foundation.

Langlois, R.N., Pugel, T.A., Haklisch, C.S., Nelson, R.R. and Egelhoff, W.G. (1988) *Micro-Electronics: An Industry in Transition*, London: Unwin Hyman.

Martin, R. (1989) 'The Growth and Geographical Anatomy of Venture Capital in the United Kingdom', *Regional Studies* 25(1): 389–403.

Morse, R.S. (1976) 'The Role of New Technical Enterprises in the US Economy', Report of the Technical Advisory Board to the Secretary of Commerce, Washington, DC: January.

Oakey, R.P. (1984) *High Technology Small Firms*, London: Frances Pinter.

Oakey, R.P. (1985) 'British University Science Parks and High Technology Small Firms', *International Small Business Journal* 4(1): 58–67.

Oakey, R.P. (1991a) 'High Technology Small Firms: Their Potential for Rapid Industrial Growth', *International Small Business Journal* 9(4): 30–42.

Oakey, R.P. (1991b) 'High Technology Industry and the "Peace Dividend": A Comment on Future National and Regional Industrial Policy', *Regional Studies* 25(1): 83–86.

Oakey, R.P. and Cooper, S.Y. (1991c) 'The Relationship Between Product Technology and Innovation Performance in High Technology Small Firms', *Technovation* 11(2): 79–92.

Oakey, R.P., Rothwell, R. and Cooper, S.Y. (1988) *The Management of Innovation in High Technology Small Firms*, London: Frances Pinter.

Oakey, R.P., Faulkner, W., Cooper, S.Y. and Walsh, V. (1990) *New Firms in the Biotechnology Industry: their Contribution to Innovation and Growth*, London: Frances Pinter.

Office of Technology Assessment (1984) *Commercial Biotechnology: An International Analysis*, Washington, DC: Government Printing Office.

Rothwell, R. and Zegveld, W. (1981) *Industrial innovation and public policy*, London: Frances Pinter.

—— (1985) *Reindustrialization and Technology*, Harlow: Longmans.

Storey, D.J. (1982) *Entrepreneurship and the Small Firm*, London: Croom Helm.

DISCUSSION

Charlie Karlsson

Oakey's contribution to this book is certainly a provocative one. Its main purpose is to create a case for a technology policy in a developed market economy, with the United Kingdom as the prime example. One could have wished that Oakey had supported his case with a little more relevant data on R&D, patents, new products, market shares, etc., but nevertheless he has produced an interesting case.

His chapter deals with manufacturing industry in general and high technology industries in particular and their potential to create employment. One could, of course, ask why he has neglected the service industries and their potential to create employment. Anyone visiting the United Kingdom is certainly impressed by the development of the tourism industry. It is, for example, no longer possible to visit St Paul's cathedral as a tourist without paying an entrance fee.

Turning to the major purpose of the chapter I feel that it lacks a general discussion of the rational basis for a technology policy, i.e. of market failures such as monopolies, problems with property rights, risks and uncertainty, lumpy investments, external effects, etc. The discussion also ought to include questions such as the effects on employment, military power, and national pride and prestige.

However, it is not enough to discuss the rational basis for a technology policy. There is also a need for discussion of the relevant policies. Which are the effective measures, if there is a need for a technology policy? What do we know and what advice can we give the politicians? What should be the balance between supply and demand side policies? And looking on the supply side, which stages of the process from basic research to commercialization should a technology policy target? Certainly, the author could have dealt in a little more detail with these issues. In particular, I think that he should have discussed the role of higher education. One important element of Mrs Thatcher's policies was their severe neglect of the role of higher education in the modern knowledge society. I would argue that the major reason behind the difficulties for manufacturing industries – high tech or not – to compete during the 1980s was this neglect. The ability to compete on international markets was fundamentally circumscribed by lack of people with higher education. I will pursue this line of argument any further but I hope that the author will consider this hypothesis.

My last comment concerns the issue of strategies. How are we to find the balance between new and old sectors? How should we determine at the national level which technologies should be developed? What advice can we give to our politicians?

Hence, a number of questions could be raised in relation to Oakey's contribution, but this does not reduce its value. On the contrary, one could say that the large number of questions emerging from his chapter is an indication of its value, since good science always raises more questions than it answers.

Index